Erik Loomis is an associate professor of history at the University of Rhode Island. He writes on labor, politics, and the environment at the blog *Lawyers, Guns, and Money*. His work has also appeared in the *New York Times*, the *Washington Post*, *Dissent*, and the *New Republic*. The author of *Out of Sight* (The New Press) and *Empire of Timber*, he lives in Providence, Rhode Island.

A HISTORY OF AMERICA IN TEN STRIKES

Also by Erik Loomis

Out of Sight: The Long and Disturbing Story of Corporations Outsourcing Catastrophe

Empire of Timber: Labor Unions and the Pacific Northwest Forests

A HISTORY OF AMERICA IN TEN STRIKES

ERIK LOOMIS

NEW YORK
LONDON

First published in the United States by The New Press, New York, 2018
This paperback edition published by The New Press, 2020
Distributed by Two Rivers Distribution

ISBN 978-1-62097-627-2 (pb)
ISBN 978-1-62097-162-8 (ebook)

LIBRARY OF CONGRESS CATALOGING-IN-PUBLICATION DATA

Names: Loomis, Erik, author.
Title: A History of America in Ten Strikes / Erik Loomis.
Description: New York : The New Press, 2018. | Includes bibliographical references and index.
Identifiers: LCCN 2018017580 | ISBN 9781620971611 (hc : alk. paper)
Subjects: LCSH: Strikes and lockouts—United States—History. | Labor disputes—United States—History.
Classification: LCC HD5324 .L56 2018 | DDC 331.892/973—dc23 LC record available at https://lccn.loc.gov/2018017580

The New Press publishes books that promote and enrich public discussion and understanding of the issues vital to our democracy and to a more equitable world. These books are made possible by the enthusiasm of our readers; the support of a committed group of donors, large and small; the collaboration of our many partners in the independent media and the not-for-profit sector; booksellers, who often hand-sell New Press books; librarians; and above all by our authors.

www.thenewpress.com

Book design and composition by Bookbright Media
This book was set in Bembo and Gotham

Printed in the United States of America

To my departed mentors:
Richard Maxwell Brown,
Susan Becker,
and
Tim Moy

Contents

A HISTORY OF AMERICA IN TEN STRIKES

Introduction: Strikes and American History

Everyone has a limit. West Virginia teachers had struggled for years to make ends meet, finding themselves the butt of lawmakers' attacks on the budget. They worked in underfunded school districts, in buildings that were falling apart, and for less money than any teachers in the country except for three other states. Despite their pathetic salaries, they bought school supplies out of their own pockets.

While the teachers had unions, those institutions had struggled to fight back and were tired. West Virginia became a so-called "right to work" state in 2016, allowing workers to opt out of their unions and still receive all the benefits the unions won. This reduced union power, but it did not mean that workers considered themselves powerless. Seeing that the union officers would not lead a counterattack, teachers Emily Comer and Jay O'Neal started a secret Facebook group to organize their fellow workers throughout the state's schools. Comer said, "We thought this would be an easier way to get in touch with people, and keep people updated on what was going on."[1]

The Facebook group caught on like wildfire, attracting even

teachers who had left their union. After Governor Jim Justice signed legislation capping teacher pay well below the cost of living increases, teachers across West Virginia went on strike on February 22, 2018. They didn't want to go on strike. But they felt they had no choice, not if they wanted to be able to teach their students effectively. Rebecca Diamond, an elementary school teacher who spends her weekends working a second job at the local Hardee's, said, "I have lived in West Virginia my whole life. I have two children who I don't want to leave the state. What I'm fighting for is the future of West Virginia."[2] She joined thirty-four thousand teachers who put down their chalk and their grading pens and decided to fight for themselves and their students. This strike was illegal. The teachers figured it didn't matter. What did they have to lose when conditions were this bad?

West Virginia's parents saw the conditions of their schools. They knew and liked the teachers. Many parents joined the rallies. Huge marches on the state capitol in Charleston by teachers wearing red T-shirts, which has become the symbol of the teachers' movements nationwide, gained national media attention. Some had signs reading, "Will Teach for Insurance."[3] Even when an initial agreement convinced leadership to send workers back on the job, teachers from all of the state's fifty-five counties rejected it and stayed on strike.

After nine days the teachers won all their major demands. They pushed back against a state proposal to expand the charter schools that undermine public education. Governor Justice agreed to veto all anti-union legislation and create a health care task force with representatives from organized labor. Teachers won a 5 percent pay raise—very small, but a step in the right direction. Most importantly, as teacher Jay O'Neal said, "We made it so thousands of eyes will be watching everything the task force does."[4] The fight is nowhere near over. Teachers want a reversal of the corporate tax breaks that have underfunded schools in their state, a problem across the country. They are fighting for themselves, their students, and the future of their state. Though they won their immediate demands, they know that their strike was one skirmish in an endless push and pull between workers and bosses in America.

Only a few experiences tie us all together as people. One is that we almost all work or have worked. Whether in a factory, on a farm, at McDonald's, or as an unpaid housewife, work is as much a central experience to human society as eating and family. For the unemployed, the absence of work not only impoverishes but shames and isolates. Work fills the hours of our lives, it provides us with sustenance, and it can give us satisfaction with a job well done. Work is so central to human existence that we hardly know what to do without it. We long toward a well-deserved retirement, but when we get there, most people have to find new things to do, and that often includes part-time work.

The workplace is a site where people struggle for power. Under a capitalist economy such as that of the United States, employers profit by working their employees as hard as they can for as many hours as possible and for as little pay as they can get away with. Their goal is to exploit us. Our lives reflect that reality. Many of us don't enjoy our work. We don't get paid enough. We have to work two or three jobs to make ends meet if we have a job at all. Our bosses treat us like garbage and we don't feel like there is anything we can do about it. We face the threat that machines will replace us. Our jobs have moved overseas, where employers can generate even higher profits. Sometimes a job at Walmart is the only option we have.

In our exploitation, we share common experiences with hundreds of millions of Americans, past and present. Our ancestors resisted. So do we, sometimes by forming a union, sometimes by taking a couple extra minutes on our break or by checking social media on the job. All of these activities take back our time and our dignity from our employer. Class struggle—framed through transformations in capitalism, through other struggles for racial and gendered justice, and through changes in American politics and society—has played a central role in American history. Future historians will see this in our lives as well.

This book places the struggle for worker justice at the heart of American history. This is necessary because we don't teach class conflict in our public schools. Textbooks have little material about workers. As colleges and universities have devalued the study of the past in favor of emphasizing majors in business and engineering, fewer students take any history courses, including in labor history. Labor unions and stories of work are a footnote at best in most of our public discussions about American history. Most history documentaries on television focus on wars, politicians, and famous leaders, not workers. Labor Day was created as a conservative holiday so that American workers would not celebrate the radical international workers' holiday May Day. Yet today, we do not remember our workers on Labor Day like we remember our veterans on Veterans Day. Instead, Labor Day just serves as the end of summer, a last weekend of vacation before the fall begins. That erasure of workers from our collective sense of ourselves as Americans is a political act. Americans' shared memory—shaped by teachers, textbook writers, the media, public monuments, and the stories about the past we tell in our own families, churches, and workplaces—too often erases or downplays critical stories of workplace struggle.

Instead, our shared history tells myths about our economy meant to undermine class conflict. We are told that we are all middle class, that class conflict is something only scary socialists talk about and has no relevance to the United States today. Our culture deifies the rich and blames the poor for their own suffering. "Why don't they pull themselves up by their bootstraps?" so many people say. This ignores the fact that millions of Americans never had boots to pull up. Most of us are not wealthy and never will be wealthy. We are workers, laboring for a few rich and powerful people, mostly white men who are the sons and grandsons of other rich white men. We have a hierarchical society that has used propaganda to get Americans to believe everyone is equal. We are not equal. The law routinely favors the rich, the white, and the male.

During the twentieth century, workers fought and died to solve some of these problems, even though white men still benefited more than women or people of color. Workers formed unions, joined them by the millions, and convinced the government to pressure companies to negotiate with them. Unfortunately, the period of union success ended in the 1970s. So did the rising tide for American workers that created the middle class. With the decimation of unions, the fall of the middle class and the evisceration of the working class have followed. Politicians talk about the middle class during elections, but they too often pursue policies that increase inequality and give power to the rich. This has transformed the fundamentals of the American Dream. The idea of getting a job and staying with it your whole life, working hard to feed your family and educate your children, and then retiring with dignity is gone. Now, we are expected to take on massive student debt, enter an uncertain job market, and change jobs every few years, all the while being told by our parents and the media that we should stop eating avocado toast and instead buy a house, as if a $7 appetizer and not $50,000 in student loan debt is why young people suffer financial instability. Pensions are dead, and the idea of retiring seems impossible even for many baby boomers, who have significant consumer debt and shaky finances as they reach their later years.

We cannot fight against pro-capitalist mythology in American society if we do not know our shared history of class struggle. This book reconsiders American history from the perspective of class struggle not by erasing the other critical parts of our history—the politics, the social change, and the struggles around race and gender—but rather by demonstrating how the history of worker uprisings shines a light on these other issues. Some of these strikes fought for justice for all. Sometimes they made America a better place and gave us things we may take for granted today, such as the weekend and the minimum wage. But we also should not romanticize strikes. Some workers went on strike to keep workplaces all white. Sometimes strikes backfire and hurt workers in the end. Working Americans do not always agree with each other. Race, gender, religion, region, ethnicity, and many other identities divide us. Just because a Mexican immigrant and a fourth-generation Italian American work in the same place does not mean that they like each other or see eye-to-eye on any issue, including their own union, if they have one.

Taking a hard look at the history of strikes helps us in the present. This book argues for two interlocking necessities for workers to succeed in the past, present, and future. First, workers have to organize collectively to fight employers. Through American history, workers have fought to make their jobs better paid, fought for the right to negotiate a contract with their employer, fought to feed their children or have the chance to send them to college, fought for a completely new society that valued work as it deserved. Like the Chicago Teachers Union in 2012, workers of the past two hundred years also had to strike to win their struggles. Strikes take place when workers collectively decide to stop working in order to win their goals. Usually that happens with a labor union, which is an organization that workers create to represent them collectively. In the United States, this has usually meant the strikers have the aim of the union winning a written contract from the employer that lays out the rules of work and gives workers set wages, working hours, and benefits. But strikes happen with or without unions. They can be spontaneous acts by workers—paid or unpaid, with their union's support or without it—when they throw down their tools or their washrags or their chalk and they walk off the job for whatever reason they want.

Strikes are special moments. They shut down production, whether of manufacturing cars or manufacturing educated citizens. The strike, the withholding of our labor from our bosses, is the greatest power we have as workers. As unions have weakened in recent decades, we have far fewer strikes today than we did forty years ago. During the 1970s, there were an average of 289 major strikes per year in the United States. By the 1990s, that fell to 35 per year. In 2003, there were only 13 major strikes.[5] When a strike like the CTU action takes place, it forces people who claim to support the working class to announce which side they are on. Do they really believe in workers' rights or will they side with employers if a subway strike blocks their commute to work or a teachers' strike forces them to find something to do with their children for the day? Strikes are moments of tremendous power precisely because they raise the stakes, bringing private moments of poverty and workplace indignity into the public spotlight. And unless you are a millionaire boss, we are all workers with a tremendous amount in common with other workers, if we only realize that all of us—farmworkers and teachers, insurance agents and construction workers, graduate students and union staffers—face bad bosses, financial instability, and the desperate need for dignity and respect on the job.

We might like to believe that if all workers got together and acted for our rights, we could win whatever we want. In theory, if every worker walked off the job, that might happen. Unfortunately, real life does not work that way. Given that we are divided by race, gender, religion, country of origin, sexuality, and many other factors, class identity will never become a universal sign of solidarity. Employers know this and act to divide us upon these bases. For most of American history, the government has served the interests of wealthy employers over those of everyday workers like you and me, sometimes even using the military against us. At the local, state, and national levels, employers have far greater power than workers to implement their agenda, especially unorganized workers who lack a union. Therefore, in addition to worker action, organizers and union leaders have discovered a second requirement for success: Workers have to neutralize the government-employer alliance. After decades of struggle, in the 1930s, a new era of government passed labor legislation that gave workers the right to organize, the minimum wage, and other pillars of dignified work for the first time. While employers' power never waned in the halls of government, the growing power of unions neutralized the worst corporate attacks until the 1980s. Since then, the decline of unions and a revived, aggressive lobby attempting to drive unions to their death have rolled back many of our gains. Once again we live in a country where the government conspires with employers to make our work lives increasingly miserable. Unions are the only institution in American history to give working people a voice in political life. This is precisely why corporations and conservative politicians want to eliminate them.

There is simply no evidence from American history that unions can succeed if the government and employers combine to crush them. All the other factors are secondary: the structure of a union, how democratic it is, how radical its leaders or the rank-and-file are, their tactics. The potent and often interlocking strategies of the state and bosses build a tremendous amount of power against workers. That was true in the late nineteenth and early twentieth centuries and it is true under the Trump administration. Workers were and are denied basic rights to organize, income inequality is rampant, and the future of unions seems hopeless. Workers and their unions have to be as involved in politics as they are in organizing if they are to create conditions by which they can win. To stop involvement with the two-party political system would be tantamount to suicide. Having friends in government, or at least not having enemies there, makes all the difference in the history of American workers.

In Donald Trump, we face the most racist and misogynistic president in a century, a fascist Islamophobe who has demonstrated his utter contempt for the Constitution and the values that have made the United States the best it can be, even if it was never great for many of its citizens. Trump won in 2016 in part because he tapped into white Americans' anxiety about their unstable economic futures. Video footage from Carrier's announcement that it would close its Indiana heating and air-conditioning manufacturing plant to move its production to Mexico touched home for millions of Americans who do not see a path to a better future. For them, the American Dream is dead. Of course, African American, Asian American, Native American, Middle Eastern, and Latino workers also share those economic anxieties. But as has happened so often throughout American history, Trump managed to divide workers by race, empowering white people to blame workers of color for their problems instead of pointing a finger at who is really responsible for our economic problems: capitalists.

Capitalism is an economic system developed to create private profits. Within that broader definition, there are many forms of capitalism, some with socialist tendencies to ensure that the benefits of the economy are distributed relatively equally throughout all of society. In the modern United States, business and the government have dedicated themselves to a more fundamentalist version that uses the state to promote profit and keep workers subjugated under employer control. That has led to the income inequality that defines modern society. Whether some form of capitalism can work for everybody is a question people have debated for nearly two centuries. Some radicals reject capitalism entirely as a system that will never treat workers fairly. Others believe the state, businesses, and unions can all work together to create a form of capitalism where everyone benefits. We should be debating what the future of American and global capitalism looks like, or whether we should replace it entirely. I argue that at the very least we can use the government to create equitable laws and regulations to ensure that everyone lives a dignified life under a broadly capitalist economy. But that can only happen when workers reject the fundamentalist capitalist propaganda, such as from Ayn Rand and Fox News, and instead stand up for the rights not only of themselves, but of their friends, families, and co-workers. Solidarity is the answer for the future, which means sacrificing for others as they sacrifice for you. The extent that we will stand up for the rights of others, including at the workplace, will determine whether we will continue to see growing inequality and political instability in our world or we will see the world get better in our lifetimes.

This book focuses on ten major strikes in American history to tell the story of the United States through an emphasis on class and worker struggle. Combined, they weave a tale of a nation that promised life, liberty, and the pursuit of happiness, but that routinely denied that to workers, whether slave or free, men or women, black or white. They tell a story of a nation divided by race, gender, and national origin, as well as by class. They place work at the center of American history. This book sees the struggles for the dignity of workers, the rights of people of color, and the need to fight racism, misogyny, and homophobia as part of the same struggle.

Each chapter centers on one strike that accounts for about one-third of the chapter. The rest of the chapter places that strike in context of the broader issues affecting Americans at the time. The first chapter, on the Lowell Mill Girls strikes of the 1830s and 1840s, demonstrates how the Industrial Revolution transformed life for the new nation. Chapter 2, on slave self-emancipation, establishes the centrality of slave labor in American history and shows how slaves themselves helped win the Civil War for the Union, even if racism undermined their economic freedom after the war. The third chapter, on the 1886 eight-hour-day strikes, explores how workers responded to the rapid growth of capitalism that created a shocking world of inequality and exploitation after the Civil War. Chapter 4, on the 1902 anthracite coal strike in Pennsylvania, explains the central role of the government in deciding the fate of a strike, with both great possibilities and great peril for workers. Chapter 5 examines the Bread and Roses strike in Lawrence, Massachusetts, in 1912 as a window into those fighting for an alternative to capitalism entirely.

The sixth chapter investigates the Flint sit-down strike of 1937 to demonstrate what workers can win when conditions and organizing allow them to elect politicians who will help them and how small numbers of brave people can transform the world. Chapter 7 examines the Oakland General Strike of 1946 to show how workers won a fair share of the economic pie after World War II but also how fears of radicalism and unions' inability to organize nonunion parts of the nation laid the groundwork for the repeal of labor rights later in the twentieth century. Chapter 8 focuses on the Lordstown, Ohio, autoworkers strike of 1972 as a window into the tumultuous years of the 1960s and 1970s. Chapter 9 surveys the air traffic controllers strike of 1981 and how President Ronald Reagan reoriented the American government to crush unions instead of acting as a neutral arbiter between unions and employers, laying the groundwork for the attack on labor that continues today. Finally, chapter 10 discusses the Justice for Janitors actions in American cities during the late 1980s and early 1990s, focusing on the rise of immigration and how unions transformed from opposing immigration to being on the front lines of fighting President Trump's attacks on immigrants today.

We all want to live the American Dream. That can happen only if we combine organizing and solidarity with electing politicians who will fight for us instead of for our employers. Getting into the street to stand up for our rights must play a central role in these struggles. We cannot rely on others to fight for us. We have to do it for ourselves, in the streets and at the ballot box, at our workplaces and in our homes. The strike is the best weapon we have as everyday people to win our rights. Taken together, these strikes tell a broader story of workers in the scope of American history that I hope inspires you to fight for justice in your own life, just as so many people have done in the past and continue to do today. A better tomorrow is possible, but only if you demand it.

1

Lowell Mill Girls and the Development of American Capitalism

Outside of the very rich, everyone is a worker.

When Christopher Columbus stumbled across the Americas in 1492, he had specific ideas about work, who would do it, and who would benefit. So did the European nations that followed him: Spain and Portugal, France and England. Europeans colonized the Americas to get rich, and that would happen through other people doing work for them. In most colonies, they would enslave Native Americans and then Africans. Conquest, slavery, dispossession, and racism have defined much of American history, creating the inequalities we face today. Later chapters of this book will return to these issues repeatedly.

However, to tell American history through ten strikes, we need to examine the exception in American colonization. In New England, a different type of colonist arrived with a different type of labor system. Puritans, a Protestant separatist group seeking to reform the Church of England, settled in relatively close-knit communities revolving around their churches. The land of New England was rocky and soil poor. This led to a work culture centered around small farming and artisanship. The Puritans had little objection to slavery, and some New England colonists did own African slaves, but the economic system did not produce the wealth required for large-scale slavery such as in Virginia or Jamaica. New England was an economic backwater; logging and fishing were its important economic contributions to the British colonial project. As the English colonies moved toward independence in the eighteenth century, the economic basis of New England changed little. Growing cities, particularly Boston, created slightly more wealth, but this was still a region of small farms. But this geography, with a dense population and significant water sources close to large ports, paid off by 1800, with the Industrial Revolution transforming American work forever.[1]

The Industrial Revolution began in Britain in the mid-eighteenth century, when small-scale manufacturing underwent a radical transformation with the development of new technology that used waterpower to generate energy that moved machines, in the process shifting work from people's homes into factories. Mechanized cotton spinning, with the development of the power loom, drastically increased the productivity of a single worker; better technologies to produce iron rapidly lowered its cost; and the development of steam power provided energy sources to run the new factories. The British, realizing the enormous economic advantages these new technologies provided, banned their export and even limited the foreign travel of those familiar with the processes.[2]

But the British could not keep their technology under wraps. Americans, wanting to compete with their former motherland in the years after the American Revolution severed those ties, looked to build factories of their own. More than anyone else, Samuel Slater, a British factory worker who migrated to the United States with a memory full of how English mills worked, made this happen. He made a deal with a Rhode Island investor named Moses Brown, who wanted to replicate the British factory system. By 1793, Slater had a fully operational factory in Pawtucket, and American textile production was on the precipice of a revolution.[3]

That revolution required a second technological advancement:

the cotton gin. Invented by Eli Whitney, this simple machine could separate cotton seeds from the boll where they grew far faster than human hands could. This allowed for the mass production of cotton on southern plantations to feed the ever more powerful textile mills of New England. It meant the transition from agricultural to industrial labor in the North and the rapid expansion and intensification of slavery in the South to produce the cotton. The cotton gin went far to create the nineteenth-century American economy and sharpened the divides between work and labor in different regions of the United States, problems that would eventually lead to the Civil War. Its impact still shapes the global cotton and textile industries today.[4]

For New England, mass production meant child labor in the mills. Children worked during the eighteenth century, usually on their parents' farms, but sometimes as apprentices to craftsmen in cities. Benjamin Franklin, for instance, worked as his brother's apprentice in a print shop in Boston starting at the age of twelve, before he ran away to Philadelphia, eventually becoming one of the most important Founding Fathers. Slater had started working in a British mill as a child and hired children in his own mills. Child labor scaled up with the factory system. It placed thousands of people in cities with no care to their living or working conditions. Americans feared importing the filth, dire poverty, and crime of the British industrial city along with its factory system. Those fears quickly became justified. The entire labor system of the American economy soon revolved around an ever more exploitable labor force, both in the North and in the South, setting the stage for the justice movements that would slowly transform the lives of working people throughout American history.[5]

By 1815, 140 mills had opened within 30 miles of Providence, employing 26,000 people. The mill owners demanded incredible levels of work from their new, young laborers. Farmers labored hard, but they controlled their own time. Factory owners demanded punctuality and submission to the clock. Samuel Slater enforced his seventy-two-hour workweek by firing laborers who resisted. And resist they did. As early as 1817, mill workers possibly invented the idea of overtime by demanding extra pay for even five minutes of extra work over their allotted seventy-two hours.[6]

With the Industrial Revolution, young workers began moving to the mill towns from the farms where they had labored turning the raw products of nature into economic survival. These children often faced physical punishment. By the late 1830s, factory overseers faced criminal charges for the brutal beatings of child workers. It became the American version of the British factory-town nightmare. These children could not attend school; as Seth Luther, a former carpenter turned educational reformer said of his tour of Rhode Island mill towns in the 1830s: "In Pawtucket there are at least *five hundred children* who scarcely know what a school is . . . and to add to the darkness of the picture . . . in all the mills which the enquiries of the committees have been able to reach, books, pamphlets, and newspapers are *absolutely prohibited*."[7]

The factory system and cotton gin began the industrial age in the United States. New technology advanced it. Robert Fulton's commercial adaptation of the steamboat in 1807 began a revolution in transportation and communication. Using steam energy to move upriver meant the new industrial goods could easily travel anywhere in the country. The completion of the Erie Canal in 1825 magnified this revolutionary moment. The canal was an engineering marvel that connected the Great Lakes to the Hudson River using an ingenious system of locks that allowed boats to travel up- and downstream, connecting two great waterways and what was then the American West with the East. The sheer size of this project awed people around the world. It lowered consumer costs and allowed farmers in places such as Ohio to send their goods cheaply by boat to New York instead of all the way downriver to New Orleans and then to New York, which itself was far less expensive than dragging the goods across the barely passable roads of early America. The canal had enormous impacts on the future of American work, including spurring ever-greater industrialization, helping cement the Great Lakes region as a center of American industrialization, and ensuring New York would be the long-term capital of American commerce.[8]

Building the Erie Canal also killed a thousand workers. Workers' lives were cheap, and employers did not concern themselves with safety. Many died from the epidemic diseases that periodically ravaged the United States in this era. But the use of gunpowder to blow through rock also blew up or crushed a lot of workers. Canal wall collapses buried workers. Workers fell to their deaths building the locks and aqueducts. Exhausted, Orrin Harrison fell asleep resting against a beam on a lock. He fell into eight feet of water, where his legs were caught in the lock's gates and he drowned. This was just a standard event, happening with very little notice. The death toll rose daily from these sorts of incidents.[9]

The sheer brutality of the labor made most native-born Americans avoid working on the canal, so it became a prime job site for the nation's growing numbers of immigrants from Wales and Ireland. Throughout American history, foreign workers have entered the United States to escape economic desperation or political and religious oppression in their home countries. The United States attracted significant Irish immigration after an 1817 famine, exploding during the famous Great Famine in the 1840s. Employers quickly learned they could import cheap, exploitable labor rather than improve working conditions for native-born laborers. When early nineteenth-century immigrants arrived from Ireland or Wales and found the conditions terrible, their American Dream was shattered. Welsh immigrant William Thomas found work on the Erie Canal, but when he wrote back home, he despaired of the horrible conditions he faced and urged his friends not to repeat his mistakes: "I beg all my old neighbors not to think of coming here as they would spend more coming here than they think. My advice to them is to love their district and stay there." Thomas considered returning to Wales, although we do not know if he did.[10] The Irish took the most difficult and dangerous jobs in the pre–Civil War North. Conflict arose between native-born workers and immigrant workers, foreshadowing how race and immigration would block worker solidarity throughout American history. Anti-Irish agitation later led to the Know-Nothing Party, a major political movement of the early 1850s dedicated to ending Irish immigration.[11]

The introduction and development of the railroad in the United States during the 1820s only increased the death tolls of early industrial work. Fast trains, poor safety precautions, and many moving parts made riding the early trains deadly for the passengers. European travelers constantly noted the intense dangers of American trains versus those in their home nations. Most early trains even lacked effective brakes. Working for the railroads was even more dangerous than riding the trains. The work was associated with working-class cultures of manliness and risk-taking, creating an atmosphere of independence and indifference to safety from both workers and bosses. Supervision was light and working or production standards nonexistent.[12]

The injury or death of thousands of rail workers tore apart families. They began seeking compensation for their losses in the courts. Did employers have legal responsibility for dead or maimed workers? Or did the workers take on the risk themselves by agreeing to such a job? On October 30, 1837, Nicholas Farwell, a train engineer toiling for the Boston and Worcester Rail Road Corporation, fell off a train after a switchman made a mistake. The train ran over his hand, forcing an amputation. In an era without workers' compensation or any economic safety net, Farwell had no guarantee that he could work or eat. He sued the company for $10,000. In the 1842 case of *Farwell v. Boston and Worcester Rail Road Corporation*, Massachusetts chief justice Lemuel Shaw claimed that Farwell agreed to take on the risk of work by laboring for the railroad. He called the $2 a day Farwell made a "premium for the risk which he thus assumes." Shaw might sue his "fellow servant" who made the mistake that led to his fall but the company was immune to lawsuits of this kind.[13]

The *Farwell* case was part of a larger transformation in the American legal code to facilitate employer rights at the expense of everyone else. Citizens sued textile mills for damming rivers that ended age-old fish runs people upstream relied upon for food. The courts consistently found in favor of the new corporations, claiming these businesses promoted "progress" in the justification for the courts' decisions. This led to corporations with the right to pollute at will and timber companies with the right to destroy the stream banks that farmers owned, with courts backing up corporate domination of anyone who got in the way of their growth.[14] *Farwell* directly led to tens of thousands of dead workers and millions who suffered from tuberculosis, lead poisoning, electrocution, severed limbs, hair ripped from workers' scalps after being caught in machinery, suffocation in coal mines, and other workplace hazards and diseases in a nation where corporations had no responsibility for their workers' safety and health. Workers might receive compensation from companies—but the average for the 149 workers injured on the Boston and Maine Railroad in 1891 was all of $21. The roots of capitalist exploitation go to the system's very beginning.[15]

Early railroad unions sought to provide some benefits upon injury or death. Labor organizations formed soon after 1800 to promote the collective interest of fellow workers, usually laborers who did the same job across different workplaces or sometimes all the workers in a given workplace. During the 1830s, perhaps 44,000 Americans were union members, around 2.5 percent of the nonagricultural free labor force. The center of American unionism was New York City, with perhaps 11,500 union members out of an overall population of 218,000.[16] However, those unions could do little to battle a poorly regulated economy that impoverished them. During the Panic of 1837, up to one out of three workers in New York lost their job.[17] Economic dislocation combined with industrialization to undermine the master craftsmen and apprentice system that had long dominated urban work relations. Shoemakers, coopers, ironworkers, and other shop workers valued their independence, controlling their time and pace of work. The Industrial Revolution had no place for these inefficiencies, and companies began eroding workers' independence.

Class consciousness, or the belief that workers should band together for mutual interest based upon their status as workers in an exploitative economic system, slowly developed. Strikes, or "turnouts" as they were called, were rare in the early nineteenth century.[18] In 1827, workers at Samuel Slater's mills went on strike when he cut their pay rates—an action built upon years of growing grievances—but the strike failed.[19] In 1831, Providence workers started a movement for a ten-hour day that caught fire across the factory towns of Rhode Island and Massachusetts. Factory owners responded with mass firings and considered demanding the state militia protect them from this supposedly radical threat. Yet throughout early 1832, machinists, mule spinners in the textile factories, and carpenters struck, refusing to work more than ten hours. But poverty, the fact that many of them were children supporting their families, and intimidation largely killed this early workers' movement by the middle of 1832. Such movements continued well into the 1840s, with a big push in 1844 by the building trades in Fall River, Massachusetts, that led to the creation of the New England Workingmen's Association later that year. The association combined working-class organizing with the reform movements of the era to stress both individual morality and mutual aid in promoting workers' rights.[20]

In 1835, coal heavers in Philadelphia walked off the job and twenty thousand other workers in the city's General Trades Union joined them. This early "general strike" included everyone from those coal heavers to people who worked for the city government. The strikers won a ten-hour day, which still meant that the workers were on the job from six a.m. to six p.m., with two hour-long meal breaks. Even early union victories meant hard labor and long days.[21] Like these coal heavers, most workers in the nascent industrial economy saw wage labor as a specifically male realm. Men felt that the growth of the market economy challenged their ability to provide for their families, and they acted politically as workers to fight that. The Loco Focos, an 1830s splinter movement of the Democratic Party in New York, fought to bring down the price of food, arguing that men laboring to take care of their families had moral authority to fight for the rights of workers, which built on two decades of New York workers organizing for a family wage and the right to spend time away from their jobs with their families.[22] Yet the idea of the single-family wage, where a man earned enough to support his family, was already more myth than reality. Women worked in all sorts of occupations to support themselves and their families in the early industrial economy, not only in unpaid labor on farms, but as sex workers by the thousands in cities such as New York, as domestic servants, and in factories.[23] In fact, women would lead the way in protesting unfair working conditions as the Industrial Revolution transformed the nation.

The Mill Girls Strike

In 1822, textile manufactures started an experimental town in Lowell, Massachusetts. They wanted to avoid the conditions of the hellish British textile cities. Visitors to the British city of Manchester repeatedly expressed shock both at its rapid growth and the foul, dreadful, degraded lives of the people laboring there. Americans wrote books defining the United States as superior to Britain precisely because their nation did not have these cities. Yet Americans also wanted the industrial expansion and money that the textile mills brought.[24] Lowell's founders wanted to prove that factories and respectable labor could coexist. They recruited young New England farm women to work, have a bit of an adventure, and live under supervision. The short-term nature of the work, to be undertaken before the women became wives and mothers, meant the avoidance of a permanently degraded working class. Employers housed the so-called Mill Girls in boardinghouses under the watchful eyes of older women. Ralph Waldo Emerson, Henry Wadsworth Longfellow, and other writers gave talks to the workers. The Mill Girls produced their own magazines, took classes, and, in the eyes of the factory owners, prepared themselves nicely for marriage while producing profit for their employer. The town's founders hoped they'd created a model for labor in the industrializing age.[25]

Young women came to the mills for a number of reasons. Mary Hall made $115 in eight months in 1834, more than enough for her to live on comfortably. Harriet Hanson Robinson moved to Lowell as a child and found upward mobility in the mills, rising into skilled positions before leaving when she married at the age of twenty-four. Sally Rice left her village of Somerset, Vermont, in 1838 and worked in mills in New York and Connecticut to make enough money to earn a dowry and get married, which she finally did in 1847. Sisters or cousins came together, while many workers came and went periodically, going to the mills when they needed money and back to the farms when they fell ill or got homesick.[26]

These women were used to hard farmwork, but the factories were notably unpleasant. They were hot and humid to keep the cotton fibers workable and reduce fires. Enormous glass windows allowed sun to pour in on the hottest days of the year. The machines were loud in a way that's difficult to imagine today unless you are a factory worker yourself. They worked twelve- or fourteen-hour days, six days a week, locked up in that factory tending those machines minute after minute, day after day, month and month. Historians have argued that working-class Americans began to see the natural environment as something romantic during this era, something to escape to rather than tame. Reflecting the transcendentalist thinkers who spoke to them, the workers wrote longingly of the beauty of the forests and fields of New England—a striking transformation from the matter-of-fact style of writing about the New England land before the factories opened.[27]

It did not take long before the Mill Girls moved from intellectual pursuits during their limited free time to political organizing. They began demanding better conditions in the factories, and since they came from respectable families, they had the social status to demand a response. The first strike among textile workers was in Pawtucket, Rhode Island, in 1824 when Samuel Slater reduced wages and extended hours. Male and female workers fought together, the mills closed, and Slater agreed to compromise.[28] Occasional strikes took place over the next decade. In February 1834, Lowell saw its first strike. Eight hundred women quit work to fight against a reduction in their piece rates, the wages paid per piece of cloth produced. The Mill Girls held organizing meetings to resist the pay cut. When one employer fired an organizer, the women walked out and the strike began. It failed quickly, with the mills returning to near-capacity production within a week. Yet, this early effort was an important pioneering stand against exploitation. In a statement titled "Union is Power," the workers connected their struggles to their ancestors resisting oppression from the English, whether Puritans escaping religious oppression or fighting King George III's taxes during the American Revolution: "We circulate this paper wishing to obtain the names of all who imbibe the spirit of our Patriotic Ancestors, who preferred privation to bondage, and parted with all that renders life desirable and even life itself to procure independence for their children." They rejected the assertion that employers could exploit them at will and demanded an equal say in the burgeoning industrial economy.[29]

In 1836, the workers walked off the job once more, again protesting a reduction in their earnings, in this case due to an increase in the cost of room and board in the boardinghouses. Business was booming, but the companies sought to capture all the profits instead of sharing them with the workers. One of the strikers was Harriet Hanson Robinson, who remembered:

> Cutting down the wages was not their only grievance, nor the only cause of this strike. Hitherto the corporations had paid twenty-five cents a week towards the board of each operative, and now it was their purpose to have the girls pay the sum; and this, in addition to the cut in the wages, would make a difference of at least one dollar a week. It was estimated that as many as twelve or fifteen hundred girls turned out, and walked in procession through the streets. They had neither flags nor music, but sang songs, a favorite (but rath-

er inappropriate) one being a parody on "I won't be a nun."

"Oh! isn't it a pity, such a pretty girl as I—
Should be sent to the factory to pine away and die?
Oh! I cannot be a slave,
I will not be a slave,
For I'm so fond of liberty
That I cannot be a slave."[30]

Probably fifteen hundred to two thousand workers went on strike, up to one-third of the workforce. Unlike in 1834, they kept up the struggle for several months, making it impossible for the mills to run at full capacity. They would turn off all the machines in a given room before walking out, effectively shutting down an entire mill. At least two mills gave in and revoked the boarding-house rate increases.[31]

Lowell was not the only site of these strikes. In Paterson, New Jersey, more than two thousand workers from twenty mills, largely young girls, walked off the job on July 3, 1835. Their workday was 13½ hours. For this, they made $2 a week. Employers fined workers for mistakes or not working hard enough. The mills also opened a company store and forced workers to shop there. Some of the tradesmen in Paterson, including the fathers of some of the mill workers, had organized earlier that year and successfully won a ten-hour day. The Paterson mill workers decided to make this their prime demand, with the fines, wage withholding, company store, and pay as less central issues. Support from workers around the region allowed the strike to continue for nearly two months. Donations came in from workers in Newark and New York City, and the Paterson Association for the Protection of the Working Class formed to organize relief. Workers in Newark created an investigating committee to look into the working conditions in the cotton mills, described as "more congenial to the climate of the autocrat of all the Russias than to this 'land of the free and home of the brave.'" Employers refused to negotiate and did bust the strike, but only after giving in to several of the workers' demands, including reducing the workday to twelve hours Monday through Friday and nine hours on Saturday, a sixty-nine-hour workweek. That's still a very long week, but it also meant about twelve hours returned to workers each week, a significant improvement in their lives.[32]

The Lowell Mill Girls did not win their strike either, but they continued fighting. As the mills began to hire men as well as women, male and female workers tried to find common ground. In 1844, a petition demanding a ten-hour day was signed by three hundred mill workers of both genders. In Worcester, Massachusetts, a similar petition simply stated, "Ten Hours per day as a day's labor for all Adult Persons."[33] The ten-hour day became a major fighting point for the Lowell workers, especially as employers sped up the work, increasing the rate of the machines without hiring new workers. One worker had the speed of her two looms increased by 70 percent over a two-year period, with her wages only increasing 16 percent.[34] Stopping the speedup was much harder than limiting the number of hours workers toiled, a concrete demand that compensated workers rather than limiting production. Huldah Stone wrote, "Is it necessary that men and women should toil and labor twelve, sixteen and even eighteen hours, to obtain mere sustenance of their physical natures?"[35] For Stone and her fellow workers, the answer was clearly no. But the conditions of work continued to decline. Between 1840 and 1854, the workload of spinners at the Hamilton Corporation in Lowell more than doubled, while wages declined.[36]

Some of the Mill Girls developed into long-term fighters for economic justice. In 1835, Sarah Bagley, age twenty-eight, began working in the mills. She quickly became politically aware and started working to reform the conditions. She asked the Workingmen's Convention in 1844, "When our rights are trampled upon and we appeal in vain to our legislators, what shall we do but appeal to the people? Shall not our voice be heard and our rights acknowledged here; shall it be said again to the daughters of New England, that they have no political rights and are not subject to legislative action?"[37] Bagley, who held to many of the gender norms of her day, saw women as taking a subservient role to men in the overall labor movement, but she also saw them as agents who needed to stand up for themselves. Bagley believed women should operate within the women's sphere of society that Victorian-era reformers had created by the 1840s, staying at home if possible, but given that the reality of factory work degraded the morals of women, they also needed to speak out to protect themselves.[38]

Bagley helped found the Lowell Female Labor Reform Association in 1844. Other mill towns such as Manchester, New Hampshire, formed their own branches of the Female Labor Reform Association. Bagley led a campaign to demand that the Massachusetts government hold hearings about conditions in the mills. By 1845, 1,150 Lowell workers had signed petitions to demand the hearings, about three-fourths of them women.[39] On February 13, 1845, Bagley's organizing paid off and the state of Massachusetts held hearings on reducing the workday in the state's textile mills to ten hours a day. Six women testified, including Bagley. She said, "The chief evil, so far as health is concerned, is the shortness of time allowed for meals. The next evil is the length of time employed."[40] Bagley and others would use their perceived vulnerability as women to make the ten-hour argument. Said E.S., a Mill Girl, a shorter workday would lead "to the improvement of the condition of women in particular" that would allow them to become educated and then become better mothers.[41] Bagley built on these arguments by arguing that Sunday work undermined women's morality because they could not go to church.[42] But in 1846, the Massachusetts legislature voted to reject the workers' demands. As in the *Farwell* case, Massachusetts prioritized the desires of employers over any form of social justice. However, the owners did agree to reduce the hours to eleven a day in 1853 as the women continued pressuring them. States did respond to pressure to pass ten-hour legislation, including New Hampshire in 1847 and Rhode Island in 1853, but these laws were ineffective and not enforced, a major problem in this era when even the federal government was small and weak.[43]

The long hours and ever harder work undermined the Mill Girls' culture. The *Lowell Offering*, the main journal of the Mill Girls, stopped publication in 1845 because the women who wrote it quit as the work became ever more intense and degrading.[44] The response of the factory owners to the Mill Girls agitating was to find more easily exploitable workers. The Great Famine meant 780,000 new immigrants to the United States from Ireland in the 1840s alone, with another 914,000 following in the 1850s. These workers were in no condition to turn down hard industrial labor; any work was better than starvation at home. During the 1850s, Lowell employers shifted decisively toward immigrant labor. By the early 1860s, the Lowell operators no longer had any illusions about a model labor force. They gave up on supervising their workers' behavior or treating them with paternalist concern, with nine companies stopping production in 1862 and throwing ten thousand workers out of a job.[45] It's possible that the Lowell experiment never really had much chance of working, given the lack of government-mandated employment standards and an ever more competitive market with factories seeking to undercut each other. But eliminating what we can call a privileged labor class—workers with options and access to political levers—proved incredibly profitable for the textile industry.

Free Labor in a Capitalist Nation

The Industrial Revolution transformed women's work outside the factory as well. Both in terms of personal cleanliness and modern housework, Americans still lived basically medieval lives. Bathing was rare, farm animals lived in close proximity with people, and the separation of spaces we find in modern homes was largely unknown. The economic and social upheavals of the Industrial Revolution spawned a series of reform movements based in New England and New York, including abolitionism, temperance, religious revivals, the creation of new religions such as Mormonism, the public education movement, creating solitary confinement in prisons so that prisoners could theoretically reflect on their moral failings, and more. Each of these attempted to make sense of a new and rapidly changing world.[46]

New middle-class values created the modern definition of housework, which became unpaid women's work. In 1841, Catharine Beecher, from the nation's foremost reformer family, published *A Treatise on Domestic Economy*, the first major tract to promote the idea of cleanliness and housekeeping as specifically women's work that would civilize men and raise proper children. She believed housework was a legitimate profession and thus women should be educated for it as they would be educated for teaching. Her book attempted to teach these qualities to American women. She focused on practical advice around childcare, cleaning, training servants, cooking, sewing, nursing, gardening, and other skills a proper middle-class woman needed to create a new generation of moral Americans. She called for a redesign of houses to create an architecture of cleanliness. Every room would have a fireplace, a kitchen needed a good sink, and homes needed wells or cisterns nearby for the vastly increased amount of laundry required to be clean. She emphasized bathing and rejected the common idea that dirt was healthy. By the 1870s, her ideas had caught on, creating new forms of women's work and giving workingwomen what was essentially a second unpaid job when they returned home from earning wages.[47]

Northern men responded to the Industrial Revolution by promoting the idea of "free labor," wherein workers would direct themselves in productive labor that created economic and therefore political independence, allowing white males to govern the nation as a collective body with similar interests. Free labor would create a white male democracy that would put small farmers, skilled workers, employers, and entrepreneurs in a society of relative equality, albeit one that excluded people of color and women of all races. Despite the stresses factory workers faced, this dream remained prominent well into the late nineteenth century. But the system of slavery expanding across the southern United States, as slaveholders' demands for power grew ever more strident, increasingly seemed to threaten white northern free labor. More northerners saw a South dominated by an elite plantation class with slaves and widespread poverty among everyday white farmers.[48]

This was at the core of why Republicans opposed slavery after the party's 1854 founding. While abolitionists who called for the immediate end of slavery because it was immoral did exist, they were a minority even in the Republican Party until well after the Civil War began in 1861. Rather, slavery threatened the white male democracy of the northern free laborer because a system of forced black labor left no place in society for the middling whites who made up northern society. The expansion of slavery into the territories recently acquired by the United States, through war against Mexico and Native American peoples, further threatened the future of white male democracy by cutting off the land and labor seen as necessary to its continuation. As one Iowa Republican stated, "Slavery is a foul political curse upon the institutions of our country; it is a curse upon the poor, free, laboring white man."[49] Abraham Lincoln's opposition to slavery was similarly based upon the opportunities it denied to white men. He stated, "Men, with their families . . . work for themselves on their farms, in their houses, and in their shops, taking the whole product to themselves, and asking no favors of capital on the one hand nor of hired laborers or slaves on the other."[50] Industrial capitalism would later make this ideology of control over one's labor antiquated, but it drove northern white opposition to slavery and continued as an ideal for the American working class for decades.

The beginning of the Civil War in 1861 reinforced industry's growth. Inflation rose rapidly and wages did not keep up. Unions expanded in response to the growing dissatisfaction. Republican governors began to use armed forces to suppress strikes, such as at an arms factory in Cold Springs, New York, and intervening to stop war workers from forming a union in St. Louis.[51] After the war's 1865 conclusion, workers organized the first large unions in American history. At a Baltimore convention in 1866, workers founded the National Labor Union (NLU), the first attempt to create a labor federation of unions from around the nation. It was led by William Sylvis, an iron molder from Philadelphia who had been involved in unions from an early age. He had a vision for a national organization and in 1859 had created the National Union of Iron Molders, becoming its first president. The NLU had one major goal: the eight-hour day. It got a bill passed in Congress in 1868 mandating it for federal employees. Several states also passed eight-hour laws by 1868, but enforcement lacked at both the federal and state levels. The NLU grew to perhaps three hundred thousand members by 1869. However, the NLU was also cursed with the core problem of the American working class: racism. While it claimed to represent all workers, it called the freedom of African Americans "unpalatable" in its foundational document. A Colored National Labor Union formed for black workers and attempted to work with the NLU, but without a great deal of success. Sylvis died in 1869 and the NLU fell apart without his leadership.[52]

Women continued organizing as well. One of women's hardest jobs was washing clothes, whether at home or in laundries. Workers who cleaned collars washed them in harsh, caustic chemicals and boiling water. Women working in commercial laundries labored twelve- to fourteen-hour days in extraordinarily hot workplaces for $3 a week. Rapid technological advancements came at the price of worker safety. New starching machines were known for causing horrific burns for workers. On February 23, 1864, Kate Mullaney, head of the all-women Collar Laundry Union (CLU), led three hundred workers in Troy, New York, out on strike. Mullaney entered the labor force in the early 1860s when her father died, and with her mother an invalid, she became the family's primary breadwinner. Like the vast majority of the collar workers, Mullaney was a young unmarried woman. Ninety-two percent of Irish collar workers were single, and another 5 percent were widows. The CLU wanted higher wages and better working conditions.

Within a week, twenty Troy laundries increased workers' pay by more than 20 percent and agreed to work on safety issues. The strike made the union successful. The CLU lasted for five years, which may not seem long to us today, but in an era of embryonic labor organizations, that was a pretty good run. In 1866, the CLU went on strike again, forcing employers to raise wages to $14 a week, over four times what workers had made just two years earlier. In March 1869, the CLU won another strike, but this convinced operators to destroy the union. That May, workers again walked off the job. But the owners chose a strategy that would prove very effective at forestalling unionization: they organized themselves to collectively resist the union. They pressured smaller operators to hold out against the CLU, began to recruit scab laborers, and worked to control press coverage of the strike in Troy. The workers protested the bad press coverage, but while the Troy *Times* published a letter by the workers, it refused to endorse their actions. Perhaps the most effective action was to lock out union members. The owners offered higher wages, but only if workers abandoned their union. This proved effective in the face of poverty. The strike was lost and the union destroyed. Mullaney faded from view after 1870. We know she married at some point and that she died in 1906 in Troy. She remained poor and was buried in an unmarked grave until the 1990s, when women's rights and labor rights advocates fought to create a National Historic Landmark to remember Mullaney and the CLU.[53]

The early strikes by American workers most often failed. They were responses to new industrial systems workers had only begun to understand. Yet these stories make us remember how workers have always struggled against oppression. They remind us that despite the media image of workers as men, women's work played an equally central role in American life, even if male workers added to the oppression women faced from their bosses. Unions are the prime way workers have organized to improve their lives, but even outside of unionization campaigns, workers fight for their rights. These early strikes should serve as an inspiration today, showing us that our ancestors, much like us, faced a rapidly changing world by seeking justice for their brothers and sisters.

2

Slaves on Strike

The slaves freed themselves.

The contemporary uprisings of African Americans against police violence, systemic racism, low wages, and poverty over the past few years have inspired many people to action. Black Lives Matter, the fight for the $15 minimum wage, the struggle against mass incarceration, and many other movements have led the way in a new era of activism in the United States. These are the latest examples of centuries-long resistance by people of color to white domination and exploitation. From the beginning of European colonization of the Americas, European Americans have sought to exploit people of color, especially their labor. These latest protests are part of a continuum of black resistance in the United States that began with the first slaves imported into Virginia in 1619. The biggest labor strike in American history took place during the Civil War, when slaves simply stopped working for their owners at the first opportunity. They did not wait for Abraham Lincoln to free them. Rather, they took their lives in their own hands through withholding their labor from their masters, fleeing to Union lines, and forcing Lincoln and the North to recognize the new reality of their lives. The self-emancipating slaves are true heroes of working-class struggle.

Slavery is fundamentally a labor system. Slaves lived unimaginable horrors every day. They also fought back any way they could. Whether through slowing down their work, stealing from their masters, running away, or rebelling, whenever slaves saw an opportunity to improve their lives, they took it. When opposing soldiers arrived in the South—whether British soldiers during the Revolutionary War and War of 1812 or American soldiers during the Civil War—slaves ran to the arriving armies, hoping for freedom. The black scholar and civil rights leader W.E.B. DuBois identified this phenomenon in his seminal 1935 book *Black Reconstruction in America*, when he called slave self-emancipation a "general strike," which is a moment when workers across employers and industries collectively stop their labor. DuBois's insight was ignored by generations of historians imbued with white supremacist ideas, but in recent decades, historians have built upon DuBois to demonstrate the complex ways that slaves sought freedom.[1]

When the Civil War began in 1861, African Americans, slave and free, knew what was at stake: the future of slavery. By walking away from the plantations, withholding their labor from masters who increasingly could not control them, the slaves undermined the southern economy and morale. By fleeing to Union lines and then fighting for the freedom of themselves and their families, they helped Abraham Lincoln and the northern public understand the true meaning of the war. By demanding labor rights after the war, they challenged white supremacy, including that in the North.

Slavery: The Foundation of the American Economy

When the English settled in Virginia in 1607, they demanded native peoples serve their every whim. In doing so, they reflected the overall European view of indigenous peoples when they colonized the Americas. The Spanish conquest of Hispaniola in 1492, Mexico in 1521, and Peru in 1533 all included the enslavement of indigenous peoples. The English, French, and Spanish who came to the United States also brought race-based slavery with them.[2]

Led by Powhatan, the native peoples of Virginia resisted the

English, and the colony nearly collapsed when the colonists, too scared of Indian attacks to leave their fort, starved to death and left the survivors eating the human dead. But in 1612, John Rolfe introduced tobacco into the colony and Virginia had an economic basis to survive and expand. Tobacco is a labor-intensive crop, and no one who could pay their own way to Virginia would toil for someone else. Large-scale plans to enslave Native Americans failed in the face of the diseases that quickly reduced indigenous populations; additionally, native peoples had the ability to escape into the nearby forests. Planters first recruited white indentured servants from England, who took the chance to escape poverty at home. In return for a five- to seven-year contract, indentured servants would eventually receive land. Planters frequently abused these workers, including with whippings and overwork. Many contracts for women included clauses that if a woman became pregnant, time would be added to her indentureship. If a master raped and impregnated his servant, he could keep her under his control. Fifty thousand English men and women migrated to Virginia for a chance at a new life between 1630 and 1680. But the cruel conditions and better opportunities at home reduced the supply by the 1670s.[3]

Virginians turned to Africans as a permanent labor force in the late eighteenth century. The first African slaves came to Virginia in 1619. They did not, however, pioneer the transatlantic slave trade. The Spanish and Portuguese were already using African slaves in large numbers. But they had been too expensive for early Virginia planters. However, rising supplies of slaves by 1700 lowered prices and made them available to Virginians. Early Africans had ambiguous legal status in Virginia; some gained freedom and a very few even bought their own slaves. However, Virginia courts began laying the groundwork for permanent slave status. In 1662, after a slave sued for freedom by claiming his father was white, Virginia decided that slave status was confirmed by the mother. This gave masters the right to rape their slaves and keep their own children as property. Forced sexual labor became central to a system that denied slaves basic human rights. The new era of chattel slavery, that is, slaves who could be bought, sold, and traded, had begun.[4]

Slavery spread around the North American colonies. The New England Puritans did not have a plantation economy, but those with the money bought a few slaves. New York became a center of slavery. Slaves did the work of rice and indigo growing in South Carolina and Georgia. The French colony of Louisiana grew sugar, the most labor-intensive slave crop of all and the basis of European fortunes. To acquire these slaves, slave traders, often operating out of northern colonies such as Rhode Island, bought slaves from Africans. Over 12 million Africans were sent to the Americas, the vast majority between 1701 and 1810. Slave merchants stacked thousands of slaves inside of ships for long journeys to the Americas, in what came to be known as the Middle Passage. If weather delayed the ship and supplies were low, the ship captains would throw live slaves into the ocean to drown. Slaves faced lives of endless toil and exploitation, under the complete control of masters who saw them as beasts of burden, as sex slaves, and as breeders for future profit.[5]

These slaves did not accept their new lives if they could help it. In 1739, a group of twenty recent arrivals from Africa under the leadership of a man named Jemmy started the Stono Rebellion in South Carolina. Arming themselves by robbing a gunsmith, they had no intention of accepting their status as slave laborers. They hoped to reach the Spanish fort at St. Augustine, Florida, believing that the enemies of the English would grant them freedom. Gathering more followers as they marched, they killed perhaps twenty-five whites before engaging in a final bloody battle with the South Carolina militia; twenty whites and forty-four blacks died that day. Some of the rebellious slaves were executed, others sent to the Caribbean. South Carolina cracked down by banning slaves from reading and limiting the rights of slaves to assemble in groups, raise food, or earn money; the state also allowed slave owners to kill their slaves.[6]

The ideas of the eighteenth-century Enlightenment convinced some white Americans that slavery was wrong. If people had the right to life, liberty, and the pursuit of happiness, did that also include slaves? After the American Revolution, northern states moved toward freeing slaves, sometimes immediately but usually after a period of gradual emancipation. Vermont abolished slavery in 1777, before it became a state, while the rest of the New England states, along with Pennsylvania, followed in the 1780s. By 1804, all northern states had either barred slavery or had plans in place to eventually free slaves, although New York still had some slaves in the 1820s. Talk of emancipation even reached southern states. George Washington freed his slaves when he died in 1799, and Thomas Jefferson bemoaned the existence of slavery and hoped for a way to be rid of it, even though he exploited his slaves for both plantation and sexual labor.[7]

Slaves also took matters into their own hands. When they could, slaves used the Revolutionary War to free themselves. While some free blacks and slaves fought for the colonists, the British found that offering freedom to slaves in exchange for fighting was an effective tool to punish southern revolutionaries. Thousands of slaves fled to British lines, as they would during the War of 1812. After both wars, many of those now freed slaves settled in Nova Scotia, the West Indies, Britain, and Africa. They faced hard lives, poverty, and racism, but they were no longer slaves. Fleeing to British lines, refusing to labor any longer for a planter and instead selling their labor to free themselves and then make their own lives, was a prelude to slaves' response to the Civil War.[8]

While slavery slowly withered in the North after the Revolution, it exploded in the South thanks to the rapid expansion of cotton production. The rise of the Industrial Revolution fueled by cotton capitalism transformed the South as much as the North, enmeshing slave owners in a global economy based around commodity production, transnational markets, and debt to fund more slaves and land. Slave owners in states such as Maryland and Virginia who had considered freeing their slaves after the Revolution suddenly found themselves buying up land on the western frontier as fast as wars of genocide pushed the Native Americans off it. This had a brutal effect on slaves, as planters split up slave families, sending some west to work in the cotton fields and keeping others on the original plantation.[9]

As the cotton economy developed, planters bred new strains that vastly increased the crop. At harvest time, overseers drove slaves to the point of death to pick every possible boll of cotton. Masters balanced this brutality with maximizing the harvest, often with slaves dying of exhaustion in the fields or being beaten into submission.[10] Violence was at the heart of slave labor. Said the escaped slave and abolitionist legend Frederick Douglass, "I have often been awakened at the dawn of day by the most heart-rending shrieks of an aunt of mine, whom he used to tie up to a joist, and whip upon her naked back till she was literally covered with blood. He would whip her to make her scream, and whip her to make her hush; and not until overcome by fatigue, would he cease to swing the blood-clotted cowskin."[11] Such beatings occurred daily on many plantations. Owners could murder slaves at will. Harriet Jacobs, who hid in her grandmother's attic for seven years after escaping from her master, wrote of a story of a slave locked in a cotton gin until he died. By the time the gin was opened, rats had eaten much of the body.[12]

Slaves rarely rose up in violent rebellions, but owners lived in constant fear of it. Stono remained in the memory of the slaveholders. In 1791, slaves in Haiti revolted against their white masters, leading to the nation's independence in 1804. Slave owners feared a similar revolt in the United States. On January 8, 1811, it seemed that their fears might come true when the German Coast uprising began in Louisiana. Charles Deslondes led this rebellion, with men named Quamana and Harry playing major roles. Quamana and another slave named Kook were Asante warriors, imported from Africa around 1806. Deslondes was the son of a white planter and a black slave. As they marched toward New Orleans, hundreds of slaves joined them. Armed with hand tools, knives, and a few guns, they came close to New Orleans before being crushed near modern-day Norco, Louisiana. Forty-four slaves were tried and executed and around ninety-five died in all. Slave owners cut off the heads of the slaves, placed them on pikes, and lined the roads with them.[13]

Slave owners began fearing rebellion everywhere they looked. In 1822, South Carolina cracked down with vicious violence once they uncovered a plot by Denmark Vesey, a freed slave and minister, to lead a slave rebellion.. Even more terrifying to slave owners was Nat Turner's Rebellion in August 1831. Turner and a trusted group of fellow slaves began a war of extermination against whites. Armed with axes, knives, and blunt instruments, they went house to house in Southampton County, Virginia, killing between fifty-five and sixty-five whites. More slaves joined them and their force grew to forty. Although they moved swiftly and silently, the rebellion was suppressed within forty-eight hours. Turner eluded capture for over two months before he was found and executed in November. Fifty-six slaves were executed, while mobs murdered perhaps one hundred innocent slaves in an orgy of anti-black terrorism. Harriet Jacobs remembered the fear slaves in North Carolina felt in the aftermath, when white mobs entered their cabins and threatened their lives. Virginia and other states passed laws making it illegal for whites to teach blacks how to read, as Turner's apocalyptic visions based on the Bible represented a very real threat. Each of these moments of heroic resistance laid the groundwork for slaves' actions to free themselves during the Civil War.[14]

Rebellions dramatically demonstrate the power of collective action. Far more common were everyday acts of resistance. Slaves taught their children to never reveal their true selves to their owners, creating outer masks to contain their inner thoughts from their masters. They held on to African traditions and developed their own forms of religion in defiance of owners attempting to foist an approved form of Christianity upon them. They faked illness or broke farming equipment. Reading was resistance. They fought to keep what they saw as their customary rights. When a new overseer at Bowler Cocke's Virginia plantation tried to end the slaves' traditional five-day break at the end of 1769, the slaves beat him up and whipped him. This led to a localized rebellion that left two whites dead.[15] Domestic slaves dealt with the tyranny of slaveholding women, who might slap them or burn them with an iron. They resisted too, by laughing at their mistresses, slowing down the work, burning food, or otherwise infuriating their owners. These actions might not have led a rebellion, but they helped slaves retain their dignity.[16] Slaves also escaped. Usually these desperate actions consisted of fleeing to a forest or swamp and only lasted a few days before the hungry slaves returned. A few achieved permanent freedom. Slaves who lived on the border with the free states or near waterways had more opportunities. Slaves in Texas could get to Mexico. But if a slave lived on a cotton plantation in Alabama, the opportunities to run to freedom were few. The Underground Railroad helped a lucky few slaves escape, but most did not have that opportunity.

Sometimes, slaves killed their owners rather than subject themselves to mistreatment. In 1855, a nineteen-year-old slave in Missouri named Celia murdered her master rather than allow him to rape her. He had bought her in 1850 when she was fourteen. He first raped Celia before they returned to his plantation. She eventually had two children by him. Celia did everything she could to stop it. She asked his daughters to intervene. She pleaded with him. Nothing helped. One night, she smashed his head with a brick and burned his body. Her crime was discovered the next day and she was executed, after delivering her master's stillborn child.[17]

This was the "peculiar institution" southern whites committed treason against the United States to defend in 1861. After decades of expansionist policies that included stealing half of Mexico in the Mexican-American War, after demanding increased protection for their human property that included the Fugitive Slave Act of 1850 and the ability to take their slaves into free territories—the result of the Supreme Court's infamous *Dred Scott* decision—and after justifying these actions with an intellectual framework that declared slavery a "positive good" that created the ideal society, southern nationalists decided to leave the United States. What they did not anticipate is that their own slaves, who they sincerely believed were loyal to them, would destroy their way of life by walking off the plantations.[18]

The Slave Strike and the Civil War

On April 12, 1861, Confederate forces in South Carolina fired on American troops at Fort Sumter, off the coast of Charleston. The Civil War had begun. Eleven southern states made up the new Confederate States of America, a nation explicitly founded on slavery. Their documents of secession repeatedly stated the need to defend slavery. Abraham Lincoln believed that most southern whites were unionists at heart and that a moderate policy could entice them to rejoin the United States. He was wrong. The Republican Party was deeply divided over slavery in 1861; abolitionists urged immediate emancipation but conservatives feared the loss of the border states to the Confederacy. Lincoln took a moderate tone and delayed doing anything about slavery except reassuring border states he would not interfere with their human property.[19]

Southern whites had convinced themselves that their slaves were happy and content with their lives. The *New Orleans Crescent* wrote of the "absurdity of the assertion of a general stampede of our Negroes."[20] Other southern papers talked of how the loyal slaves would allow the whites to fight the war while keeping masters wealthy. When Confederate president Jefferson Davis left his Mississippi plantation to take office, his wife wrote that he "assembled his negroes and made them an affectionate farewell speech, to which they responded with expressions of devotion."[21]

Slaves proved their owners wrong. They started fleeing, showing up at Union lines almost immediately. A few generals quickly realized the military potential of the slaves. Some abolitionist generals used their power to end this national evil. General John C. Frémont, the Republican candidate for president in 1856, declared slaves free in Missouri. General David Hunter, working on the South Carolina coast, freed all the slaves who could make it to his lines and created the first black regiment of troops in U.S. history. Lincoln, fearful of the regiment's impact upon both slave-owning border states that remained in the Union and a northern population largely nervous about ending slavery, reversed both decisions.[22]

Slaves taking freedom into their own hands forced the issue. Eight slaves escaped and arrived at U.S. lines at Fort Monroe, at the very spot where the first slaves arrived in Virginia in 1619. The commanding officer, Benjamin Butler, immediately recognized the value of the slaves to his forces. Rather than free them and risk Lincoln's ire, he declared them contraband and, realizing that he could take the Confederacy's labor force, he put the escaped slaves to work in the fort. When slaves heard about this, more showed up. Lincoln appreciated Butler's justification: if the South considered slaves property, then taking property was acceptable by the standards of war. No racial radical, Butler even had his troops keep track of hours the contraband worked so their masters could be paid at the end of the war. Butler's actions outraged Confederates, who had the gall to demand the return of their escaped slaves by invoking the Fugitive Slave Act, even though they had renounced the United States. For slaves, who understood this was a war about slavery even if northern whites did not, working for the military furthered their freedom, even if Butler did not pay them. By June 1861, over five hundred slaves had fled to Fort Monroe. Other commanders began following Butler's lead. Slaves changed the national strategy over the relationship between slavery and the war.[23]

What the slaves had done is strike in the form of self-emancipation. When they fled to the Union army, the now ex-slaves undermined the Confederate war effort. The Confederate elite needed slaves to grow the cotton they hoped to sell to the British for weapons and other war material. When slaves refused, they freed themselves and withheld their labor from their oppressors. Even when they could not run away, with many of their masters away at war, slaves took more control over their lives and slowed or even stopped their work. Without their labor, the Confederate war effort melted.

To quote DuBois, "It was a general strike that involved directly in the end perhaps a half million people. They wanted to stop the economy of the plantation system, and to do that they left the plantations."[24] Whenever the Union troops arrived, slaves just left their plantations, as they had done when British forces gave them the opportunity in the American Revolution and War of 1812. South Carolina slave Robert Smalls used his knowledge of the Charleston waterways to commandeer a ship, pick up the families of himself and his crew, and sail the ship to the North.[25] Meanwhile, as the journalist Charles Carleton Coffin wrote, when the Union army began shelling the South Carolina Sea Islands, a planter ordered his overseer to round up the slaves to move them inland. But as soon as the slaves heard the shells, they fled into the woods and the overseer found "his drove of human cattle gone." The planter left without his human property.[26] Another planter lost seventy-five slaves in one night in March 1863.[27]

With many men away, slaves who did not have the opportunity to run took more control on the plantations. Virginia slave owners complained constantly about slaves slowing down in the tobacco fields after the war began.[28] The radical secessionist Edmund Ruffin was shocked when 70 percent of his slaves walked away from his Virginia plantations in 1862. He could not understand how there was "not an indication of disobedience or discontent" and then immediately nearly every male over the age of twelve disappeared. For someone such as Ruffin, who had convinced himself that his slaves were happy, the expression of slave self-emancipation was shocking.[29] One slave coachman, freed in 1862, went into his master's bedroom, dressed himself in the master's finest clothes, and walked out the door.[30] Slaves on one plantation sixty miles southwest of New Orleans simply announced that they would take Christmas off and erected wooden gallows to ensure the owner knew they were serious.[31]

Escaped slaves proved critical to the American war effort. Many of them went to work for the U.S. military. By cooking, digging latrines, and burying soldiers, they freed up the military to fight the war at the same time that Confederate plantations lost their labor force, leading to declines in cotton and food production. Even when they could not escape, they provided intelligence to Union troops, guiding them through swamps and informing them of the state of Confederate defenses. But they wanted more: the right to pick up a gun against their former masters. Immediately after the war commenced, Frederick Douglass and other abolitionists urged Lincoln to enlist black troops. In May 1861, Douglass wrote an editorial that argued that "carrying the war into Africa" was the ticket for victory over the Confederacy.[32] But Lincoln did not think blacks would make good soldiers and he continued to fear the impact on the slave-owning border states that had remained in the United States. Lincoln, a white man of his time, questioned whether whites and blacks could live together peacefully. Well into the war, he toyed with colonization schemes to send slaves back to Africa or to Central America, struggling to imagine a nation with a large free black population.[33]

Yet the bravery of the slaves pushed a reluctant Union toward abolition. By mid-1862, with pro-Union forces in control of the border states, Lincoln reconsidered his position on slavery and black troops, signing new laws that moved the nation toward ending slavery. Finally, on September 22, 1862, Lincoln announced the impending Emancipation Proclamation. This groundbreaking announcement freed all slaves in areas of rebellion beginning on January 1, 1863. Slaves could not have ended slavery without the help of the federal government, but without their own actions, it's highly unlikely the Lincoln administration would have issued the proclamation. It did not free any slaves in most, though not all, areas controlled by the United States. But if slavery was eliminated in Mississippi and South Carolina, it could not survive in Delaware and Kentucky. By 1864, slavery in the border states began to wane, and with the passage of the Thirteenth Amendment in 1865, slavery was legally dead, an amazing achievement.[34]

The Lincoln administration began to arm black soldiers in 1863. African Americans, both freedmen in the North and slaves who had recently freed themselves, rushed to join the military. Confederates were furious; Robert E. Lee called it a "savage and brutal policy."[35] Frederick Douglass traveled across the North to recruit black troops. Around two hundred thousand African Americans served in the Union military during the Civil War; around 81 percent of them originated from slave states, where they fought for their own freedom and that of their families, albeit always under white officers. Some were recruited from the northern free black population, including the Fifty-Fourth Massachusetts Volunteer Infantry Regiment, made famous by the film *Glory*. Confederates often executed black soldiers they took as prisoners of war, most notoriously at the Fort Pillow Massacre in Tennessee in 1864, when regiments commanded by Confederate general and future Ku Klux Klan founder Nathan Bedford Forrest murdered surrendering black troops in one of the war's worst atrocities.[36]

As the war reached its bloody conclusion, slaves became ever braver in demanding their freedom. One slave in Georgia shoved her mistress into a fire and fled to Union lines. A group of slaves near Pineville, South Carolina, started burning plantation homes to the ground. When Union troops arrived at the Cherry Grove Plantation in South Carolina in March 1865, the slaves urged them to burn it so their hated mistress could never return. Rice planter Charles Manigault wrote in outrage how his slave Peggy confiscated anything she could carry from the man who had stolen her labor for her entire life. Each of these individual actions undermined white morale in the South, with slave owners now worried as much about slave rebellions on the plantations as about declining fortunes in battles against Union armies.[37]

When William Tecumseh Sherman marched through Georgia in 1864, destroying the heart of the Confederacy, he knew slaves would follow his forces. They poured toward Sherman's lines. Sherman himself had little interest in black welfare; a racial conservative, he found his status among the slaves as a Moses bemusing. Some of his soldiers committed atrocities against the freed slaves. But wanting to crush the treason of the slaveholding South, Sherman sought to help the slaves, if for no other reason than to get them to stop following his army, which was slowing them down and forcing him to feed the slaves at the same time his own forces were foraging off the land. He met with black leaders on the South Carolina and Georgia coast and asked what they wanted. Their leader, a sixty-seven-year-old Baptist minister named Garrison Frazier, replied, "The way we can best take care of ourselves is to have land, and turn it and till it by our own labor."[38] So, on January 16, 1865, Sherman issued Special Field Order No. 15, which granted forty-acre plots of land to African Americans and the use of an army mule in the coastal areas of those states. The idea of forty acres and a mule became a powerful demand for freed slaves because it meant control over their labor, and their independence from whites.[39]

Slaves wanted their masters' lands confiscated and redistributed as subsistence plots. In March 1865, now freed slaves took over the Keithfield rice plantation in South Carolina. During the next year, 150 people worked it on their own. When the owner returned in early 1866, she asked her neighbor Francis Parker to help her recapture it. Parker had executed escaped slaves during the war. He hired a former slave driver named Dennis Hazel to be the new overseer. When the ex-slaves saw Parker and Hazel, they erupted in a bloody riot. Led by the plantation's women, they threatened to kill the interlopers. The freedpeople beat them with their working tools and then attacked a soldier accompanying them. A former slave named Becky hit Parker in the right eye with a club, causing blood to gush across his face. Finally, they dove into the river to escape. Former slaves would fight to the death to control their land and labor.[40]

But despite Sherman's plan, the U.S. military had already developed different ideas. On November 7, 1861, the U.S. Army occupied the South Carolina Sea Islands, rich cotton land laced with wealthy plantations that Confederate elites fled from because they could not be defended. Suddenly having to deal with the existence of thousands of slaves with no masters, the military engaged in what became known as the Port Royal Experiment. By January 1862, the government was working with the black population to grow cotton for the army for $1 for every four hundred pounds they harvested, and philanthropists had recruited northern teachers to come and work with the freedpeople. The army ended the slave system of gang labor, gave workers garden plots for themselves, and provided a variety of incentives for the workers. The freedpeople hoped to own their own land. But the U.S. Treasury officials running the revived plantations saw potential profit paying black workers low wages. In 1863, Lincoln instituted a plan to sell some abandoned Confederate lands in the Sea Islands. Although most of the ex-slaves could not afford the price of $1.25 per acre, they pooled resources to buy about two thousand acres of land. Northern whites also bought the land, creating new plantations for themselves worked by paid laborers. Other military leaders instituted similar labor regimes on land their forces occupied, such as General Benjamin Butler's use of paid black field hands to grow sugar. Yet northern whites who leased the plantations routinely stole African Americans' wages, an omen of the struggles the freed slaves would face after the Civil War ended.[41]

African Americans achieved their freedom because their actions forced the hands of the Lincoln government and the army. When their demands no longer coincided with the federal government's needs, could freedpeople control their own labor?

The Triumph of White Supremacy

The Confederacy finally surrendered in 1865, in no small part because so much of their labor force had walked away. The Thirteenth Amendment banned slavery. But what did freedom and slavery mean? Most southern *and* northern whites believed black laborers should toil on plantations for white landowners. The North needed cotton for its factories and to sell overseas to pay off war debts. The South wanted to force black laborers to provide that cotton in conditions as near to slavery as they could.

The period of Reconstruction, lasting from 1865 to 1877, would determine the fate of the emancipated slaves and the new labor system to replace slavery. When Abraham Lincoln was assassinated five days after the war ended by a southern sympathizer from Maryland, the Tennessean Andrew Johnson ascended to the Oval Office. A white supremacist replacing Lincoln is one of the greatest tragedies in American history. Johnson opposed the Confederacy, but he also fervently opposed black rights. This gave the former slaveholders the initiative to reestablish their control over their former laborers. Johnson reversed Sherman's Special Field Order No. 15—the promise of forty acres and a mule—and the army took back the land distributed to ex-slaves. On the plantations, former owners sought to either force workers back into total subservience, kick them out, or murder them. Ex-slave Henry Adams, remembering the postwar days near Shreveport, Louisiana, reported "over two thousand colored people killed trying to get away, after the white people told us we were free."[42] Calvin Holley, a black soldier serving in Mississippi, wrote, "Some are being knocked down for saying they are free, while a great many are being worked just as they ust to be when Slaves, without any compensation."[43]

The freed slaves had a very different idea about their life and labor in the postwar world. Thousands left the plantations for cities, including Atlanta, New Orleans, Memphis, and Richmond, where they found jobs and built free communities. By the 1890s, African Americans filled 90 percent of the unskilled positions in Birmingham's rapidly growing steel industry, but whites forced them into the most dangerous, toxic workplaces with high death rates.[44] That fact sums up much of postwar southern labor history.

On the plantations, ex-slaves resisted white attempts to force women and children to work in the fields, preferring that women avoid that hard labor and children go to school. They sought full autonomy over their labor, under no control from whites. They wanted land on the farms and they demanded good wages in the cities. Associating cotton with the detested slave labor, many fought to grow subsistence crops instead, even if they remained poor. In the countryside, as in the cities, they built schools and churches and fought for the vote.[45]

This infuriated the former slave owners. They demanded compliant black labor, and they used violence to ensure it. They instituted the Black Codes, laws re-creating slavery in all but name. Building upon the slave codes regulating black behavior before the war, blacks in rural areas had to labor for a white under one-year contracts. The Mississippi code used the category of "vagrancy" to control black workers. This was a term long used in the United States to crack down on workers, white or black, who did not have a job. In this case, it meant not working for a white person. A vagrant could be thrown into prison or rented out to work for free. Mississippi did not allow blacks to rent land for themselves, and black workers did not have the option to quit working. If a black worker did not work for a white, the state would contract that person out to a private landowner and receive a portion of their wages. If a black person could not pay high taxes levied on them by the state, they received a vagrancy charge and the same process resulted. As during slavery, any white person could legally arrest any black person. It was illegal for whites to assist a black person in an escape from their landowner. That provision also stated that blacks caught running away from their employer would lose their wages for the year. Children whose parents could not take care of them would be bonded to their former owners. Other forms of black behavior were also criminalized, such as preaching without a license or using "insulting" language toward whites. Interracial marriage, it almost goes without saying, was banned as well. Terrorist organizations such as the Ku Klux Klan, founded in 1865, formed to ensure black compliance with white demands.[46]

A disgusted Republican Congress quickly declared the Black Codes invalid and instituted the Freedmen's Bureau, a federal agency dedicated to untangling postwar southern race and labor relations. Its designers hoped to help freedpeople negotiate contracts with planters and to intervene in cases of violence against black workers. Ex-slaves saw the Freedmen's Bureau as their best hope for the government to enforce their labor rights. At times, it worked well, but it was always underfunded and often staffed by politically appointed agents more sympathetic to slaveholders than African Americans. Some bureau agents barred freed slaves from entering cities, requiring them to sign contracts to work on plantations. Ultimately, it had far too few agents to counter the violence faced by ex-slaves. Employers routinely broke contracts with freedmen if they registered to vote and tried to deny them their contractual compensation at the end of the harvest. It also made many northern conservatives uncomfortable because it set a precedent of government interference in labor relations. Congress slashed the bureau's funding in 1869 and killed it in 1872.[47]

The demise of the Freedmen's Bureau demonstrates the limited interest of most northern policymakers in helping blacks achieve economic self-sufficiency. A group of politicians and abolitionists known as the Radical Republicans wanted to expropriate planter land and distribute it to ex-slaves, but most Republicans disagreed. They valued the former slaveholders' private property over autonomy for black laborers. Northern banks had loaned millions to indebted planters and wanted repayment. Northerners wanted to apply their free labor ideology to the slaves, even though they lacked the capital or education to win equal rights on the job market. Colonel Orlando Brown made this clear to ex-slaves in his 1865 published address "To the Freedmen of Virginia," in which he told them: "You are to direct and receive the proceeds of your own labor and care for yourselves." Brown also instructed ex-slaves to save their wages and be frugal if they wanted to succeed.[48]

The ex-slaves largely ignored these "moral" lessons and continued to claim their own rights as they defined them. Black women hired as domestic servants, sometimes in the houses where they used to be slaves, quit over everything from low wages and bad working conditions to wanting to spend more time with their own families. Women working in laundries in Jackson, Mississippi, organized in 1866, presenting an open letter to the mayor that stated they would charge a uniform rate to everyone who hired them, taking the power to set wages into their own hands. These sorts of actions angered southern whites, who even appealed to the Freedmen's Bureau to try to keep black workers under control.[49] In Florida, black workers alternated between working on the railroad, in phosphate mines, and going to labor in Alabama coal mines, often leaving the cotton fields entirely. In response, white employers wanted to find more pliable workers, even considering schemes to import Chinese immigrants to work for next to nothing. By the late nineteenth century, the southern police state turned to convict labor to provide its black unpaid labor. In the late 1860s, Virginia convicted a young black man named John Henry of a minor theft and turned him over to a railroad to labor in tunnel building, where he would soon die of disease and become the subject of a legendary set of songs about a heroic black man laboring faster than a machine.[50]

Despite all of these barriers to true freedom, former slaves took command over their own lives in ways unthinkable before the war. Black Virginians acquired up to one hundred thousand acres of land by the early 1870s and perhaps 1 million acres by 1900.[51] But only about one hundred thousand of the 4 million former slaves managed to buy their own land. Many ended up sharecropping. White landowners rented land and supplies such as farm animals, plows, and seed to black workers in return for between 25 and 50 percent of the crop. Landowners routinely cheated often illiterate sharecroppers out of their crop, forced them into debt, and those who complained were forced off the land, beaten, or lynched. Generation after generation remained in dire poverty. Yet sharecropping was also a compromise that reinforced a limited freedom. White landowners wanted to replicate slavery after the war. That meant keeping black labor under watch from the plantation house. But African Americans refused to live under white eyes and built houses scattered around the old plantation. They would not work under the gang labor system of slavery. They demanded access to their own plot of land—even if they could not own it, they would rent it and work it on their own. Whites had little choice but to acquiesce to these demands and find new ways to cheat black workers.[52]

Sharecropping was not slavery, but it was pretty horrible. Whites, both northern and southern, deserve the blame for suppressing black economic equality. For northerners, ending slavery opened the South for greater economic growth on northern terms, but black demands remained secondary to economic development. Northerners thought black laborers' place in the new economy was producing cotton for New England textile factories, not food for their own tables. In the immediate aftermath of the Civil War, many Republicans moved to supporting black rights, but this faded by the early 1870s as economic questions took greater precedent over race in northern politics. When southern whites violently retook control over blacks in the 1870s, northern Republicans, politically weakened by economic troubles, let them do so. Reconstruction ended with a whimper in 1877, as Republicans pulled all troops out of the South in exchange for their presidential candidate Rutherford B. Hayes taking the Oval Office after a contested election.

The end of Reconstruction did not mean the end of black workers taking their destiny into their own hands. They continued to press for political and labor rights. They tried forming unions, whether among Richmond dock workers, Alabama farmers, or factory workers anywhere they found a job. They organized in the Colored National Labor Union, a short-lived union of black industrial workers of the early 1870s. But with no interest from northern whites in protecting black workers, the white South, now controlling politics with violence, crushed black labor movements. The rise of Jim Crow would lock African Americans out of legal rights in the South, and black expressions of power would be met with brutality. In 1887, a group of white vigilantes violently suppressed a strike of black sugar workers in the fields around Thibodaux, Louisiana. The black sugar workers made 60 to 65¢ a day, paid in company scrip instead of cash to keep them dependent on their white employers. But they had never accepted white attempts to re-create dependence, and they had protested every year since 1880. In 1887, the workers issued a list of demands that included a raise to $1.25 a day, biweekly payments, and cash pay instead of the company store scrip. Former slave Junius Bailey sent a letter to the sugar planters that read, "Should this demand be considered exorbitant by the sugar planters . . . we ask them to submit such information with reason therewith to this board not later than Saturday, Oct. 29 inst. or appoint a special committee to confer with this board on said date." The sheer existence of such demands and such a letter infuriated the white elite, who still considered slavery the rightful status of black labor. Up to ten thousand workers went on strike.[53]

Mary Pugh, owner of the Live Oak Plantation, said that unless this strike was repressed, "white people could live in this country no longer." On November 22, the white Peace and Order Committee closed the roads into Thibodaux and decided to deal with the strikers as violently as possible. That morning, the state militia walked into town and started killing black people at random. The militia went house to house, executing them in cold blood. Black workers fled the city and the strike was suppressed. At least thirty-five were killed. But some have estimated that number could be as high as three hundred. The editor of the *Thibodaux Star*, who had been a member of the murderous militia, wrote of "negroes jumping over fences and making for the swamps at double quick time. . . . We'll bet five cents that our people never before saw so large a black-burying as they have seen this week." Mary Pugh wrote, "I think this will settle the question of who is to rule[,] the nigger or the white man? For the next 50 years but it has been well done & I hope all trouble is ended."[54]

The racial dispossession and oppression that drove people into deep poverty during the late nineteenth century was not limited to African Americans either. Native Americans, driven off their land and conquered by the United States in genocidal wars that culminated on the Great Plains in the 1870s and 1880s, faced continued attacks on their own ways of work. The erasure of wildlife such as the bison forced them into dependence on the United States. With white Americans seeing native peoples as lazy and undeserving of help, they were driven to desperation. Even after the conquering of their land, whites used the Dawes Act of 1887 to dispossess them of their reservation land. Granting individual people only 160 acres of land and then selling the rest to white settlers undermined what was left of their traditional economies. They still labored—making baskets for tourists, working as agricultural laborers, or serving the needs of local white residents—but within a racial caste system that doomed them to endemic poverty, and which still plagues the tribes today.[55]

Black labor and political organizing challenged white supremacy, and violence was the result. Black workers would not achieve true freedom in the United States after the Civil War, and they never have, still facing poverty, doomed to low-wage jobs and high levels of unemployment, and, in many states, struggling against political restrictions on black voting put in place by a new generation of racist Republican legislators. This is all a legacy of slavery and the racism at its base. And yet, the slaves' general strike transformed the United States, perhaps more than any other labor action in American history. It ended the nation's original sin—slavery. It challenged racism and it showed what workers can do by withholding their labor from their employer. The black struggle for economic, political, and social equality has remained a central part of the larger struggle for worker rights throughout American history, and it must remain so today if economic and racial justice will ever be achieved.

3

The Eight-Hour-Day Strikes

Industrial capitalism betrayed American workers.

The Civil War changed the course of American history. Beyond ending slavery, the single most revolutionary movement in all of American history, it also led to unprecedented growth in the size of the government; the first federal income tax; the creation of land-grant colleges; unprecedented laws to spur national development, including the Homestead Act and the Pacific Railway Act, which led to the transcontinental railroad; and the development of military tactics used after the war to defeat Native American tribes in genocidal campaigns.[1] The Civil War also radically transformed the American economy, setting in motion the Gilded Age, the name Mark Twain gave to a society plagued by rampant corruption, enormous income inequality, and monopoly capitalism.

Gilded Age profits came on the backs of working Americans, many of whom were Civil War veterans who believed strongly in free labor. They believed capitalism should work for them. They felt their hard work would create a nation of relative equality among independent white men based around economic and political independence from masters of any type. But the new industrial capitalism made a few millionaires the new masters, and white workers compared themselves to slaves because their free labor ideology had proven false. Worker resistance in this period dealt with figuring out how to deal with the betrayal of this free labor ideology. As late as 1900, many believed capitalism was a just system if they could fix what allowed the monopolists to dominate their lives. Workers thought if they could fix one thing—whether eliminating Chinese immigration, creating a cooperative economy, or taxing property—free labor could be salvaged and the nation would get on the right track.

The most successful of the responses to industrial capitalism was the struggle for the eight-hour day. To achieve this, workers joined the nation's first big union, the Knights of Labor, culminating in the strikes of 1886. These strikes came to a violent conclusion at Haymarket Square in Chicago, when an anarchist threw a bomb at the police during a march against the police murder of three strikers. The state arrested the city's leading anarchists, then convicted them of murder without evidence and executed their leaders. The bombing turned public opinion against the Knights of Labor, and employer opposition to negotiating with the union led to defeated strikes and declining membership. The government's role in crushing radicalism and employer schemes to keep their workplaces union-free meant that successfully organizing the masses of American workers would remain an uphill battle, as it continues to be today. A more limited unionism developed in the wake of Haymarket, one that largely accepted the new economic system and asked far less of employers, creating a legacy of moderate unionism that has dominated American workplace organizing to the present. That unionism both acquiesces to the political limitations of radical change in the United States and has held back the American working class's ability to control its own destiny.

The Gilded Age

The roots of the corruption that dominated post–Civil War America went back to years before the war, when powerful people began to realize they could get rich off the changes transforming the nation. During the war, the government worked closely with financiers like Jay Cooke to sell war bonds—associating with men who equated self-interest with patriotism and who after the war would engage in dangerous financial speculation that routinely sabotaged the American economy. The wartime economy launched the careers of men such as John D. Rockefeller, who ran a profitable Cleveland shipping business, invested in refineries for Pennsylvania oil, and became the richest man the nation had ever seen, controlling more than 90 percent of the nation's oil supply in the late nineteenth century.[2]

These capitalists made their fortunes on the backs of workers suffering through increasingly brutish and nasty lives. By 1900, New York had 3 million people and Chicago more than 1.5 million, a population that had tripled since 1880 and made that city the Midwest's great metropolis. These cities teemed with immigrants from eastern and southern Europe crammed into substandard housing, desperate to find a better life for themselves than the poverty and religious persecution they faced at home. They provided a huge mass of cheap labor that capitalists could use in the increasingly large factories, some of which, such as Andrew Carnegie's mill in Homestead, Pennsylvania, employed up to ten thousand people. Workers died by the hundreds in mine accidents, by the dozens in factory fires, and one at a time in meatpacking plants and sawmills. The smoke and fumes of the factories choked workers' lungs and poisoned their bodies. For some women, prostitution paid far more than the factories. This was the world in which swelling numbers of workers found themselves by the 1880s. It was not the America they wanted.[3]

Gilded Age capitalists and their allies in the media and in government cared little what workers, immigrant or native-born, thought about the new society. Newspapers and politicians claimed each new strike was the arrival of a dangerous revolutionary movement. Abolitionists turned against organized white labor with a fury when factory workers called themselves slaves, comparing their increasingly desperate lives to those of the recently freed African Americans. Social Darwinist writers took Charles Darwin's theory of evolution and applied it to human relations. Calling corporate behavior the "survival of the fittest" provided an intellectual justification for exploitation. Many native-born Americans assumed that Jews, Italians, Chinese, Mexicans, and African Americans filled a natural place lower on the economic scale as appropriate to their race. Writers and speakers such as Horatio Alger and Russell Herman Conwell portrayed an America where to work hard was a moral calling that ignored or downplayed the brutality of workers' lives.[4]

The Civil War also brought an unprecedented period of corruption to American life. The role of shady financiers and politicians on the take grew rapidly. Much of this centered around the railroads. In 1872, the greatest political scandal in American history to that time shook the administration of Ulysses S. Grant. Major stockholders in the Union Pacific Railroad created a sham company called Crédit Mobilier of America, gave it contracts to build the railroad, and then personally profited from those contracts. They used stock in the company to pay off their allied politicians, which included Grant's vice president Schuyler Colfax and future president James Garfield. It was open fraud, and such theft was the order of the day in both national and state legislatures. Politicians were for the rich to buy.[5]

Workers resented this corruption and blamed the railroads for the increased inequality they faced. They had good reason to do so. In building the Northern Pacific Railway, the financier Jay Cooke overextended himself. When Cooke's company declared bankruptcy in 1873, it started a downward spiral that sent the economy into a severe depression. Eighteen thousand businesses went under during the Panic of 1873 and unemployment reached 14 percent.[6] Workers responded by taking to the streets to demand jobs, especially in New York, where unemployment reached 25 percent. Tompkins Square Park became the center of organizing, with over one thousand workers attending rallies there. Peter J. McGuire, later the longtime president of the United Brotherhood of Carpenters and Joiners of America, led this movement. He called for a mass demonstration on January 13, urging the city to quit evicting unemployed tenants and instead to provide public aid.

Newspaper editors and capitalists exploded in indignation over class-based organizing. Calling the demonstration the American version of the Paris Commune, the 1871 socialist uprising in France that briefly ruled Paris before its brutal suppression, the capitalists demanded police repression of the workers. On the day of the demonstration, over eight thousand workers met at Tompkins Square Park. Sixteen hundred police officers attacked them, savagely beating the protestors with clubs while horse-mounted police cleared the streets. Samuel Gompers remembered, "Mounted police charged the crowd on Eighth Street, riding them down and attacking men, women, and children without discrimination. It was an orgy of brutality. I was caught in the crowd on the street and barely saved my head from being cracked by jumping down a cellarway."[7] The police arrested forty-six workers, mostly unemployed immigrants who could not afford bail, and the movement died under the weight of oppression.[8]

Violent suppression of workers became employers' preferred response to organizing. When workers such as the Molly Maguires—an Irish secret society that migrated with immigrants to Pennsylvania—committed violence themselves, state violence was even starker. After the Civil War, membership in the Mollies increased in response to the terrible labor conditions they faced in the mines of northeastern Pennsylvania. A union formed in the area called the Workingmen's Benevolent Association (WBA). Probably 85 percent of the workforce joined the union by the mid-1870s. The WBA had some initial success, and wages increased. Franklin Gowen, president of the Reading Railroad, responded by hiring Allan Pinkerton to crack down on the union and the Mollies. The Pinkerton National Detective Agency was one of several private strikebreaking and security firms that served employers in the Gilded Age.[9] To this day, the term *Pinkerton* is synonymous with violent strikebreaking. In December 1874, Gowen announced a 20 percent pay cut, knowing the union would strike. He fed newspapers invented stories about Mollie violence and Pinkertons killed several strikers and their families. The strike and the WBA collapsed after six months, with arrests of the strike leaders. But the Mollies took the fight underground and killed two police officers they particularly hated. In addition, a mine boss, bartender, and justice of the peace all died, possibly killed by Mollies, although the facts of these cases are unclear. The police conducted mass arrests. Gowen named himself special prosecutor for the trial, a complete farce of justice. Twenty men were given death sentences. Ten were executed on Black Thursday, June 21, 1877. An additional ten were executed over the next year. The Molly Maguires became synonymous with violent unionism and were used to gin up anti-unionism for decades.[10]

The sudden worker uprising of 1877 was more widespread and

caused more hysteria among the nation's elites. It began in Martinsburg, West Virginia, when the Baltimore and Ohio Railroad forced its workers to accept their second pay cut in a year. Workers walked out, stating that they would have to "steal or starve."[11] Rail workers had a lot of power, because if they refused to allow trains to move, they could shut down the nation's transportation network and thus halt business. The strike spread quickly across the nation. Within days, one hundred thousand workers were on strike from Iowa to New York to Texas, many unemployed working on the picket line in support. In most places rail workers were outnumbered by citizen protestors who were angry at how railroads ran them down when crossing through cities, polluted their neighborhoods, corrupted their politics, controlled the prices of goods, and made their homes filthy, sooty, and noisy.

The Great Railroad Strike lasted six weeks. It was the first mass action of industrial workers in American history. Workers completely unrelated to the railroad were inspired to take action on their own, such as the New York cigar makers who walked out and won wage increases.[12] Newspapers called the strikers "communists" and warned of revolution. Thomas Alexander Scott, president of the Pennsylvania Railroad, said that strikers should receive "a rifle diet for a few days and see how they like that kind of bread."[13] He got his wish in Pittsburgh on July 21, when militiamen fired on strikers, killing twenty. In response, workers burned thirty-nine buildings and more than fourteen hundred railcars. The next day, the militia struck again, killing another twenty workers. In Reading, Pennsylvania, state troopers killed twelve people. In Chicago, approximately twenty died after the mayor called for a volunteer militia to crush the strike. In Baltimore, the railroad and state authorities filled the city's streets with hundreds of soldiers. When protestors started throwing stones, the soldiers opened fire and nearly a dozen people died, all everyday citizens who came out to protest the impact of the railroads on their lives. Over one hundred people died from the railroads suppressing the protests.

The federal government also decisively stepped in on the side of the railroads, setting a strong precedent for the law to tip the balance of power away from workers and toward companies, a theme that runs through most, but not all, of American history. Judge Thomas Drummond of the United States Court of Appeals for the

Seventh Circuit ordered federal marshals to protect the railroads, writing, "A strike or other unlawful interference with the trains will be a violation of the United States law, and the court will be bound to take notice of it and enforce the penalty."[14] Finally, President Rutherford B. Hayes called on the U.S. military to end the strike, setting another precedent: that the federal government would openly side with corporations over workers, no matter how legitimate their grievances. This was the first time the U.S. government had directly backed management's position with troops. In the aftermath, hundreds of workers were fired for union activities and blacklisted from the railroads.[15]

The strikers of 1877 did not want a revolution. They wanted a return to a free labor society that respected the nobility of toil—a nation of smallholders and entrepreneurs. Many of these workers were Civil War veterans. They saw low wages, brutal working conditions, and employer violence and compared themselves to the slaves the Union had recently freed. The state and employers had placed chains around these white men who believed they were the legitimate heirs of the American Revolution. The comparison between wage labor and slavery went back to the radical writer Thomas Skidmore, whose 1829 pamphlet *The Rights of Man to Property!* called for the confiscation of all property and its redistribution to the people. Skidmore died in 1832, but after the Civil War, growing numbers of workers came around to believing that something was wrong with capitalism. They believed it was fundamentally a good system, but something had gone wrong and a few men had too much money and power.[16]

Finding a solution to this spawned a wide array of ideas. Joseph Ray Buchanan, Denver's most prominent labor activist, would later write that in the early 1880s he "had been reading everything dealing with social conditions that I could get hold of. I had devoured the writings of the leading political economists and had formed opinions of a just and equitable social and industrial system."[17] Buchanan and other activists and publishers would disperse these ideas to thousands of readers, creating a national debate about how to fix the problems of workers.

One of the most prominent solutions came from Henry George's 1879 book *Progress and Poverty*, in which he argued for a "single tax" upon property as the surest way to bring corporations under control. He believed people earned the value of their own labor, but land was a common resource for all and thus large landowners should have to pay very high taxes to reduce the era's inequality. George ran for mayor of New York City on a single tax platform in 1886. He came in second in a three-man race. The Republican candidate, Theodore Roosevelt, came in third. The simplicity of George's idea appealed to Americans who still believed that they could avoid class conflict. Others followed the ideas of Edward Bellamy, who in 1888 published *Looking Backward: 2000–1887*, a novel detailing how a visitor from 1887 wakes up in 2000 and finds all the problems of the Gilded Age solved through a peaceful revolution that replaced competitive capitalism with a cooperative society. Reading and discussion groups known as Bellamy societies popped up around the country to implement his ideas. By 1891, the book had sold nearly half a million copies, making it the biggest bestseller of its era. Other Americans, especially in rural areas, thought the ticket to fixing the corruption and greed of America was to get rid of the gold standard and instead issue paper currency based on credit. "Greenbackers," as they were called, hoped that expanding the currency away from gold-backed money would increase inflation and give workers and farmers the ability to pay off their debts, taking power away from the corporations that controlled the economy.[18]

These responses were productive. Far less so was the white working class demonizing nonwhite workers and constructing a white identity that excluded other workers, whether black, Irish, or Chinese.[19] These workers believed that immigrants and people of color undermined white workers' wages and that eliminating the competition would reset the system to work for them. Racial divisions have long plagued working-class solidarity in the United States, and continue to do so today. By the 1870s, this led to both racial violence and the opportunity for employers to break unions by importing groups of workers that strikers hated.[20] When white Americans arrived in California to mine gold in 1849, they found Chinese and Mexican miners already there. Whites seized the mines. The Chinese then filled service jobs for whites in laundries and restaurants and worked brutal jobs building the railroads under near-slave conditions. San Francisco workers responded to the 1877 railroad strikes by forming mobs not against railroad companies but against Chinese workers.[21] The Workingmen's

Party of California adopted the banning of Chinese immigration as its sole issue. Congress responded by passing the Chinese Exclusion Act in 1882, the first law barring immigration to the United States based on national origin. A law enshrining racism was the American labor movement's first major legislative victory. Violence continued against Chinese workers through the rest of the century, most notoriously in Rock Springs, Wyoming, in 1885, when a rampaging mob of whites committed an act of ethnic cleansing by murdering at least twenty-eight Chinese miners.[22] In later years, whites in the American West would continue lobbying to eliminate unwanted foreign labor, such as by pressuring the federal government to stop Japanese immigration. They succeeded in 1907, undermining the cross-racial organizing of such organizations as the Japanese-Mexican Labor Association, a pioneering farmworker organization that California's white-dominated labor movement rejected because it refused to accept Asian Americans.[23] Whether through getting rid of the Chinese or embracing Edward Bellamy's ideas or implementing the single tax, most working Americans in the 1880s still fundamentally believed the capitalist system could be tweaked and fixed.

However, a few native-born Americans, and a lot more German immigrants, began rejecting capitalism entirely and developing ideas around socialism and anarchism to replace a system that so exploited workers. The writings of Karl Marx were the most important influence, but he was far from the only important theorist. Anarchist thinkers such as Johann Most and Mikhail Bakunin also gained large followings. Many German socialists fled to the United States to escape political repression after 1870; Jewish radicals from Russia would do the same a decade later. Native-born socialists such as Peter J. McGuire traveled the nation speaking about a cooperative society in which workers received the benefits from their own labor. These new socialists would split into innumerable factions, argue about the use of violence versus nonviolence, denounce each other for believing in the political system or refusing to support socialist political candidates, and debate obscure theoretical points. They never united into one cause, but they would influence generations of activists and also reshape the course of the strikes to come.[24]

The 1886 Strike Wave

The one issue that united most reformers of capitalism was the eight-hour day. The National Labor Union's brief rise in the 1860s had placed the eight-hour day on the national agenda. In the 1880s, workers built an organization to promote this desperately desired shorter workday. Founded in 1869 by four Philadelphia garment cutters as a secret society to remake the labor movement, the Knights of Labor began its rise to prominence in 1879, when Terence Powderly, the mayor of Scranton, Pennsylvania, became its leader.[25] He turned the Knights into an organization that fought for the economic rights of the white workingman. Powderly was a superb organizer, and he began uniting the nation's workers around the eight-hour day. Like other reform organizations, the Knights believed in a natural balance of power between employer and employee, but recognized that the massive aggregation of capital into the hands of the few had thrown this out of whack. Workers had become wage slaves to corporate masters. The Knights used the language of war but the strategy of peace. The Knights' manifesto claimed an "inevitable and irresistible conflict between the wage system of labor and the republican system of government."[26] Yet at the same time, Powderly and other leading Knights believed that peaceful arbitration, not striking, was the best method for solving labor disputes. Seeing the organization as representing the interests of most Americans, the Knights invited all "producers" into their fold, which meant everyone except bankers, speculators, lawyers, liquor dealers, and gamblers; that is, groups it considered leeching off productive workers. It believed that through reform, it could re-create the democratic smallholder republic of pre–Civil War America.[27]

For a period when whites were establishing legal segregation and mobs frequently tortured and killed African Americans, the Knights had a remarkably inclusive attitude toward black workers, attempting to build alliances for mutual benefit, even in the South. In Richmond, Virginia, African American workers flocked to the Knights by 1884, with black workers organizing several assemblies. The Knights, careful to walk America's race line so as not to alienate white workers, created segregated assemblies that allowed for labor solidarity without racial mixing. Black workers used the Knights to build racial pride and to fight the growing system of segregation, and blacks and whites worked together in ways almost unheard of during this deeply racist period, for instance both gaining wage increases through simultaneous quarry worker strikes in Richmond.[28] Its Alabama chapter urged white workers to "set aside all prejudices against the colored laborer," and in some southern areas, up to half of Knights membership was African American.[29] Sometimes, white and black workers struck together, such as in a January 1887 strike in Pensacola, Florida, in which black and white longshoremen walked to support a strike of black fertilizer workers.[30] Like most workingmen, the Knights opposed women working outside the home. Their idealized society had women in the home, no longer needing to toil for wages, which also delegitimized all the women in the workforce as having a voice in union politics. By 1887, about 10 percent of Knights members were women and about 10 percent were African American.[31]

Still, the Knights' coalitions with black workers were tenuous, strained, and often temporary. Moreover, Knights wanted the Chinese expelled from the nation, and they also strongly doubted Polish, Hungarian, and Italian immigrants' ability to be good Americans. They believed black workers had the capacity for republican self-government because of their long period in the United States and thus could be allies, if not racial equals, but these immigrants could not be part of the Knights' idealized America because they lacked the capacity for republicanism.[32]

The fight for the eight-hour day was a fight for workers to take control of their own lives. The Knights adopted the great line from I.G. Blanchard and Reverend Jesse H. Jones's popular song "Eight Hours" as its own: "Eight hours for work, eight hours for sleep, eight hours for what we will."[33] Workers routinely labored ten, twelve, fourteen hours in the Gilded Age. Steelworkers had to work a twenty-four-hour shift twice a month in an extraordinarily deadly workplace with no safety protections. In 1867, the Illinois legislature passed an eight-hour law, but business ignored it; workers struck and lost. The federal government passed a limited eight-hour-day law for a few workers in 1868; again, it lacked enforcement. In 1872, nearly one hundred thousand workers in New York City struck for nearly two months to demand that the state enforce its recently passed eight-hour law.[34] An 1880 survey of New England textile and paper mill workers demonstrated that most workers wanted to use their leisure time, often quite a bit less than eight hours, to just live—visit family, take a walk, go outside, do whatever they wanted.[35] Eight-Hour Leagues sprung up across the nation, and workers joined the Knights of Labor and other labor organizations in the 1880s to fight for the eight-hour day.

Powderly's leadership created a mechanism for workers to find the Knights appealing. But being open to nearly everyone meant that people joined who did not understand the Knights. The open nature of the union laid the groundwork for its demise. The organization was extremely loose, and Powderly had no real control over what individual lodges did. Powderly and the Knights' leadership believed that peaceful action could transform the nation back to its rightful small-producer orientation. They ran candidates for office and wanted labor conflicts settled with arbitration, hoping to avoid strikes.[36] Even these moderate positions alarmed the nation's elites. The *New York Sun* opined that the Knights could "array labor against capital, putting labor on the offensive or the defensive, for quiet and stubborn self protection, or for angry, organized assault, as they will."[37]

The great strike year of 1886 began on the western railroads of the rapacious investment capitalist and railroad magnate Jay Gould. Gould had already earned a reputation as an enemy of everyday people, and he was portrayed in the popular media as a near monster who destroyed honest men on Wall Street. His control over the railroads made him a popular target. In 1885, railroad workers on the Missouri Pacific struck after he cut their wages. Powderly helped settle the strike, and workers won a settlement that included rehiring strikers and paying back wages. This victory gave the Knights legitimacy as an effective union, and hundreds of thousands of workers joined over the next few months. In the next year, membership grew from 110,000 to 700,000 members, or so the Knights claimed. Overnight, the Knights became the first mass organization in American workers' history. The strike worked, but Powderly's discomfort with direct action remained.[38]

Gould had the money to play the long game against the Knights. In Marshall, Texas, a Knights member working for a Gould railroad was fired for attending a union meeting on work time. His fellow workers walked off the job to demand his rehiring, as well as more pay. The strike spread among workers infuriated with Gould over the terrible wages, long hours, and dangerous working conditions they endured. Starting in Texas and moving into Arkansas, Kansas, Missouri, and Illinois, upwards of two hundred thousand workers walked off the job, making the Great Southwest Railroad Strike the largest of the nation's fourteen hundred strikes in 1886.[39]

The strike showed the great militancy of workers in 1886 but also exposed the Knights' problems. First, other rail unions, such as the Brotherhood of Locomotive Engineers, refused to recognize the strike and continued to work. Battles between unions often hurt strikers as much as battles with employers or the state. Solidarity between different sections of the working class is a great goal but incredibly hard to achieve, then and now. Second, Terence Powderly still resisted mass strikes. He wanted to quickly settle it with Gould. But the plutocrat refused, sensing his opportunity to sweep organized labor from his railroads. Perhaps apocryphally, he said about the strikers, "I can hire one half of the working class to kill the other half."[40] Like the rail barons in 1877, Gould could rely on corporate-friendly politicians to crush the strike. The governor of Missouri called out the state militia, and the governor of Texas by mobilized the Texas Rangers. U.S. Marshals assisted these forces. Gould also hired the Pinkertons. At least nine workers died in shootouts between workers and trains running through the strikers. Gould's violence forced workers back on the job. The media helped, painting the strike as the ultimate battle between capital and labor, raising the stakes for an already nervous public. The strike died at the beginning of May, at the moment the membership of the Knights crested.[41]

The Knights' growth and the eight-hour day's appeal brought a huge diversity of workers into the organization. Some did not believe in the Knights' principles at all. Some were anarchists, who rejected the power of the state entirely and argued for the use of violence in fomenting revolution. Among them was Albert Parsons. Born in Alabama, Parsons grew up in frontier Texas in the 1850s. Although he volunteered for the Confederacy, Parsons later repudiated his past and supported black rights. He married a former slave named Lucy Gonzalez (as Lucy Parsons, she would have a long radical career on her own that extended into the 1930s), and they left Texas for Chicago to protect themselves from intolerance to their political beliefs and their interracial marriage. Parsons first became a socialist newspaper editor and later immersed himself in anarchism, beginning an anarchist newspaper in support of the eight-hour day in 1884.[42] By this time, many anarchists argued for the "propaganda of the deed." Johann Most promulgated this idea in his visits to Chicago, arguing that anarchist violence against class war enemies would convince workers to revolt, even if innocents died in the process. In 1885, Most published a pamphlet titled *Revolutionary War Science*, which was a manual on how to make explosives and use them to promote revolution.[43]

Parsons played a key role making Chicago the center of the eight-hour movement, giving radical talks around the city. The Knights, uncomfortable with this radicalism and the potential for violence that the anarchists embraced, kept their distance from the growing protests in that city. Terence Powderly began to speak against anarchists within the Knights and urged members to stay away from the planned May 1, 1886, protests. But on that date, between 300,000 and 500,000 workers walked off the job around the nation to fight for the eight-hour day. At least 30,000 of those workers were in Chicago, where strikes had increased from an average of thirty-five per year between 1881 and 1885 to 307 in 1886.[44] Prominent Chicago anarchists such as Parsons and August Spies worked within the Knights because they wanted to be connected to a real workers' movement. They also set much of the local agenda, including demanding their hours be reduced from ten to eight with no reduction in pay.[45]

This was a tenuous time for the Knights. Just as the Chicago protests peaked, word came that Gould had won the railroad strike, a major blow to labor's morale. One major Chicago factory did not close during the eight-hour strikes—the McCormick Reaper Works, one of the city's largest employers, continued to run, with police-guarded strikebreakers. Its workers had fought for justice for a year, after its head, Cyrus McCormick Jr., instituted a 10 percent wage cut at the same time the company earned record profits. He fired angry workers and brought the Pinkertons in to protect nonunion iron molders. This infuriated the largely Irish workforce, who assaulted a trolley of Pinkertons. The rest of the business community convinced McCormick to reinstate the wages to forestall a larger strike throughout the city. The war continued inside the factory, with McCormick firing union activists, but unionists were able to organize most of the workforce into the Knights of Labor by February 1886. Tensions continued to heighten as May approached. The police responded with what had become predictable violence. As August Spies gave a speech in front of the McCormick plant on May 3, some of the strikers began to confront strikebreakers as the workday ended. The police responded by brutally attacking the strikers with both clubs and guns. As the workers ran away, the police shot them. As many as six workers died that day.[46]

Responding to the murders, Spies and the other anarchist leaders called a march to protest police violence the next day at Haymarket Square. About fifteen hundred people attended, not a particularly large rally compared to many eight-hour strikes. The language was angry, but the rally was initially peaceful. Albert Parsons gave an hour-long speech, and by the time he finished, only around five hundred people remained. As Samuel Fielden closed the rally with one last speech, the police marched into the square to end it by force. At that moment, someone threw a bomb into a crowd of police officers. The police responded by firing into the marchers, killing a disputed number, probably between four and eight, and causing most of their own seven casualties. About fifty people were wounded.[47]

The media reacted with antiradical hysteria. The *Chicago Tribune* called to bar any "foreign savages who might come to America with their dynamite bombs and anarchic purposes."[48] Unsure who actually threw the bomb but assuming it was a conspiracy, authorities tried eight of Chicago's leading anarchists for the murders. That included Albert Parsons and August Spies, both of whom definitely did not throw the bomb. Parsons was actually in a nearby bar drinking a beer after his speech. Louis Lingg openly admitted making bombs but said he would have admitted it had he thrown it.[49] Parsons argued that someone working for the corporations threw the bomb to provide an excuse for police violence and repression.[50] The most likely candidate was anarchist named Rudolph Schnaubelt, who fled the nation immediately after the killings and perhaps lived the rest of his life in Argentina. Yet no one knew for sure. Despite the lack of evidence, seven of the defendants were sentenced to death and another, Oscar Neebe, was sentenced to fifteen years in prison for conspiracy to commit murder. Two of the defendants, Samuel Fielden and Michael

Schwab, would later have their sentences commuted to life in prison. Lingg committed suicide the day before his execution, while Parsons, Spies, Adolph Fischer, and George Engel were hanged on November 11, 1887. The hangings did not break their necks and they were left to strangle to death over the next several minutes.[51] When Illinois governor John Altgeld, elected as a reformer, freed the three remaining prisoners in 1893, the backlash from conservatives destroyed his political career.

Haymarket did not immediately end the eight-hour movement in Chicago, but by May 15, the strikes had ended and workers returned to their jobs without a victory. Haymarket and the failed eight-hour strikes brought the ascendancy of the Knights of Labor to a screeching halt. Powderly immediately denounced the anarchists. Some workers were horrified by the violence, others disgusted that Powderly did not denounce the trial of the radicals. At the same time, employers began conspiring to resist the Knights everywhere they operated. This was not a new phenomenon. As early as the Civil War, employers had begun to form trade groups to ensure that workers would not unionize, blacklisting strikers and forcing workers to sign "yellow-dog contracts" that forbade union membership.[52]

In 1887, Newark, New Jersey, leathermakers destroyed the Knights membership in their factories through locking out workers until they left the union. As the Knights did not charge high union dues, it had no money to give to the workers, leaving them impoverished and desperate. In the face of overwhelming employer opposition, this once-strong center of Knights membership collapsed within three weeks of the lockout. As the leather employers demonstrated, American employers organized a much more effective, coordinated, and well-funded anti-union strategy than employers in Britain or France, and thus unions succeeded more in those nations.[53] This helped set the precedent of the United States as a nation where employers would never accept unions and made unionization extremely difficult for workers to accomplish—a situation that still affects American workers today. Knights' membership in Chicago rapidly fell from 400,000 to 17,000 after Haymarket. Nationwide, an organization that had 750,000 members in 1886 plummeted to 80,000 by 1893.[54] But workers continued to seek any organization that would help them lead dignified lives and fight the inequalities of the Gilded Age.

The Gilded Age's War on Workers

The same year that the Knights began its decline, a more conservative union federation began. The American Federation of Labor, led by Samuel Gompers, an immigrant cigar maker, offered a very different model of unionism. It concentrated on what Gompers called "pure and simple unionism," focusing on skilled white male workers who organized to promote better wages, shorter hours, and more control over working conditions, without trying to transform society or get involved in politics. Negotiating a union contract was the goal, not challenging capitalism. Gompers eschewed federal involvement in labor issues, such as laws to protect workers, because the courts could overturn the laws or the government would not enforce them. Only a union contract would ensure worker power. The AFL was a collection of independent craft unions, mostly of skilled Anglo-Saxon workers whose control over their work and their status as elite laborers were slipping in the face of the industrial factory, the growing diversity of the American workforce, and employers seeking to take control over production processes. These unions still believed in the archetype of the independent, free white male laborer, the world of pre–Civil War America. By 1897, Gompers had 264,000 of those skilled workers in his federation. These workers battled owners over control of their work, mechanization, speeding up the work process, and employer prerogative in controlling the shop floor. These were privileged workers, proud of the hard, dangerous jobs they accomplished. Their culture represented that pride.[55]

The AFL refused to organize and often demonized any worker who was not a white male, either native-born or from western Europe. Millions of immigrants poured into the United States from eastern and southern Europe after 1880, filling industrial jobs the AFL had no interest in organizing. It despised radicalism in all its forms and yet sought to crush any rival that would organize the industrial workers. There was little place in the AFL for African Americans and none for Asians. In 1897, the AFL endorsed a literacy test for immigrants to stem the tide of people entering the nation, and in 1898, the AFL convention passed a resolution opposing women holding wage-earning jobs rather than organize the growing number of women in the workforce.[56] While solutions such as Bellamyism, the single tax, and Chinese exclusion would fade from importance, the AFL's vision of reinforcing the skilled white male worker would limit industrial organizing for a half century.

Yet for most employers, even the conservative unionism of the AFL was too much to accept. They desired to break the culture of the working class and they craved union-free factories. They wanted to take away skilled workers' control over their jobs and subject them to greater discipline. They did so through the combination of technological advances and brutality. New technologies in the steel mills, specifically the Bessemer process that allowed for the mass production of steel at low cost with little labor, eliminated the need for puddlers, and so the highest paid and most militant skilled workers could be fired or demoted. A group of puddlers had won perhaps the nation's first union contract in 1865. Deskilling the work gave control of labor back to the employers. Workers fought to keep their jobs. Occasionally they won. In 1889, workers at Andrew Carnegie's Homestead Steel Works organized by the Amalgamated Association of Iron and Steel Workers (AA) struck and won a union contract with wage gains for the next three years. This was the latest in a long history of battles between Carnegie and unions that dated back to a strike in 1867 when he tried to reduce puddlers' wages. Over and over, Carnegie and his fellow steel employers sought to throw workers out of a job when they fought for the dignity a union can bring; in 1874, Carnegie forced local store owners to not advance strikers credit so they would be starved back to work.[57]

When the contract ended in June 1892, Carnegie decided to destroy the AA. He traveled to his native Scotland and gave his right-hand man, Henry Clay Frick, carte blanche to deal with the union in any way he liked. Frick despised unions. He once personally evicted a striker from company housing by throwing him in a creek.[58] Workers asked for a wage increase; Frick responded with an offer of a 22 percent pay decrease while making military preparations around the factory to provoke the workers. They hanged Frick in effigy. He locked out workers on June 28. The workers united to keep out scabs. Craft union members controlled the Homestead city government, so Frick could not rely on local police forces. He called in the Pinkertons. When they arrived on July 6, an armed force of workers ready to fight for their jobs met them. For thirteen hours, the two sides traded gunfire. Eventually, the Pinkertons surrendered. But Pennsylvania governor Robert Pattison sent in the National Guard to break the strike. Frick had strikers evicted from company homes and arrested repeatedly so they would have to put up bail they could not afford.[59]

Again, anarchists decided to act on their own without consulting the workers. On July 23, Alexander Berkman, an anarchist in a political and romantic relationship with the legendary anarchist activist Emma Goldman, walked into Frick's office, fired two shots, and stabbed Frick three times. Although armed with a gun and knife, Berkman failed to seriously wound Frick, who was back at work within a few days. In taking it upon himself to revenge the Pinkerton invasion, Berkman undermined public support for the strike and earned himself a twenty-two-year prison sentence. The taint of radicalism helped doom the strike by November. The company welcomed workers back without their union, while blacklisting union leaders. Well known for his vanity and concern about his public image, Andrew Carnegie later regretted his actions at Homestead, writing, "It is expecting too much to expect poor men to stand by and see their work taken by others. . . . The Works are not worth one drop of human blood. I wish they had sunk."[60]

Carnegie's actions were more typical of the Gilded Age than his later regrets. The continued corporate domination of the economy and politics led to repeated bubbles of speculation that burst and threw workers into poverty. Caused by another round of irresponsible railroad speculation, the Panic of 1893 led to the worst economic crisis in American history prior to the Great Depression. Over the ensuing five years, unemployment reached as high as 18 percent, and banks failed across the country. President Grover Cleveland's administration did nothing to alleviate the deepening poverty. The post–Civil War economy had its ups and downs, but the Panic of 1893 convinced many Americans that capitalism and the government would never allow workers to live dignified lives.[61]

With employers continuing to respond to workers' reasonable demands with repression, the appeal of violence grew, and not just from anarchists. In 1892, silver miners in Idaho struck when employers demanded they work longer hours for no additional pay. The mine operators hired the Pinkertons to infiltrate the strike. Outraged when they realized Pinkertons had infiltrated their meetings, the miners turned to violence. Miners tried to halt a trainload of scabs from entering the mines. Union men climbed above the Frisco Mill, where Pinkertons had opened fire, and dropped a box of powder down a flume. It exploded upon impact, killing one mine employee. The Pinkertons ran out and hid in another building. The miners fired into the building, killing another and forcing the Pinkertons to surrender. This led Idaho governor N.B. Willey to declare martial law and send in the Idaho National Guard to break the union. Martial law continued for four months. Yet another strike of desperate workers was brutally defeated.[62]

While the working class struck for their rights when possible, for millions of Americans during the Gilded Age, life was dreary toil. That was especially true for women, who had few options to make a living. Many women labored as sex workers. Sex work had long provided women economic opportunities in American cities. Women who had suffered sexual abuse or rape, or became pregnant and were abandoned by their families, often had few options for survival. Brothels proliferated in the cities, and red-light districts were established where sex work would remain quasi-legal. African American women, with even fewer economic options, often worked in the sex trade. In 1890, black women made up only 1 percent of Chicago's population but 15 percent of the city's sex workers. The work was exploitative, dull, unhealthy, and often dangerous. But how was that different from working in a Gilded Age factory?[63]

The sudden growth of labor violence combined with the deep poverty of the working class and rise in sex work disturbed many middle-class Americans. Employers had a simple answer: violence and coercion. Cities built armories to put down the domestic insurrections they feared from striking workers. But a growing number of people realized that the laissez-faire attitude of the Gilded Age had created such extremes of poverty and wealth that perhaps the government needed to intervene before a revolution upended the nation. The 1901 assassination of President William McKinley by the anarchist Leon Czolgosz only made people feel this more strongly.[64] The middle class increasingly believed that something needed to be done in order to save the United States from the turmoil caused by its industrialization. Before 1900, the government routinely sided with employers, serving as the strikebreaker of last resort. Workers could not overcome this hostility. After 1900, the role of government in deciding the fate of workers' struggles would become even more clear.

4
The Anthracite Strike and the Progressive State

Each major strike forces the state to decide whether it represents workers or employers.

The Gilded Age was a very bad time for American workers. Capitalists' unquenchable thirst for profit and their power to control the state meant striking workers faced almost unbeatable odds. The desperation and violence that boiled over during the Great Railroad Strike and at Haymarket continued as workers had no redress for their demands for dignity. The government routinely sided with employers—through legislation that backed capitalists, through court decisions that impeded unions, or through police forces that busted strikes. However, in the early twentieth century, a growing concern with inequality and disorder led a new generation of middle- and upper-class political and social reformers known as Progressives. Combining a complex and overlapping series of reform movements, Progressives broadly agreed that a stable nation required workers to have something more than despondency in their future. Both the violent deaths of workers at the hands of employers and the violent responses by increasingly desperate workers framed this change. Progressive-controlled governments could alleviate some of the most extreme exploitation of American capitalism in response to worker activism.

The turning point in the state's response was the 1902 anthracite coal strike in Pennsylvania, when President Theodore Roosevelt shocked corporate America by using the federal government to mediate a strike. This new attitude was critically important, for strikers could almost never win without state neutrality. However, this strike, as well as strikes before and after 1902, also demonstrates the stark limitations of Progressive interventions into the workplace. The strikes of the 1890s through the 1910s reveal the absolutely critical role government played in American labor history, how the middle class could unite with workers to create positive change, and how working-class outrage and violence could provoke state responses that combined both repression and reform. However, Progressives largely did not believe in promoting the power of unions and thus did not change the fundamental balance of power between workers and employers.

Pullman and Cripple Creek: Two Stories About the State

In the years after the eight-hour strikes of 1886, there was little reason to think that government would change its fundamental antilabor position. The courts continued backing employers at every step. Even when the government passed the rare bill to limit the power of corporations, right-wing courts interpreted it to stop unions from succeeding while ignoring anticorporate provisions. Congress passed the Sherman Antitrust Act of 1890 to limit the growing monopolies that, as portrayed in popular political cartoons of the time, squeezed the nation like an octopus. Courts rarely enforced it against corporations. But in 1908, the Supreme Court used the law to bust unions in *Loewe v. Lawlor*, deciding that the United Hatters of North America, attempting to organize a hatmaker's shop in Connecticut, had violated the Sherman Act by calling for a nationwide boycott of the company's products, unlawfully restraining trade. If courts interpreted laws that had nothing to do with workers to defang unions, what hope did workers have to organize?[1]

Employers expected workers to sacrifice when profits lagged. George Pullman owned the Pullman Palace Car Company, which made sleeper cars for the railroads. He created his own company town south of Chicago, where he lorded over his workers. William Carwardine, pastor of the Pullman First Methodist Church, wrote of the total company domination: "It is a civilized relic of European serfdom." Of Pullman, he wrote: "He is the King, and he demands to the full measure of his capacity all that belongs to the insignia of royalty."[2] Pullman charged workers high rents for his company housing, would not employ someone if they did not rent from him, and evicted workers if they quit or were fired. When the Panic of 1893 hit, Pullman lowered wages by 25 percent while refusing to lower rent. In protest against this, as well as against working days that sometimes reached sixteen hours, Pullman workers attempted to meet with their boss and present their grievances. Pullman refused to talk to them and fired three of the leaders. Outraged, his workers walked off the job on May 11, 1894.[3]

A young organizer named Eugene Debs started the American Railway Union (ARU) in 1893. Debs believed in an industrial union that represented all white workers on the railroad, skilled and unskilled, as the key to improving their conditions. The ARU opposed the traditional railroad brotherhoods that represented only elite workers and had helped break the Great Southwest strike against Jay Gould in 1886. That the ARU still discriminated based upon race represented the overwhelming racism of white workers toward nonwhite competition. Solidarity might extend across the working class, but it hit a brick wall on the issue of race. Despite this and despite dislike from the brotherhoods, the ARU quickly found its legs, defeating the powerful James J. Hill and his Great Northern Railway in a strike; the ARU had 150,000 members within a year of its founding.[4]

The ARU did not represent the Pullman strikers. But acting in solidarity with their fellow railroad laborers, ARU members refused to move any Pullman cars. An official boycott began on June 26, and like the Great Railroad Strike of 1877 and the eight-hour strikes of 1886, it generated its own momentum as a larger protest against corporate domination. By June 29, 150,000 workers were on strike, and the American train system, vital to the nation's economy, ground to a halt. American labor leaders saw it as a battle not just against Pullman but all their corporate enemies. The president of the Chicago Federation of Labor said, "We all feel that in fighting any battle against the Pullman company we are aiming at the very head and front of monopoly and plutocracy."[5]

President Grover Cleveland's attorney general was Richard Olney, former general counsel for the Chicago, Milwaukee, and St. Paul Railway. Citing the Sherman Antitrust Act, Olney ordered federal attorneys to issue an injunction against the ARU to protect his railroad friends. An injunction is a court order that compels a union to stop its action, often through hefty fines that quickly bankrupt the union; it is the classic state intervention on behalf of employers. The ARU refused to obey the injunction. Cleveland and Olney then called in the military to squash the strike. Commanded by General Nelson A. Miles, known for his role in crushing the last Native American resistance in the West, twelve thousand U.S. troops, aided by U.S. Marshals, cracked down on the strike, using the pretense that it interfered with the delivery of the mail. Miles hated Debs, thought the strikers were defying the federal government, and followed through on his orders with relish. As Debs proclaimed in a speech the following year, "the American Railway Union challenged the power of corporations in a way that had not previously been done."[6] This was why the government would not let them win.

The Pullman strike was largely nonviolent until the military intervened. On July 7, soldiers fired into a crowd, killing at least four strikers and wounding around twenty. The same day, the military arrested Debs and other ARU leaders. Facing unbeatable state repression, the strike fell apart. After thirteen strikers were killed and fifty-seven wounded, the Pullman plant reopened on August 2. Eugene Debs served six months in prison for violating the injunction and spent his time reading Karl Marx. He became a socialist and emerged as the greatest leader for working-class rights the country had ever seen.[7]

Pullman showed yet again that the government would assist corporations in destroying working-class movements. But it did not have to be that way. If the government responded to strikes more favorably, how might workers fare?

By the 1890s, the center of Colorado gold mining had settled around Cripple Creek, where prosperity bloomed. Miners desperate for work moved there during the Panic of 1893. The glut of workers led the owners to increase the workday to ten hours from eight, with no pay raise. Disgusted, the workers joined the Western Federation of Miners (WFM), a new industrial union organizing the hard rock miners of the American West. They went on strike on February 7, 1894, just a few months before Pullman. By the end of February, nearly every gold mine in Colorado had shut down. A few owners restored the eight-hour day and their workers came back. However, most brought in scab labor. At first, the WFM tried to organize these men into the union, but the strikebreakers kept working and the strikers upped the ante. On March 16, a group of armed miners captured and beat six sheriff's deputies heading up to a mine at Victor, where they were to assist in the protection of scabs.

At that point, El Paso County sheriff M.F. Bowers requested the governor send the state militia to break the strike. But Colorado voters had recently elected a reformer named Davis Waite. The rare pro-worker governor during this era, Waite refused. Bowers arrested the strike leaders, but a jury found them not guilty of the trumped-up charges. Strikers continued attacking the strikebreakers, throwing bricks and getting into fistfights with them. When the miners rejected an offer to return to work for eight hours but with reduced pay, and with Waite's refusal to use the militia as the personal army of the mine owners, the owners decided to raise a private army of mostly ex-policemen to become sheriff's deputies. On May 24, miners took over the Strong Mine, near Victor. When 125 deputies marched to take it, the miners blew it up. The deputies fled, but the miners wanted blood. Many of the miners wanted to systematically blow up the mines. They filled a railroad car with dynamite and sent it down the track, hoping to cause an explosion in the deputies' camp, but it derailed. Tensions rose even further when the mine owners paid for an additional twelve hundred deputies for their private army.

At that point, Governor Waite did intervene: he declared the owners' army of deputies illegal and ordered them to disband it. He sent in the state militia as a peacekeeping force and won the miners' approval to be their bargaining agent with the mine owners. The owners were apoplectic. Supporting workers is not what government did during the Gilded Age. When Waite called a meeting of the union and owners in Colorado Springs, a mob whipped up by the companies formed outside and threatened to lynch Waite and the unionists. Despite this, Waite forced the owners to restore the eight-hour day at the previous wage of $3 a day (about $73 today, the equivalent of a little more than $9 an hour for extremely dangerous work). But the owners refused to disband their forces. In Cripple Creek, they arrested hundreds of miners, formed a gauntlet, and forced townspeople to run through it while being beaten. Finally, the state militia rounded up the private police force. The governor stated he would keep the militia in Cripple Creek until the owners followed the rule of law, meaning they would have to keep paying their forces to do nothing. The employers caved and the workers won.[8]

This was organized labor's biggest win in the entire Gilded Age. Like the Pullman strike, the government played an absolutely crucial role in deciding its fate. Davis Waite showed that government could stand on the side of workers. This also led to the end of his political career. Mine owners made sure he lost his reelection campaign in 1894. Then they had their revenge on the miners. In Leadville, one hundred miles west of Cripple Creek, 1,200 miners struck in 1896 when owners refused to raise their wages back to the 1893 standard. The strike led to owners locking out the rest of the town's miners by June 22. After its great victory at Cripple Creek, the WFM believed it could wait the owners out. When the owners hired armed strikebreakers, the union dynamited a mine. But the new governor, Albert McIntire, was a friend to the employers and reverted to using the state militia for their interests. He sent a military guard to Leadville to reopen the mines. The WFM could not defeat armed state militiamen. Its resistance crumbled in March 1897 after half the miners had returned to work. Western state governments took a hard line against the WFM after this; it responded by growing increasingly radical, believing that only through direct action could the working class rise to power in the United States.[9]

Progressives and the Anthracite Strike

Waite's actions at Cripple Creek did not lead to a new era of power for the WFM, but they did preview a new attitude politicians increasingly took toward corporations. Gilded Age excesses led to many protest movements, not only from workers but also farmers organizing themselves to escape control from eastern banks and railroads, first in the Farmers' Alliance and then the Populist Party.[10] The anarchists at Haymarket, Alexander Berkman's attempted murder of Henry Clay Frick, and the assassination of President William McKinley alarmed the nation about the rising violent opposition to capitalism. Many younger people, often the sons and daughters of the Gilded Age capitalist class, wondered if the extreme income inequality of the period portended more political violence. The terrible working conditions, the poverty of the millions of immigrants coming to work in the nation's factories and sweatshops, and the children working instead of going to school deeply concerned the growing middle class.

The general disorder of American society, ranging from political corruption and the waste of natural resources to poverty and unsafe food, led to rise of Progressivism after 1885. This was a series of movements led by middle- and upper-class people who believed Americans should come together to solve society's problems, using government when necessary, but with an emphasis on voluntarism, scientific study, and investigative journalism. Jane Addams opened Hull House in Chicago to provide desperately needed services for the city's immigrants. After working there, Florence Kelley moved to New York and fought to end child labor. Theodore Roosevelt used his money and ambition to promote the conservation of the nation's resources. Not all of these reformers responded to workers' demands, but many of them did. The growing number of strikes increased the pressure. In 1896, American workers engaged in 1,026 strikes. That number rose to 3,495 in 1903, when over 531,000 workers struck. The total number of union members in the United States increased from 447,000 in 1897 to almost 2 million by 1903.[11] Even Mark Hanna, the Gilded Age Ohio political boss and president of the National Civic Federation, admitted in 1901 that unions were here to stay.[12]

The nation's growing industrial capacity had an almost limitless appetite for coal to fuel everything from railroads to steel mills. The number of miners in the coal country of northeastern Pennsylvania grew from 35,600 in 1870 to 126,000 by 1890, more than tripling as factories transformed the nation.[13] Even compared to the many other brutal, dangerous jobs of the period, coal mining was notorious for the lives it took. In 1869, a fire killed 110 miners at the Avondale Colliery in northeast Pennsylvania. In 1907, a fire at the Darr Mine in the same state killed 239 workers. In 1909, a fire at the Cherry Mine in Illinois killed 259 workers. In December 1907 alone, more than seven hundred coal miners died in disasters in West Virginia, Pennsylvania, Alabama, and New Mexico.[14]

The coal operators ran their mines like medieval fiefdoms, paying workers in company scrip instead of cash, forcing them to shop at company stores, and driving out or murdering union organizers. In Pennsylvania, anthracite miners worked a minimum of ten hours a day. They lacked access to fresh air from the mine shafts. Instead, dangerous gases built up, leading to deadly explosions. Mine owners rarely repaired problems unless workers died. Companies took back as much of the measly wages they paid out as possible through a series of fines for impurities in the rock, through paying by the "ton" with a weight more than the standard two thousand pounds, and by forcing workers to spend their own unpaid time shoring up mine ceilings to keep them from collapsing.[15]

Responding to these conditions, miners created the United Mine Workers of America (UMWA) in 1890. In a hypercompetitive industry suffering from overproduction and low coal prices, organizing was hard going. If the UMWA raised wages in Illinois, those mines had to compete with nonunion mines in Pennsylvania and West Virginia. In 1897, the UMWA won a big victory in the Midwest, leading to improved wages and working conditions as well as shorter hours. Led by its president, the dapper and handsome John Mitchell, the UMWA sought to organize Pennsylvania and West Virginia, allowing the Illinois win to take hold. The UMWA grew from 10,000 to 150,000 members by 1900 and thus gained more union dues to organize more miners.[16]

The mines of northeastern Pennsylvania had produced coal for the market since the early nineteenth century. This once-remote region soon attracted significant capital to develop some of the largest mines in the United States. In 1842, fifteen hundred men walked off the job to protest wage cuts. This was the home of the Molly Maguires and of generations of unionization attempts. Each loss taught workers something: that strictly ethnic associations were not sufficient, that organized political action was more effective than spontaneous protest, and that solidarity across the coal workforce was necessary for victory. These were hard-learned lessons and often relearned as unions rose and fell. The Knights of Labor briefly organized here, but Protestant miners, largely from England, Wales, and Scotland and wanting to preserve their own ethnic privileges, created the Amalgamated Association of Miners and Laborers as an alternative to the broad-based unionism of the Knights. Over time, these miners coalesced in the UMWA. By 1894, it had become an important presence in northeastern Pennsylvania, even though English-speaking miners held their co-workers from southern and eastern Europe in contempt.[17]

The mine owners responded to strikes with state-sponsored violence. In 1897, when strikers marched to shut down a mine near Lattimer, Pennsylvania, the police opened fire and killed nineteen workers by shooting them in the back.[18] Hardly an isolated incident, the Lattimer Massacre summed up employers' feelings about mine worker organizing. George Baer, president of the Philadelphia and Reading Railroad, headed the Anthracite Operators' Association. Baer was notoriously arrogant, almost a comic stereotype of a Gilded Age plutocrat. He explained his view of labor relations in a letter titled "Divine Right of Capital." He wrote, "The rights and interests of the laboring man will be protected and cared for—not by the labor agitators, but by the Christian men to whom God in his infinite wisdom has given the control of the property interests of the country."[19] Somehow, the Pennsylvania miners disagreed with sentiment.

Thanks to committed organizers such as Mary Harris "Mother" Jones, rank-and-file activism, and John Mitchell's leadership, a small strike led to a victory in the mines of northeastern Pennsylvania in 1899. In 1900, the UMWA launched another strike, this one lasting six weeks and leading Mark Hanna to convince the mine owners to settle and pay a 10 percent wage increase in order to not hurt President McKinley's chances during his reelection campaign. With increased confidence but facing operators furious at concessions already granted, the UMWA increased its demands. By 1902, Mitchell pressed for union recognition, a pay raise of 20 percent, the eight-hour day, a new system to weigh coal that would not cheat the miners, and the establishment of a grievance system that would allow resolution of disputes between employers and workers. Baer and the coal operators rejected it completely. They wanted to take back control of their mines. Baer said, "There can not be two masters in the management of the business."[20]

Mitchell did not want to strike. He hoped to mediate the conflict as he had in 1900. But with workers ready for a fight and the coal operators rejecting everything the union offered, he had little choice. On May 12, 100,000 miners walked off the job. It soon rose to 150,000. It would last for more than five brutal months, as impoverished miners took on the nation's most powerful corporate elites. The UMWA managed to hold the strike together, raising money and building political support for their actions. Mitchell immediately took on a conciliatory tone, discouraging other workers from walking out in solidarity (an action known as a "sympathy strike") and calling for mediation. Meanwhile, the miners themselves enforced the picket line. Polish workers threw rocks at their countrymen who tried to scab, while other strikers captured scabs imported from elsewhere, stripped them, and paraded them through town.[21] Calls grew in eastern newspapers to crush the strike, playing up the antiscab violence and complaining of the "utter disregard of the property rights either of corporations or of individuals" by strikers digging small amounts of coal to heat their own homes.[22]

The miners had more power than other workers because American cities were heated on coal. Anthracite coal burns cleanly, with little smoke, so consumers bought it to heat their homes, as opposed to the dirtier bituminous coal used to fuel industry. As the summer went on, the impending coal shortage worried policymakers. Pressure grew for a settlement. Mark Hanna once again called for negotiations, and even ex-president Grover Cleveland, notorious buster of the Pullman strike, agreed. As winter approached, Americans worried how they would stay warm.

President Theodore Roosevelt found the strike alarming. He also worried about the impact the coal shortage would have on congressional Republicans in the fall's midterm elections. Roosevelt first looked into mediating the strike in early June, but Attorney General Philander Knox told him he had no authority to do so. Indeed, no president had attempted this. But Roosevelt had different ideas than the presidents before him. He was a Progressive, and he believed that government could act as a moderating force in the raucous Gilded Age, serving not only the interests of capitalists but those of workers and citizens too. Roosevelt frequently broke new ground in expanding the role of the president. He invited John Mitchell and the coal operators to the White House on October 3 to talk and settle the strike.[23]

Mitchell jumped at Roosevelt's unprecedented action. He offered to call off the strike if the owners agreed to full presidential mediation and a small wage increase to show good faith. The coal bosses flatly refused Roosevelt's entreaties, even refusing to talk directly to Mitchell at the meeting. The coal barons' refusal to arbitrate combined with Mitchell's conciliatory tone to move public opinion against the mine operators. The *Scranton Times* stated, "We have no hesitation in placing the responsibility for this industrial war where it justly belongs, upon the coal carrying companies."[24] This was a new era that caught the coal companies off guard, one in which an aroused public wanted some level of fair treatment of workers when unions had moderate demands. That included Roosevelt. He was no friend of unions. In 1907, he would use the military to crush a strike in Nevada mines he considered dangerously radical. His goal in Pennsylvania was to mediate a difficult strike that impacted millions of Americans, not unionize the nation.

Roosevelt saw the mine owners' haughty refusal to talk as a crisis of presidential authority and knew Americans wanted action.[25] His infuriated response to the coal operators was a threat to nationalize the industry, sending in the U.S. military to open the mines and employ the workers to get coal to eastern customers. Roosevelt appealed to the powerful capitalist J.P. Morgan, a heavy investor in the Pennsylvania mines, to force the owners to acquiesce. The president spoke of Mitchell's moderation and his behavior in the face of Baer's hatred. Roosevelt wrote of the UMWA leader, "He made no threats and resorted to no abuse. The proposition he made seemed to me eminently fair. The operators refused even to consider it, used insolent and abusive language about him, and in at least 2 cases assumed an attitude toward me which was one of insolence."[26] Roosevelt's entreaties convinced Morgan to support mediation. On October 23, the UMWA ended the strike after 165 days.[27]

Clarence Darrow, at the height of his career defending the nation's poor and oppressed against corporate power, represented the workers before the Anthracite Coal Strike Commission. He said, "When I think of the cripples, of the orphans, of the widows, of the maimed who are dragging their lives out on account of this business, who, if they were mules or horses would be cared for, but who are left and neglected, it seems to me this is the greatest indictment of this business that can possibly be made."[28] Workers testified about how mine bosses ripped them off by underestimating the weight of the coal they cut, their often fatal working conditions, the months during the year when the mines closed and they had no work, and the long, hard days when they did have work. They discussed the sheer physical brutality of the work—the ear-splitting noise, the scorching heat in the summer, the devastating cold in the winter, how the sharp coal cut their hands and severed their fingers.[29]

In response, Baer ranted about the natural right of employers to advance society through their monopolies, while accusing unions of creating a "monster monopoly" that produces nothing. He claimed the union was a violent organization that did not deserve legitimacy. He defended the long hours of work and coal operators' right to total control over their miners by stating "the masses of men have advanced, and are continuing to advance under the powerful stimulus which individual liberty gives to individual initiative." Any employer behavior was justified under Baer's extremist position.[30] Finally, Baer simply denied the miners' humanity, stating, "These men don't suffer. Why, hell, half of them don't even speak English."[31]

On March 18, 1903, the commission made its decision. The UMWA did not win everything, as the commission did not grant the union exclusive bargaining rights, but it did give workers a 10 percent wage increase and reduced the working day by an hour, to nine hours a day. In lieu of union recognition, the commission created a mediation bargaining board. Baer was outraged and Darrow disappointed. The commission hardly ensured industrial peace. Without the companies recognizing the union as the workers' bargaining agent, they would continue their war on the UMWA. The commission did not limit child labor in the mines, a major goal of the union. However, even this limited advancement was one of the greatest strike victories in American history to that time, thanks to Roosevelt's intervention. The sheer idea that the government would *mediate* a strike instead of serve the owners marked a new day in the history of American labor's relationship with the government.[32]

Even with government mediation in 1902, the UMWA could not continue building upon its momentum. Membership declined from 37,000 in mid-1904 to only 23,000 by the end of 1907. The constant flow of new immigrants from southern and eastern Europe entering the mines required endless organizing, and existing members dropped out and stopped paying dues or attending union meetings. The Anthracite Board of Conciliation, created to mediate conflicts between the owners and miners, usually favored employers, angering miners. Unable to press the union's agenda, Mitchell and the UMWA agreed in 1906 to a three-year extension of the status quo. An internal rebellion forced Mitchell out in 1908, in part because UMWA members saw him as too cozy with the mine owners. Ultimately, a government mediating board was more favorable than total industry control over employees, but it was no avenue for worker power.[33]

The Progressive State: Its Potential and Its Limitations

Despite Roosevelt's outsized personality, his action in 1902 was not an isolated incident. Progressivism seeped through American government by 1910. States passed new laws to limit worker exploitation. Employers challenged them in the courts, but Progressives began changing the courts as well. Unfortunately, the Supreme Court continued to embrace the right of contract created in the early nineteenth century, effectively arguing that if a worker took a job, that worker agreed to whatever the employer offered and the government should not intervene in that sacrosanct arrangement. Such a worldview completely ignored the vast disparities of power between an employer and a worker desperate to eat.

New York had one of the nation's strongest Progressive movements. In 1895, the state legislature passed the Bakeshop Act, regulating the sanitary conditions of bakeries and limiting employees to sixty-hour workweeks with no more than ten hours a day. In 1899, Joseph Lochner, a baker in Utica, was indicted for violating the act by requiring employees to labor for more than sixty hours. He drew a $25 fine. He was charged again in 1901; this time the state fined him $50 and sentenced him to up to fifty days in jail if he did not pay the fine. Lochner appealed, and the case went all the way to the Supreme Court. In

1905, the court decided *Lochner v. New York* and overturned the law. Asking, "Is this a fair, reasonable, and appropriate exercise of the police power of the State, or is it an unreasonable, unnecessary and arbitrary interference with the right of the individual to his personal liberty or to enter into those contracts in relation to labor which may seem to him appropriate or necessary for the support of himself and his family," and answering definitively for the latter, the court effectively ruled that corporations had full rights to set any conditions of employment they chose. Progressives and workers suffered a horrible defeat.[34]

Yet just three years later, in the case of *Muller v. Oregon*, the court made an exception to restrict working hours for women. In 1903, Oregon passed a law limiting women to ten hours of work a day and sixty hours a week. Progressives saw women as not only exploited workers but also mothers responsible for raising the next generation of Americans. They argued that the state had a unique interest in excepting women from the freedom of contract ideology of *Lochner* and the Gilded Age courts.[35] Curt Muller, a Portland laundry owner, sued the state over the law. Muller believed that his workers freely agreed to the terms of hours and wages when they took the job. The National Consumers League, led by the pioneering labor feminist Florence Kelley, defended Oregon's law and convinced the brilliant rising lawyer Louis Brandeis to file a lengthy brief about the terrible lives of female workers. He used four specific arguments. First, women were physically different and weaker than men. Second, damage to women's health on the job might affect their reproductive capacity. Third, the health of children might be damaged if the mother was overworked. Fourth, long workdays deprived family members of their wife and mother. The court accepted this rationale and upheld the law, shocking employers.[36] Although some feminists opposed this ruling because it treated women as different from men, creating any exception to *Lochner* opened up the court to more exceptions; *Muller* served as a first leak in the dam holding back all workers' rights. It chipped away at the freedom of contract ideology and within a decade, many industries would have eight-hour days.[37]

Workers were not helpless victims waiting for the middle class to save them. Rather, their activism attracted reformers such as Brandeis and Kelley. The young immigrant female workers in New York's apparel industry sweatshops labored sixty-five to seventy-five hours a week when there was work; if orders declined, workers could be laid off at any time. Women earned from $3 to $10 a week, poverty wages even at the higher level. Bosses required workers to supply their own materials, such as needles, and docked their pay for the slightest infraction. Factory owners locked doors so workers could not sneak outside for breaks and required that workers request permission to use the bathroom. In 1909, those immigrant young women workers went on strike in what became known as the Uprising of the 20,000. At a November meeting, New York Progressives and labor leaders, including American Federation of Labor head Samuel Gompers, urged caution. After listening to this for two hours, a sweatshop worker named Clara Lemlich stood up and spoke to the workers in Yiddish, saying, "I am a working girl, one of those who are on strike against intolerable conditions. I am tired of listening to speakers who talk in general terms. What we are here for is to decide whether we shall or shall not strike. I offer a resolution that a general strike be declared—now."[38]

This is what the angry workers wanted to hear. The strike began the next day. Over seven hundred women were arrested in the next month. Lemlich suffered six broken ribs when police beat her. A ten-year-old girl was arrested and sentenced to forced labor for "assaulting" a scab. But public opinion turned against the operators. Wealthy women, moved by the brutality these working-women faced, began joining them on the picket line and bailing the arrested women out of jail. Among them were future secretary of labor Frances Perkins and, in a sign of generational transition, Anne Morgan, the daughter of the capitalist J.P. Morgan, who had been behind coal operator resistance to the Pennsylvania anthracite strike just a few years before. The strike lasted for eleven weeks, and the workers won some slight gains. The workweek was reduced to fifty-two hours and workers received four paid holidays per year. Additionally, workers would no longer be required to buy their own work materials, and a general agreement was reached to negotiate pay rates with workers. But they did not win on the key issue of workplace safety.[39]

Owners preferred the risk of killing easily replaceable workers to investing in workplace safety. The Triangle Shirtwaist Company in New York was owned by Max Blanck and Isaac Harris, Jewish immigrants who made their fortune as the "Shirtwaist Kings" by manufacturing a woman's undergarment popular in this era. They set up a sweatshop on three floors of the Asch Building in Manhattan's Greenwich Village and hired workers, mostly young women, for very low pay. One corner of the factory was known as the "Kindergarten," where young girls sat for twelve hours, snipping thread. The average working day for all workers was twelve to fourteen hours, at least six days a week. That included Saturday, which was important because 60 percent of the workers were Jewish women. During the peak production season, workers had to labor all seven days. A sign above the elevator read, IF YOU DON'T COME IN ON SUNDAY, DON'T COME IN ON MONDAY. Blanck and Harris had led the industry opposition to the Uprising of the 20,000, criticizing smaller operations who signed contracts with the union and asserting their right to complete control over the factory.[40]

On March 25, 1911, at the end of a long shift on a Saturday afternoon, a fire broke out in the factory. Of the 250 workers on the ninth floor, 146 died, many jumping to the streets below to escape the flames. Clara Lemlich said, "If Triangle had been a union shop there would not have been any locked doors, and the girls would have been on the street almost an hour before the fire started."[41] Reporter William Gunn Shepherd, who also witnessed the fire and the horrors of young women jumping to their death, noted, "I remembered the great strike of last year, in which these girls demanded more sanitary workrooms, and more safety precautions in the shops. These dead bodies told the results."[42]

The combination of consumers witnessing the death of workers and Progressives' new ideas about government led to reforms. Investigations showed that half the city's workers labored on floors higher than fire department ladders could reach, most in factories with iron bars blocking fire escapes, overcrowded conditions, or in rickety wooden buildings. Lemlich demanded the investigating commission accompany union leaders on unscheduled factory visits to get the real story. The inspections created wide-reaching laws that began the reform of labor conditions in this country, including new standards for lighting, ventilation, and sanitation; fire exit laws; and limitations on the hours women and children could work. On the other hand, Blanck and Harris were found not guilty of manslaughter and escaped justice.[43]

The same Progressive impulse that provided mediation for the

United Mine Workers in 1902, *Muller*, and the Triangle reforms continued providing limited interventions in the workplace to alleviate the worst exploitation of workers. After the 1909 Cherry Mine fire in Illinois, which killed 259 workers, the state crafted new safety laws for mines that included safety training, certification for those in charge of safety equipment, and better firefighting equipment. It also helped convince Congress to establish the United States Bureau of Mines in 1910, to oversee mine safety.[44] States began to pass workers' compensation laws in 1911 after juries started finding in favor of injured and dead workers in lawsuits about workplace safety. Realizing a new day had dawned, industry decided to promote a system of limited liability rather than take the chance to lose large sums of money in the courts. Workers' compensation provided only a fraction of lost wages, but it was an improvement on the nothing injured workers had received earlier.[45]

The Progressive interest in workers had sharp limits. For instance, meatpackers lived lives of great brutality. The largest and most profitable sector of the Chicago economy, the packing plants employed thousands of workers, increasingly immigrants from eastern Europe, along with growing numbers of African American workers brought in as strikebreakers during the industry's frequent strikes—a strategy to divide workers by race. Many black workers, facing hostility from unions, rightfully believed the only way they could get a factory job was through strikebreaking. Once again, white hostility to workers of color interfered with class solidarity.[46]

Regardless of race, meatpackers suffered from low wages and extremely dangerous working conditions, with near-freezing temperatures leading to frigid hands using sharp tools to disassemble the animals flying rapidly through the factory. Carcasses frequently smashed workers in the head, and water on the factory floor often led to electrocution. In 1906, the journalist and novelist Upton Sinclair published *The Jungle* to expose meatpackers' lives to the public, hoping to convert Americans to socialism. However, his middle-class audience largely ignored the plight of the workers and instead focused on the unsanitary conditions of the meat, which Sinclair described in grotesque detail. His book led to the passage of the Pure Food and Drug Act, which created the U.S. Food and Drug Administration, but readers, including

Theodore Roosevelt, showed much more concern about themselves than they did the workers making the meat.[47]

Moreover, most Progressives did not support union power. They feared it and wanted a slightly regulated capitalism to undermine radicalism. Harrison Gray Otis, editor of the staunchly conservative *Los Angeles Times*, was proud of his role in keeping that city a bastion of anti-unionism. In 1910, two leaders of the International Association of Bridge and Structural Iron Workers bombed the *Times* building. Unfortunately, the bomb went off early, killing twenty-one workers. This act bewildered Progressives, who struggled to understand such violence. In response to this and other violent acts, the government created the United States Commission on Industrial Relations (USCIR) in August 1912 to investigate the conditions of work. When Woodrow Wilson stepped into the presidency in 1913, he empowered the commission to expose the realities of American work. Said the groundbreaking journalist Walter Lippmann, "The nine members of the Industrial Relations Commission have before them the task of explaining why America, supposed to become the land of promise, has become the land of disappointment and deep-seated discontent."[48]

Led by Frank Walsh, a Kansas City lawyer who determined that corporate heads would answer for their actions, the USCIR hearings became one of the most remarkable moments in American history. For the first time, industrial leaders had to testify about the conditions of American labor in front of a government committee. Between 1913 and 1915, the USCIR interviewed hundreds of people about the conditions of American work. Investigators in the Northwest discovered stories of logging camp cooks infected with venereal disease and still allowed to prepare food, loggers beaten by owners and having their money stolen, and workers getting so sick from timber camp food that they could not work for weeks. One investigator, writing about miners at U.S. Steel operations in Duluth, detailed how the police, owners, and city leaders conspired to crush a strike. Everyday workers told their stories and capitalists faced unprecedented public criticism. *The Masses*, one of the most important radical journals of the era, went so far as to call it "the beginning of an indigenous American revolutionary movement."[49]

That was an overstatement, but the relevance of the commission grew throughout the investigations. Colorado Fuel and Iron

(CF&I), a mining and smelting company owned by the Rockefeller family, treated their largely Mexican, Italian, and Greek coal mining workforce in their southern Colorado mines with the same level of contempt that coal operators did in West Virginia and Pennsylvania. Colorado had passed laws regulating coal mines, but CF&I ensured that none of them were enforced. Workers lived in company houses that CF&I agents could enter at any time, they had to shop at the company store using company scrip, and anyone associated with unions faced termination. The United Mine Workers of America organized the workers, and in 1913 they presented CF&I with a series of demands that included an eight-hour day, the right of workers to choose their own homes and doctors, a pay raise, and enforcement of mine safety laws. The company rejected it and the miners went on strike. CF&I kicked strikers out of company housing, but the union had anticipated this and had leased land nearby for tent cities.

CF&I hired the notorious Baldwin-Felts Detective Agency, a Pinkerton-like anti-union strikebreaking firm, to harass the strikers. The agency helped CF&I buy four machine guns from the West Virginia Coal Operators' Association and mounted two on an armored vehicle known as the Death Special and they set up additional snipers to shoot into the tent camps.[50] Colorado governor Elias Ammons called in the Colorado National Guard to "restore order" and gave state forces to the company for their use for the winter. On April 20, 1914, CF&I and National Guard forces opened fire on the camp and a day-long battle raged. After killing union leader Louis Tikas with the butt of a rifle, they set the camp on fire. Fearing the snipers, many camp residents dug cellars underneath the tents to hide. Four women and eleven children, including two infants named Elvira Valdez and Frank Petrucci, went into the cellars during the day. They suffocated to death. It was the death of these fifteen innocents that led to this event being known as the Ludlow Massacre.

The well-armed strikers did not meekly return to work. Furious and wanting revenge, they began their own campaign of violence against the militia and scabs. The Colorado State Federation of Labor told the strikers to "organize the men in your community in companies of volunteers to protect the workers of Colorado against the murder and cremation of men, women, and children."[51] A ten-day guerrilla war ensued with high casualties on both sides;

somewhere between 69 and 199 people died. Miners destroyed mine buildings and tunnels and even blew up the dam that provided drinking water for the Ludlow mines. Finally, Woodrow Wilson sent in the U.S. Army to end the hostilities; unlike in previous examples of federal intervention in strikes, Wilson ordered neutrality and in fact the army arrested several militia members. By December, however, the UMWA had run out of funds and the strike ended in a total defeat.[52]

After the Ludlow Massacre, Frank Walsh called John D. Rockefeller Jr. before the USCIR and publicly humiliated the powerful man for his company thugs and indifference to workers' lives. Never before had a capitalist been embarrassed publicly for his actions concerning workers. A shocked and humbled Rockefeller sought to make sure this would never happen again by creating what became known as a company union. He intended to give workers a limited voice to air their concerns and improve working conditions, while keeping power in the hands of his mine managers. For all the very real limitations of company unions that workers would chafe against and eventually reject, this was a concession to a new era of government interest in ensuring fair conditions for workers.[53]

Opinion on the final report from the USCIR was divided, with more conservative elements outraged by Walsh's criticism of capitalists. In the end, Progressives' intervention in the workplace led to only limited improvements in workers' lives, most of which came only in the aftermath of workers expressing power through strikes or dying in horrifying tragedies. For the middle class, government involvement garnered optimism in the future. However, events like those at the Triangle factory and in Ludlow also contributed to many workers seeing no hope in capitalism. Without real power, the occasional government mediation that helped coal workers in Pennsylvania or a government committee to investigate why workers blew up a newspaper building would do little for workers. Instead, a lot of workers looked at the assassination attempt on Henry Clay Frick or the *Los Angeles Times* bombing as a model for action. The radicalism that resulted would shake the nation to its core.

5

The Bread and Roses Strike

When capitalism fails workers, radicals can mobilize them to fight.

By 1910, the Progressive movement had brought middle-class reformers into alliance with workers on some issues. The United States Commission on Industrial Relations provided an unprecedented investigation into the exploitation workers faced and transformed the conversation about worker rights. American society became a little fairer.

Those changes meant very little to the daily life of a worker struggling to eat and working sixty hours a week in a dangerous factory or mine for low wages. The rank exploitation workers faced—their terrible housing, their malnutrition, the horrifyingly unsafe working conditions—meant capitalism had failed millions of workers. Lacking any hope for change, they would sometimes turn to violence in their anger and frustration, from Haymarket to the *Los Angeles Times* bombing. The American Federation of Labor refused to organize the most exploited workers, such as immigrants toiling in sweatshops and steel mills, African Americans, Asian Americans, loggers, and farmworkers.

All sorts of radical ideologies helped fill this vacuum. The anarchism that came to the nation's attention at Haymarket, the socialism embodied by Eugene Debs, and many other alternatives to capitalism appealed in a world of desperation. But none of these ideas formed a mass organization to gather the workers into a fighting force for revolution. That changed in 1905 with the formation of the Industrial Workers of the World (IWW). Unlike the AFL, the IWW (aka Wobblies), had openly radical leadership seeking direct action from workers at the point of production to create a revolution from below.[1] Directly challenging capitalism, organizing the nation's most oppressed workers, savaging the compromising AFL with savvy propaganda, and engaging in often brilliant public relations strategies, the IWW frightened employers, government, and the AFL, who all wanted to crush the organization. Wobblies spoke a language of empowerment that brought hope to thousands of workers for the first time.

It is easy for modern radicals to look at unions and see them as compromising, stodgy, and weak and therefore view a radical front as an appealing alternative. Like a century ago, current workers seem to have no avenue for power. To harness that power, though, we need to avoid romanticizing these radicals and understand when their ideas and tactics worked and when they did not. The IWW had internal flaws that undermined its own ability to sustain its worker organizing. Its cavalier talk of violence and sabotage made Americans fear this organization more than necessary. Its unwillingness to build long-term worker organizations and its attraction to the next big struggle meant that even when the IWW won a campaign, untrained workers found themselves at the mercy of employers after the IWW organizers moved on. Constant infighting and factional debates over ideology interfered with organizing workers.

None of this was fatal to the IWW. Rather, the organization's radicalism directly challenged capitalism, and the state struck back hard. The Progressive state might sometimes help workers, but it could use its power against them. During and after World War I, in the first widespread crackdown on radicals in American history, the administration of Woodrow Wilson, the military, and employers violently repressed the IWW, leading to massive civil liberties violations and the nation's first period of anticommunist hysteria. It again demonstrates how the state response to unions, conservative or radical, goes far to determine their fate.

Radical America

Despite Theodore Roosevelt's interference in the Pennsylvania anthracite strike, the state still crushed worker movements far more often than it helped them. In the aftermath of the state oppression the Western Federation of Miners (WFM) faced in the 1890s and early 1900s, that union pioneered the path to the IWW. Its leaders realized that only large-scale industrial unionism could fight the aggressive and repressive tactics of American corporations. In 1902, it named "Big" Bill Haywood its secretary-treasurer, aligning it with the Socialist Party. Haywood had started working in the Nevada mines at the age of fifteen and became a union organizer after he injured his hands working in Idaho. He wore the scars of American work across his body and would seek to redress the injustice in American life through organizing for a radical alternative to capitalism.

The WFM had ambitious goals of expanding its organizing into the South and Midwest and translated its constitution into multiple languages to attract more immigrants. It started organizing nonminers in Colorado, targeting refineries in Colorado City, where a strike took place in February 1903. The governor called in the state militia to stop the picketing and a full-blown war on the union began in Colorado. When the strike reached Cripple Creek, home of the WFM's great 1894 victory, the militia officer in charge, General Sherman Bell, said, "I came to do up this damned anarchistic federation."[2] The governor declared martial law in Cripple Creek in December. WFM president Charles Moyer was thrown in prison, and after the bombing of a train car of strikebreakers, a vigilante group rounded up dozens of WFM workers and deported them to Kansas and New Mexico.[3]

Devastated, the WFM turned to radical action nationwide, hoping to create a broad-based organization fighting for the rights of all workers. In June 1905, the WFM joined radicals from around the nation in Chicago to form the Industrial Workers of the World. Eugene Debs was there, a decade after the brutal crushing of the Pullman strike, as was the legendary matron saint of the

United Mine Workers of America, Mary Harris "Mother" Jones. Socialist Labor Party leader Daniel De Leon wanted to control this new organization so he could lead a revolutionary movement. Lucy Parsons, anarchist, African American, and widow of Haymarket martyr Albert Parsons, attended. So did Elizabeth Gurley Flynn, the "Rebel Girl" who would inspire thousands with her impassioned speeches. WFM leaders played a critical role. Big Bill Haywood stated the IWW's goal was to form a "working class movement that shall have for its purpose the emancipation of the working class from the slave bondage of capitalism."[4] The IWW rejected AFL-style craft unionism. William Trautmann, one of the new union's founders, noted at the convention, "The directory of unions of Chicago shows in 1903 a total of 56 different unions in the packing houses, divided up still more in 14 different national trades unions of the American Federation of Labor. What a horrible example of an army divided against itself in the face of a strong combination of employers."[5] Instead, the IWW called for direct action by workers, putting power in their hands to make their own battle against capitalism.[6]

The variety of radicals meant the organization had no set ideological framework. Eventually, the IWW became known for its version of anarcho-syndicalism, in which workers would win power not through violent revolution but through a general strike of all workers that would grind the economy to a halt and allow them to take over. The IWW believed that all workers should join "one big union" in order to overthrow the wage system that would run each industry through the control of workers.[7] It defined the general strike as the "most effective weapon against capitalism."[8] But the IWW had a flexible set of ideas that shifted depending on the organizer, the campaign, and the lives of workers. It proved more effective when prioritizing organizing workers around their lived experiences than when focusing on ideological consistency. It held consistently to the idea that workers signing contracts with employers would limit their power and accept a state of oppressive capitalism. While perhaps true, this undermined the IWW's ability to build on its own victories because its leaders underestimated the power of employers to win back whatever they might have lost after a brief moment of workers' organizing. And while it offered workers practical advice to avoid violence in workplace actions, many of its propagandists also had a love affair with violent rhetoric, openly talking about sabotage and dynamiting factories. Wobblies rarely did any of these things, but by embracing violent rhetoric, all employers and the police had to do to convince people of the IWW's danger was to publicize the union's own words. This cavalier attitude toward violence would haunt the IWW.

In its first years, the IWW engaged in more infighting than organizing. The reformist socialists split with the revolutionary socialists in 1906. By 1908, the Western Federation of Miners had left their national project behind as moderates gained control over that union and returned it to the Rockies. The same year, the IWW expelled Daniel De Leon for trying to tie IWW to his Socialist Labor Party; he wanted to be America's Vladimir Lenin. This moment convinced the IWW to officially state that it would not affiliate with any political party. Some of the radicals believed the union's political goal should have focused on mobilizing a working-class vote; others felt American democracy was worthless for workers. Like many radical organizations riven with divisive ideological fights and state repression, it seemed like the IWW would not lead to anything of importance. Yet the defeat of De Leon and the rise of Big Bill Haywood, who had escaped with a not guilty verdict after a false accusation of ordering the murder of the former governor of Idaho, stabilized the IWW and gave it more practical leadership.[9]

Despite these struggles, IWW organizers seeped into the workforce. Its first adherents were loggers, miners, and farmworkers in the American West, who faced brutal exploitation in dangerous and isolated workplaces. Socialist ideas already had set roots in the West, and workers were open to challenging capitalism.[10] Unsafe technologies, cave-ins, and explosions crushed miners' bodies. They became a key IWW target as their once-skilled profession now turned into an industrial process that treated them like animals.[11] The IWW's first major strike took place in the mining town of Goldfield, Nevada. On December 20, 1906, workers went on strike, and within three weeks they won raised wages, shortened hours, and several fringe benefits, marking the IWW's first important victory. By March 1907, the IWW had three thousand dues-paying members in Goldfield and demanded that all the town's businesses agree to the eight-hour day. After another strike in November, the mine owners and Nevada's governor collaborated to crush the union with force. Falsely claiming union violence, the state asked Roosevelt for troops to end this challenge to employers. He complied. The federal troops remained until March 1908, when the Nevada legislature created a special police force to replace them. Goldfield would be a union-free town. Already, state power determined the limits of the IWW.[12]

Wobblies entered the timber industry in 1907 in Portland, Oregon, with a strike over wages; the AFL worked with industry to crush it. In Bridgeport, Connecticut, Wobbly organizers briefly united native English speakers with Hungarian immigrants to force the American Tube and Stamping Company to grant several demands. Over one thousand workers joined an early IWW local in the silk mills of Paterson, New Jersey. The AFL worried about the new attention to a radical challenge to its control over American unionism.[13]

These early actions rarely grabbed the headlines. But when the IWW challenged restrictions on free speech, it received national attention. Wobbly organizers gave radical speeches in public spaces. Disgusted, police forces repeatedly violated the Constitution by refusing to allow them to speak. In response, the IWW announced it would challenge any restrictions on free speech. It urged members to flood these cities to give more speeches, forcing police to house hundreds of prisoners and challenging the power of employers and police in brave ways. The first battle took place in Spokane, Washington. In the farming and logging industries surrounding the city, workers suffered the indignities and poverty so common in this era. Logging operations and farmers contracted with employment agencies, forcing workers to pay for a job. But if they were no longer needed when they reached the worksite, workers lost their money and had to return to Spokane and pay again.[14]

The employment scam infuriated workers and made Spokane an early IWW organizing hot spot. By 1909, the city had up to fifteen hundred dues-paying members and a union headquarters. It expanded its presence through street speaking, its organizers making angry speeches denouncing the exploitation workers faced. In March, the city council passed an ordinance banning public speaking from all "revolutionists." Arrests grew through the summer and into the fall. When Wobbly leader Jim Thompson was arrested for speaking without a permit on October 25, the IWW sent speakers from around the country to flood the city jails until they could speak freely in Spokane. Soon, four hundred people were in jail, overwhelming the system. The prisoners were intentionally underfed and forced to take ice-cold outdoor showers in the winter. Many suffered long-term health problems. But the intense resistance of the IWW surprised Spokane and overwhelmed its ability to deal with the crisis of its own making. It made a deal.[15]

The city freed all prisoners and allowed the IWW to hold outdoor meetings without police harassment. The employers gave up the contract labor system. But the IWW failed to build upon this victory. It could have continued the fight in Spokane. Instead, its organizers left to take up free speech fights in new towns instead of continuing to organize Spokane. The region remained an IWW stronghold for another decade. But workers would need more than high-publicity single campaigns to win power. More free speech fights in western cities continued: Aberdeen, Washington; San Diego and Fresno, California. The Spokane free speech fight set a pattern for future IWW actions. It created public displays that attracted media attention and exposed the injustices in American life. It gave the nation's poorest and most desperate workers hope. But it also prioritized intellectual ideas of revolution and struggle over long-term worker power.[16]

However, the IWW also provided critical organizing assistance when hard-pressed workers took initiative of their own. In McKees Rocks, Pennsylvania, largely immigrant workers faced the total control over their lives from their employer, the Pressed Steel Car Company, which kept them in a state of near peonage, with crowded company housing, company stores, and kickbacks to foremen expected from meager wages. The workers spontaneously struck in July 1909 after their paychecks were suddenly reduced. IWW organizers such as William Trautmann provided critical organizing assistance. In August, a pitched battle erupted between the strikers and police, leaving six dead, but in September, the company agreed to some of the workers' demands. It seemed like the IWW's first big victory. But once again, the organization's attention was pulled away from McKees Rocks toward new struggles. When the company reneged on the agreement and instituted a company union instead, the workers were left with little to show for their struggle.[17]

The IWW may have failed to produce long-term victories, but

it also took on the most difficult aspects of organizing American workers, including the racial divide that routinely fractured workplace solidarity. In its belief that all workers shared the common enemy of capitalism, the IWW tried to organize black and white workers together. Doing so attacked the fundamental racial ideology of the nation. The IWW did not shy away from challenging its own members. When Big Bill Haywood traveled to Alexandria, Louisiana, to speak to Wobbly loggers in 1911, he chastised the all-white meeting for acquiescing to Jim Crow laws that kept public meetings segregated, telling them, "You work in the same mills together. Sometimes a black man and a white man chop down the same tree together. You are meeting in convention now to discuss the conditions under which you labor. This can't be done intelligently by passing resolutions here and then sending them out to another room for the black men to act upon. Why not be sensible about this and call the Negroes into the convention? If it is against the law, this is one time when the law should be broken."[18] Haywood may have integrated this campaign, but racism divided many IWW members. Nonetheless, the IWW catalyzed racial solidarity in several places, including the Philadelphia docks, where the radicals provided a sharp contrast to racist AFL unions. It aggressively organized both white and black workers in a 1913 strike that revolutionized the docks in that city. As one black minister noted, "The IWW at least protects the colored man, which is more than I can say for the laws of this country."[19] All of these actions, leading to many defeats and the occasional victory, helped prepare the IWW to take on some of the most powerful industries in the United States, providing an unprecedented challenge to employer domination of workers' lives.

The Bread and Roses Strike

Lawrence, Massachusetts, became a center of the New England textile industry in the 1840s. The huge cotton and woolen mills employing thousands of people dominated the city's architecture; their ruins still do today. Forty thousand Lawrence residents worked in the mills, most immigrants from Ireland and southern and eastern Europe. By 1910, 48 percent of Lawrence's 85,000 people were foreign born.[20] A small tenement apartment took $6 of their $9 weekly wage. Many of these workers were women and children. Half the workers at the American Woolen Company, Lawrence's largest employer, were girls under 18 years old, toiling for little pay and breathing in cotton dust. They suffered from diseases such as tuberculosis and anthrax. The average Lawrence manufacturer had a life span of 58 years, but the life span of the Lawrence mill worker was only 39.6 years.[21]

As early as the 1860s, Lawrence newspapers noted "woman agitators" organizing and speaking out about the exploitation in the city's mills. In 1882, the workers struck after the Pacific Main Mill announced a simultaneous production increase and wage cut. Women, outraged over management's dismissal of their concerns as both workers and women, led the strike. It attracted the attention of both employers and workers throughout New England, who saw in it the future of labor relations and wages. The strikers lost, lacking support from male workers. Gender could divide workers as much as race. The city's textile workers would continue a spiral into exploitation.[22]

On January 12, 1912, a new Massachusetts law went into effect that limited women's working hours to fifty-four a week, a reduction of two hours. The Lawrence workers thought employers would not reduce their pay. They were wrong, as they discovered with their reduced paycheck delivered the day before the new law went into effect. Within minutes, workers marched through the Washington Mill, shutting down the machines and announcing a strike. By the next day, the city shut down. This began the Bread and Roses strike that captured national attention, demonstrated the deep injustices American workers faced, and clearly showed both the possibilities and limitations of IWW organizing.

The IWW had sent organizers to Lawrence beginning in 1907 but still had only three hundred or so members in early 1912. The AFL had a tiny United Textile Workers union presence of about two hundred members, but they gave it no resources for organizing, only focused on the English-speaking skilled mill workers, and avoided organizing any of the masses of immigrants. It would do nothing. Neither union seemed ready to pounce on the strike. However, the local IWW members asked that Joseph Ettor come to Lawrence. Although only twenty-six years old, he was a veteran Wobbly organizer; was fluent in English, Italian, and Polish; and could understand Yiddish and Hungarian. This made him an ideal person to speak to the many immigrants of Lawrence.

He had come to organize for the IWW in 1910 and 1911 and was well known by the community's labor activists. His own father, a radical Italian immigrant, had been injured in the Haymarket bombing. He was the one organizer who could speak to almost all the strikers. His commitment kept the workers' spirits high in the strike's early days. He helped them develop concrete demands that included a 15 percent pay raise, overtime pay, and no punishment of strikers.[23]

The mill owners and police responded as usual, with violence and manipulation. When agents from the American Woolen Company told workers that the mills had accepted their demands and they should return to work—a lie intended to divide the workers—Ettor exploded in a righteous fury, telling a crowd, "If an overseer comes into your house and invites you to betray yourself into being either a 'scab' or a blacklisted man, throw him down the stairs!"[24] The next day, incensed workers held a mass march. The police used fire hoses to spray water from the top of the mills onto the strikers in the subfreezing temperatures. When strikers threw ice in return, thirty-six were arrested and sentenced to a year in prison. A young Syrian immigrant named John Rami was bayoneted to death by a militia member. The region's elite classes mobilized to suppress the strike. Harvard students volunteered as part of the strikebreaking militia, a tradition at the college going back to the Great Railroad Strike of 1877, when they formed an armed militia to defend the railroads if the strike reached New England.[25] This was a common phenomenon among university students in this era when only the richest American children could go college. Harvard's president allowed them to make up their final exams.[26]

This was a critical moment for the IWW. Wobbly theorists hoped mass strikes could spur a revolution. Lawrence was the first time that workers under Wobbly leadership had engaged in a mass strike of thousands. Perhaps this would be the beginning of a larger workers' movement. Big Bill Haywood came to rally the workers. Fifteen thousand strikers met Haywood at the train station when he arrived. He spoke in very simple language to this largely immigrant crowd with limited English. Avoiding the left's theoretical language made him accessible to the average worker. Elizabeth Gurley Flynn, the "Rebel Girl" who played a major role in Lawrence, remembered how watching him talk to workers shaped her organizing for the rest of her life.[27] Yet throughout the strike, it was the rank-and-file workers, especially women, who truly led the way, understanding the street politics, deciding strategy, starting confrontations with the police and militia, and humiliating scabs. For all the IWW brought to Lawrence, it was the militancy of everyday workers, developed over a lifetime of toil and oppression, that made it happen.[28]

Strikes divided communities between strikers and those who believed themselves committed to "law and order." But the latter group committed most of the violent crimes in labor disputes. John Breen, a Lawrence school board member and son of the former mayor, framed the strikers by planting bombs around town. A week before this, William Madison Wood, owner of the American Woolen Company, had paid Breen a large sum of money. This "coincidence" was not seriously investigated, no charges were brought against Wood, and Breen was released without serving jail time. The ploy worked; when the bombs were found, it led to the typical overheated rhetoric from the media worried about revolution, especially after the *Los Angeles Times* bombing two years earlier. The *New York Times* wrote, "The strikers display a fiendish lack of humanity which ought to place them beyond the comfort of religion until they have repented."[29]

On January 29, the police murdered an Italian striker named Anna LoPizzo while breaking up a picket line. They pinned the death on the strike leaders—Joseph Ettor and Arturo Giovannitti, the editor of an Italian socialist newspaper in New York who was organizing the relief effort. They were three miles away at the time of the killing. They rotted in prison for the next eight months without bail or trial. Martial law followed. Once again, the authorities denied Wobblies their civil rights.[30] Strikers began challenging the militia to shoot them and it, rather than employers, became the top target of strikers' wrath.[31] Ettor and Giovannitti hyped these challenges by using violent language themselves; the latter told workers to "prowl around like wild animals looking for blood," while Ettor threatened the use of firearms.[32] For the militia and employers, this language justified the suppression.

With this strike gaining national headlines, the IWW sent its biggest names to Lawrence. Its best organizers, Elizabeth Gurley Flynn and William Trautmann, gave impassioned speeches. Italian anarchist Carlo Tresca followed. Big Bill Haywood returned to

Lawrence and took over the day-to-day running of the strike, holding up to ten meetings a day. He ate and socialized in workers' homes to build connections with them and held mass meetings where strikers from every different language would deliver messages to their people.[33]

The IWW also developed sophisticated propaganda to nationalize this conflict. Writers came to Lawrence to tell workers' stories. Haywood visited New England textile towns raising funds, and he gave a rousing speech at Carnegie Hall in Manhattan, telling attendees the Lawrence strikers' victory "depends on you!" as ushers roamed the crowd for donations while coins and dollar bills rained down from the rafters.[34] With the strikers destitute, the IWW thought to place workers' children with sympathizers in different cities. This spread the Lawrence workers' cause. On February 10, 119 children boarded a train to New York dressed in their rags, with their name, age, address, and nationality pinned to them. The *New York Call*, a socialist paper, wrote:

> TAKE THE CHILDREN
>
> Children of the Lawrence strikers are hungry. Their fathers and mothers are fighting against hunger, and hunger may break the strike. The men and women are willing to suffer, but they cannot watch their children's pain or hear their cries for food. Workers and strike sympathizers who can take a striker's child until the struggle ends are urged to send their name and address to the *Call*. Do it at once.[35]

They all found families when they arrived, as five thousand socialists met them at the train station to celebrate their arrival.

The children's exodus was masterful propaganda. Newspaper reporters ate it up and it raised desperately needed funds. More children followed, to Boston, Philadelphia, Vermont, New York. Another group of ninety-two children arrived in New York and paraded on Fifth Avenue before going to their temporary homes. In Lawrence, the attention led to more militia violence. The militia harassed, beat, and even bayoneted workers on the street. When a militia member told a man walking a dog to hurry and the owner refused, he stabbed the dog.[36]

On February 24, another 150 children were to board a train to Philadelphia. The police blocked their path at the Lawrence train station, threatening to arrest the mothers. As the train approached, one woman pushed ahead, desperate for her child to get out. The police grabbed her and that spark set off a frantic rush toward the train. The police began beating the women and children. Mothers were dragged from their children into police wagons. The train left without a single child aboard. The brutality badly backfired. The national media excoriated the violence. Said the journalist Ray Stannard Baker, a man not sympathetic to the IWW, "If I were living in one of those miserable tenements . . . I should join any movement, however revolutionary, to put an end to such conditions." President William Howard Taft, reading about the attack, ordered the attorney general to investigate. A congressional committee held a hearing on Lawrence, giving workers the chance to tell their stories to the most powerful people in the country. First Lady Helen Herron Taft attended. Workers testified about their poor living conditions, their poverty, and how the companies docked their pay; they even told about employers who charged them for clean drinking water. One girl testified about how a spinning frame wrenched her hair and scalped her.[37]

The timing could not have been better for the IWW. The strike had begun to collapse under the weight of hunger and poverty. Nearly half of the workforce had returned to the job. But, embarrassed by the publicity, on March 12, the owners of the American Woolen Company gave in. The other companies followed. The strike was over, a huge win for the workers and the IWW. Workers received a wage increase of between 5 and 20 percent, with more going to the lowest paid. They received overtime pay for the first time, and all strikers could return to their jobs. Yet there was one more battle—the murder trial of Ettor, Giovannitti, and Joseph Caruso, an Italian immigrant and striker later added to the indictment who never understood why he was arrested. They languished in prison until September, when their trial began. This became the IWW's major cause in the months after the strike. On September 30, the workers engaged in a one-day walkout in support of their jailed organizers. All three were acquitted on November 26.[38]

Only two years later, the union created during the great Bread and Roses strike was dust. IWW membership in Lawrence fell from ten thousand after the strike to four hundred by late 1914. Layoffs due to a 1913 economic downturn explained some of it. But the IWW did not recognize the need for long-term organizing in individual workplaces if workers were to build power. It refused to sign contracts with employers because it believed contracts limited worker action to incremental gains in a system that accepted capitalism. Maybe this could have worked had the IWW kept skilled organizers in Lawrence to continue the struggle. But Haywood and other Wobbly leaders always moved on to the next big strike. The mill owners eventually repealed what they had given up in the face of public pressure. Unionization was new to the workers. They did not know how to maintain their power. Without the Wobbly leadership, the workers were divided by ethnicity—a split encouraged by the employers. Union leaders were fired and blacklisted. Ettor returned in 1916 to try to restart the union, but a mob grabbed him and put him on a train to Boston. The strike had won the workers some material gains, but it left them no union to keep up the fight.[39]

The IWW turned to another textile town, Paterson, New Jersey, where silk workers went on strike on February 1, 1913, demanding an eight-hour day and better working conditions. Again, IWW organizing errors both helped mobilize the workers and contributed to their defeat.[40] John Reed, future chronicler of the Mexican and Russian Revolutions, met Haywood when the latter came to Paterson. Reed mobilized the New York art community for the strikers. He and other artists decided to put on a performance at Madison Square Garden to show the world the great evil of the Paterson employers and the nobility of the workers' struggle, while raising money for the cause.[41] Using actual strikers telling their stories, the Paterson Strike Pageant received positive reviews. It also undermined the strike it purported to help. Reed had promised workers the pageant would pay to keep the strikers going, but it did not raise nearly enough money. Morale plummeted. As Elizabeth Gurley Flynn said, "Bread was the need of the hour, and bread was not forthcoming even from the most beautiful and realistic example of art that has been put on the stage in the last half century."[42]

Worse, the event had distracted and divided workers. With

strike leaders rehearsing a theater production instead of picketing, strikebreakers found it easier to enter the mills. Only 1,000 out of the 25,000 strikers could participate in the pageant. This led to jealousy and accusations of favoritism. In early July, the English-speaking skilled ribbon workers agreed to a shop-by-shop settlement, kicked the IWW organizers out of the decision-making process, and went back to work. The immigrant workers could not stay out without the English speakers. By July 28, the strike had collapsed in a total defeat for the workers and the IWW. Never again would the IWW organize a large walkout among the eastern immigrant working class.[43]

The IWW and Western Workers

Reeling from Paterson, the IWW returned to the West, where the extractive economy in the agriculture, mining, and timber industries sought mobile, highly exploitable workers. IWW organizers also began thinking more pragmatically than in Paterson and Lawrence, letting workers set the demands, which usually revolved around concrete material gains that meant something to workers' impoverished lives instead of cultural productions and media events. In the face of tremendous violence, workers found in the IWW a vehicle to articulate their outrage and despair, as well as their hopes and dreams.

The violence of workers' lives should shock us. Ralph Durst's hop farm in Wheatland, California, was the largest agricultural employer in the state. Durst sent flyers across the West advertising for hop pickers, telling of ample work and good wages. He lied. By late July 1913, around 2,800 men, women, and children had arrived in Wheatland. Durst recruited far more workers than the 1,500 he needed in order to lower wages to suit him. Workers could rent a tent for $2.75 a week, but a lot of people lived in the open, with a pallet for a floor. Most made less than $1.50 a day (about $37 today) for twelve hours of work. Twenty-eight hundred people shared eight toilets, resulting in predictable filth and sickness. For five days in a row, the temperature reached 105 degrees. Durst refused to provide workers water, and the nearest wells were a mile away. Workers appealed for the promised wages, free water, and better living spaces. Durst ignored them. IWW member Richard "Blackie" Ford called for a strike. The police served as Durst's private military. One cop grabbed Ford off the speaker's platform and arrested him. When a gun fired, an already angry group of people turned violent. Over the next few minutes, a fierce battle raged between the police and workers. Four people died: two workers, a deputy sheriff, and Yuba County district attorney E.T. Manwell. The state railroaded Ford and another Wobbly leader, Herman Suhr, into prison on trumped-up murder charges. That neither had killed anyone did not matter. Both received life sentences.[44]

Such violence occurred repeatedly in the West. In Everett, Washington, in 1916, vigilantes opened fire when a boat full of Wobblies attempted to dock at the logging town to protest previous vigilante and police violence against its members. Between five and twelve Wobblies were killed, some of whom were never found because they were shot off the boat into the water.[45] Time and again—in the free speech fights, at Lawrence and Paterson, at Wheatland and Everett—workers could not receive justice under capitalism. Organizers were thrown into prison for the audacity of challenging employers; street speakers were subjected to health-destroying conditions in jails for simply expressing their First Amendment rights. This treatment became a staple of Wobbly literature, demonstrating the pointlessness of acquiescing to the system.

Yet, the IWW gave the police and employers all the evidence they needed to see the union as a dangerous revolutionary threat. The IWW promoted arson and other tools of undermining production as central pillars of its strategy for defeating capitalism. Haywood insisted that revolutionary politics were impossible without industrial sabotage. Talk of blowing up buildings, setting forest fires, and destroying corporate property scared employers. The IWW did not have to do any of these things for their words to be used against them—in fact, the number of actual incidents of sabotage was surprisingly small. Elizabeth Gurley Flynn later aptly called it "infantile Leftism."[46] After Wheatland, IWW newspapers published articles calling for arson. When a cannery in San Jose burned, there was no evidence tying it to IWW sabotage, but continued Wobbly calls for a campaign of arson to free the Wheatland prisoners convinced authorities that the IWW was a terrorist organization burning businesses.[47]

The macho attitude toward violence of a few IWW organizers should not obscure the fact that thousands of workers saw the Wobblies as their best hope for their future. That became increasingly true as IWW organizers based their campaigns on winning concrete gains for workers, letting them set the agenda. The commitment of Wobbly organizers to revolution had not changed, but they did increasingly recognize the need to reach rank-and-file workers in their lived experiences and use those as an organizing technique to move them toward radical activity.

Loggers in the Northwest lived particularly brutal lives, even compared to other workers of the day. Carrying their waterlogged and flea-infested bedrolls on their backs from camp to camp, loggers suffered through respiratory illnesses, filth, and miserable discomfort. Housing was drafty, overcrowded, and abundant in vermin. Bathing facilities and sanitary toilets were almost unknown. New technologies lacking safety precautions killed and maimed workers daily. After 1912, organizers began to focus on the lived experiences of workers, slowly working towards the victories the IWW could not achieve in Lawrence and Paterson. A June 1913 strike list of demands included not only the eight-hour day and $3 a day but also towels and soap for bathing, "clean sanitary bunkhouses" with mattresses and blankets, and safety equipment around dangerous machinery in the mills. In publicizing the strike, the IWW asked, "Are you dissatisfied with living . . . in miserable bunkhouses?" If so, "refuse to work under bad conditions, demand better camp conditions and pure food." Fifty camps shut down during this brief strike. These actions slowly built IWW membership over the next two years. By 1917, the Wobblies had made themselves the single organization fighting for workplace democracy in the logging camps.[48]

The IWW made similar gains in other industries. In 1915, it created the Agricultural Workers Organization (AWO) to organize migratory farmworkers. Like the timber organizers, the AWO's chief organizer, Walter Nef, focused on concrete gains for workers, such as a ten-hour day, a minimum wage, overtime pay, and better housing. By that summer, it won better conditions for workers in Kansas and had fifteen hundred members in North Dakota. It established offices throughout the Midwest, and by the fall of 1916 it had twenty thousand members across the region. Miners in Minnesota's Mesabi Range, seeing the AWO's success, wrote to Nef asking for Italian- and Slavic-language organizers to come to the mines. Nef did not have those, but workers struck anyway, and by July 1916, the newly created Metal Mine Workers Industrial Union No. 490 had four thousand members. Even though the companies crushed the strike, they also granted many of the miners' demands, fearful of more organizing. Sometimes the workers could win even if the IWW lost.[49]

Repression

The government never really tolerated radicalism. But when the United States entered World War I in 1917, the sheer existence of the IWW became intolerable for law enforcement, for business, and for the administration of Woodrow Wilson. In 1917, one million workers struck during 4,500 strikes, alarming employers around the country. Most of these strikes had nothing to do with the IWW, but growing worker activism frightened employers and concerned the government, which was using its growing powers under Progressive presidents to coordinate production of war materials.[50] IWW leadership equivocated on the war. Haywood feared state repression if it opposed the war. He and other IWW leaders told Wobblies to make their own decisions. It made no difference. The IWW's reputation for violence, partially earned through its own rhetoric, made it a target. Policymakers drew a sharp divide between the AFL and the IWW. Wilson wanted to bring "respectable" labor into wartime planning, and the AFL saw him as the most pro-union president to date. In fact, many unionists believed Wilson more favorable to their cause than any previous president. When Wilson signed the Clayton Antitrust Act in 1914, giving labor limited protections from injunctions, AFL head Samuel Gompers called it "labor's Magna Carta," and Wilson's signing of the La Follette Seamen's Act in 1915 gave unprecedented ability to sailors to escape their oppressive conditions upon docking in the United States.[51] These were big wins for the mainstream labor movement. The AFL, the Wilson administration, and especially employers could also all agree that World War I was an opportunity to eliminate the IWW entirely.[52]

Phelps Dodge, one of the world's largest copper-mining companies, operated on both sides of the U.S.-Mexican border. In 1916, the AFL-affiliated International Union of Mine, Mill, and Smelter

Workers had about eighteen hundred mostly native-born American members in Bisbee, a town in southern Arizona near the border. There, the IWW organized the most marginalized workers: Mexicans and eastern European immigrants. On June 24, 1917, the IWW presented Phelps Dodge with a list of demands, including better living and working conditions and nondiscrimination against union workers. The copper company refused to negotiate. By June 27, about 50 percent of Bisbee miners struck. Phelps Dodge used the war as a pretext to crush the IWW entirely. On July 12, two thousand men assembled to cleanse the town of the Wobblies. They gathered 1,186 men suspected of radicalism and marched them to waiting trains and shoved them onto cattle cars knee-deep in manure. The train dumped them in the desert near the New Mexico-Arizona border. The Bisbee Deportation crushed the unions in the town.[53]

Frank Little was one of the IWW's most skilled and radical organizers. He was in Bisbee, where beatings left him physically broken but as determined as ever. Then, he left for Butte, Montana, where he attempted to organize an angry community after the Speculator Mine fire had killed 168 miners. Little had mixed results, as Butte had a long history of independent unionism, and many miners did not trust the IWW. But the Butte police and mine owners had no tolerance for this radical. His allies told Little to flee, but he refused. Six masked men came to his hotel room, tied him up, took him to the edge of town, beat him, and hanged him from a railroad trestle. A few days after Little's lynching, Montana declared martial law against war opponents, rounded up radicals of all stripes, and engaged in a massive state-sponsored violation of civil liberties. No one was ever charged for Little's murder.[54]

When Butte miners struck in September 1918, the army raided the IWW hall and other miners' union halls, beat and arrested strike leaders, and banned the printing of union newspapers. Similar repression took place in the forests: the IWW led a 1917 strike that convinced many employers to improve the housing and sanitation in the camps and to institute the eight-hour day. When it threatened a new wave of strikes to begin on May 1, 1918, the government formed a squadron of soldier-loggers called the Spruce Production Division to acquire the wood needed to build airplanes, militarizing the forest. The army then created a government-sponsored paramilitary company union. The Loyal Legion of Loggers and Lumbermen banned IWW membership for any logger wanting a job but also cleaned up the sanitation and food in the camps, which had spurred the organizing. IWW membership shriveled in the face of both repression and of the government granting much of what rank-and-file loggers demanded.[55]

The violence against the IWW was part of the larger Red Scare. The government defined criticism of the war as a treasonous act. Wilson signed the Espionage Act in June 1917 and the Sedition Act in May 1918, which cracked down on dissent, banning radical publications from the mail and allowing for the imprisonment of people who spoke out against the war. Immigrant radicals such as Emma Goldman were arrested and deported to the Soviet Union. Socialist Party leader Eugene Debs was arrested, charged with sedition, and sentenced to ten years in prison after giving a speech urging resistance to the draft. A frequent Socialist Party candidate for president, he ran for the presidency again in 1920, this time from prison, receiving over nine hundred thousand votes.

Workers went on strike in record numbers in 1919, and workers in Seattle even went on a massive general strike that shut down the city. Most of these workers did not adhere to radical ideologies, and many of the year's strikes revolved around how inflation of consumer prices seriously challenged the ability of working people to feed and clothe themselves in the aftermath of World War I.[56] Yet repression was the response, especially against the IWW. Federal agents and mobs raided IWW offices. Violent mobs tarred and feathered individual Wobblies. The government indicted 166 Wobblies for subversion. Local elites used the vigilante atmosphere to crush African American labor organizing as well, including a 1919 massacre of black sharecroppers organizing for justice in Elaine, Arkansas, that killed between twenty-five and several hundred African Americans. In some places, the Wobblies marched on, such as leading the largest strike in the history of the port of Philadelphia in 1920, but when it failed after six weeks, it gave employers the upper hand and they crushed the rare truly interracial union through a 1922 lockout. In Centralia, Washington, a small logging town, the American Legion decided to celebrate the first anniversary of Armistice Day in 1919 by raiding the IWW hall. The Wobblies fought back and killed four invaders. That night, the Legionnaires lynched Wobbly organizer Wesley

Everest from a bridge. Eight other Wobblies were sentenced to long prison terms of up to forty years. The remaining Wobblies focused on getting the class war prisoners out of prison, but the last did not leave until 1937.[57]

The Industrial Workers of the World never brought about their revolution. Despite the IWW's internal problems, the state's intolerance for even moderate challenges to employer authority, not to mention those fighting to overthrow capitalism, meant that these radicals never had a chance to create the idealized world they sought. But the IWW provided hope and organizing expertise to workers who had none. It organized across the nation's racial divisions like no union had done before. It took on the most oppressive employers and sometimes won. The IWW advanced a radical critique of American capitalism that influenced another generation of radicals to come. It played a critical role in teaching American workers how to use radical ideas to advance an agenda that effectively challenged capitalism, laying the groundwork for the working class of the next generation to finally win dignity and respect.

6

The Flint Sit-Down Strike and the New Deal

A small group of dedicated activists can transform the world through organizing and electing politicians who support them.

The IWW failed to create a workers' revolution. But by 1940, millions of workers had won rights most could only have dreamed of twenty years earlier. They could join a union and had won old-age insurance, an eight-hour day, overtime pay, and the minimum wage. In the depths of the Great Depression, workers transformed their lives through a combination of their organizing and electing politicians to office who would change the attitude of the state toward unions. After a century of largely failed struggle, how did workers win so much so fast?

Anyone trying to organize a movement today should take three lessons from the workers of the 1930s who made the modern union movement: First, a small group of people can accomplish amazing things. Second, you never know when a small movement will become a mass movement. Third, while protest movements can create mass action, they require legal changes to win. That means electing allies to office. That was crucial in the 1930s.

These lessons are crystallized in the Flint sit-down strike of 1937, when a small group of workers occupied their factory to force General Motors to recognize their union. This brave action could have cost workers their jobs and even their lives. In fact, it likely would have, but those workers, and millions like them in Michigan and across the nation, had elected pro-union politicians to the White House and statehouses in the five years prior to 1937, creating the conditions for victory.

The 1920s and the Great Depression

Popular culture portrays the 1920s as a fun time, with flappers and gangsters selling illegal alcohol in speakeasies. A booming economy meant automobiles in more driveways and new goods hitting the American market. But this façade of luxury and parties rested on the backs of impoverished workers. Steelworkers still labored an average of sixty-three hours a week in deadly factories, to provide just one example.[1] In the face of the Red Scare that crushed the IWW, the nation's employers and government turned sharply against even conservative unions. The American Federation of Labor made major gains during World War I only to lose them all in the 1920s. Seattle's labor movement pulled off a general strike in 1919, but within just a few years, employers had cowed the city's unions and reestablished dominance at the workplace.[2] Between 1919 and 1923, national union membership fell from 5 million to 3.6 million. United Mine Workers of America membership plummeted from 600,000 to 80,000 after employers declared war on it, even using airplanes to bomb West Virginia miners marching after the companies murdered a sheriff who stood up to them.[3]

Wanting to forestall the radical strikes of previous decades, many companies instituted company unions. These employer-dominated organizations enacted just as much reform as necessary to keep real unions at bay. Over a million Americans had to sign so-called yellow-dog contracts in the 1920s, making the refusal to join a union a condition of employment.[4] The courts attempted to hold the tide of Progressive legislation and ensure the continuation of the Gilded Age. Labor activists suffered a terrible defeat in 1923 with *Adkins v. Children's Hospital*, in which the Supreme Court overthrew the minimum wage law for women that Congress had mandated for Washington, D.C. And when Congress passed a constitutional amendment in 1924 to ban child labor, the states overwhelmingly refused to ratify it. The 1927 execution of the anarchists Nicola Sacco and Bartolomeo Vanzetti for a murder after an unfair trial and in the face of national and international protests demonstrated the continued lack of justice radicals received in American courts. Little in the 1920s went workers' way.

The 1920s consumer economy rested on a shaky foundation. The stock market shot up, but used shady trading practices that allowed investors to pay a small percentage of the stock price with the rest due when the price rose. This was a recipe for economic catastrophe when the bubble burst. Factories' productivity meant that they produced huge amounts of consumer goods, but their own workers could not afford them. Enormous backlogs piled up and by 1929, industries started laying off workers. Farmers struggled with debt racked up during World War I when they had bought expensive equipment, but then they had to pay it back after farm prices collapsed in the 1920s. Everyday people went into consumer debt for the first time, buying refrigerators, automobiles, and electric washing machines.[5]

The reckoning began in 1929 with Black Tuesday, when the stock market sank like a stone. The market lost one-third of its value in three weeks, beginning the Great Depression. Between 1929 and 1932, automobile production fell by 75 percent. Ford reduced its employees from 128,000 to 37,000. For those still working, wages dropped by 37 percent. There were 113 suicides in Detroit in 1927; 568 in 1931. By 1932, there were 400,000 unemployed people in Michigan. By the winter of 1933, 25 percent of Americans were out of work, and perhaps another 25 percent were underemployed or working less than full-time.[6] Local relief efforts rapidly found themselves completely overwhelmed, and the Hoover administration had nothing but bromides about self-reliance to offer. AT&T president Walter Gifford headed the President's Organization on Unemployed Relief. He called for a "great spiritual experience" in 1931 by Americans giving charity to those who were hungry. New York could provide families with only $2 a week in aid.[7] This was no answer to widespread unemployment and misery.

The labor movement was unprepared to organize the millions of unemployed workers. The AFL still refused to organize most industrial workers. A new generation of radicals filled the vacuum. Since the Russian Revolution in 1917, American radicals had largely turned away from the anarcho-syndicalism of the IWW and to the Communist Party. Communist organizers rallied unemployed workers; in Michigan, they led a march from Detroit to the Ford River Rouge Complex in Dearborn to present petitions demanding jobs. The nonviolent march had between three thousand and five thousand workers.

Henry Ford—anti-Semitic, anticommunist, and paranoid—effectively owned Dearborn. The city government, police, and firefighters answered directly to him. Ford had no intention of tolerating unemployed workers marching on his factory. The Dearborn police sprayed tear gas at the marchers and beat them with their clubs. The police and Ford's guards fired into the crowd; among the security contingent was Harry Bennett, an ex-boxer who headed Ford's private police force. Five workers died. The Dearborn killings only helped prove the Communists' point that American capitalism needed to be overthrown. Radical leftist organizing grew throughout the nation, including among African Americans in Alabama, Latino miners in the West, and factory workers in Chicago.[8]

The growth of radicalism and clashes between the unemployed and police alarmed politicians. They should have. In Germany, where the Depression hit the hardest, Adolf Hitler and his Nazi Party came to power in 1933. Fascism or communism seemed the only options for millions of Europeans. The AFL feared leftist challenges to its supremacy over the U.S. labor movement. In response, it developed the nation's most sophisticated anticommunist information network during the interwar years, more so than even the FBI.[9] Yet even the AFL expressed radical rhetoric due to the corporations' failed response to the Depression. AFL president William Green threatened to call for a "universal strike," a shocking statement from the notoriously conservative official. But he noted that it was the "only language that a lot of employers ever understand, the language of force."[10]

The government's indifference toward workers' suffering infuriated Americans. In 1924, Congress passed the World War Adjusted Compensation Act, granting World War I veterans a pension check in 1945. By 1932, these soldiers marched on Washington to demand the immediate payment of their bonus. On June 15, 1932, the House passed the Bonus Bill that would grant the bonuses immediately. But the Senate rejected it. President Herbert Hoover ordered the military under General Douglas MacArthur to destroy the veterans' camp. MacArthur hated the Bonus Army, as these veterans were known, believing they were communists. He violently evicted the residents, burning the camp. Many wondered how long Americans would put up with the violent suppression of movements aimed to give dignity to the working class.[11]

Some workers embraced communism, but more took to the ballot box to dump Hoover. In 1932, they elected Franklin Delano Roosevelt president in one of the largest landslides in American history. Roosevelt's New Deal sought short-term employment programs and long-term structural changes to stabilize the economy. It created the Tennessee Valley Authority, a dam-and-power agency intended to lift an entire region out of poverty. The Civilian Conservation Corps took young men out of the cities, building their bodies and the nation's rural infrastructure. The Works Progress Administration and Public Works Administration employed Americans in everything from building post offices to interviewing the last survivors of slavery.[12]

The New Deal not only gave workers confidence in the government again but also spurred them to take action. Roosevelt signed the National Industrial Recovery Act (NIRA), creating the National Recovery Administration (NRA), in 1933. The NRA sought to set industry codes to eliminate unfair trade practices and the destructive competition and overproduction that helped bring on the Depression. During the 1920s, some corporations, unable to control their own brutal competition, had begun to accept politically moderate unions to set labor costs across an industry. The NIRA extended this principle, and the AFL supported it.[13] Critics accused it of promoting monopolies because it supported large operators over small business, and it had limited success before the Supreme Court declared it unconstitutional in 1935. Section 7(a) in the law granted workers the right to form a union free of employer interference. AFL president Green said it created a "compete and almost instantaneous change in the union situation" that would allow workers to have real representation on the job.[14] However, it turned out that the government could do nothing when employers ignored Section 7(a) and fired workers for union activity. Yet workers acted on their belief in Roosevelt and Section 7(a). In 1934, 1.5 million workers went on strike. Mexican American dressmakers in Los Angeles, spurred by hope in the NRA, joined the International Ladies' Garment Workers' Union, went on a strike, and won union recognition.[15]

Four strikes in that transformative year of 1934 changed American history. On April 12, workers at Toledo's Electric Auto-Lite Company struck and united with the city's unemployed to create a movement against the poverty that afflicted them all. The courts granted Auto-Lite an injunction, limiting picketers to twenty-five at each of the plant's two entrances, but that did not apply to the unemployed, who continued to block the entrances. Between May 23 and 28, strikers battled the Ohio National Guard and two workers died. On June 2, the autoworkers came to an agreement, winning only a 5 percent wage increase but also union recognition, the critical tool to have a voice on the job.[16]

West Coast longshoremen, who loaded and unloaded ships, started the next of 1934's great strikes on May 9. Longshoremen came to the docks every day in hope of getting chosen to work. The "shape-up" system shamed workers and lowered wages by bringing out everyone who needed a job. It also led to kickbacks and corruption. As labor historian Irving Bernstein wrote, "Aside from slavery itself, it is difficult to conceive of a more inhuman labor market mechanism than the shape-up."[17] Led by the radical Australian immigrant Harry Bridges, the strike spread from San Francisco up and down the West Coast. On July 5, police attacked the strikers in San Francisco, firing tear gas into the picket line and then charging with horses. That afternoon, a cop fired a shotgun into the strike kitchen, killing two workers. California governor Frank Merriam called in the National Guard to open the docks. In response, Bridges called for a general strike, shutting down the city. When it fell apart a few days later, the strike died too. The longshoremen returned to work without a victory, but the National Longshoremen's Board mediated the conflict and gave the union effective control over hiring, ended the shape-up, and granted them a 95¢-an-hour pay increase. Again, a government agency mediating a strike fairly could transform the opportunity for unions.[18]

A week after the longshoremen walked out, the International Brotherhood of Teamsters Local 574 went on strike in Minneapolis. This communist-led local inside a politically conservative union brought the city to a standstill. On May 21, the police attacked strikers trying to stop a truck. Hundreds of strikers ran over to help their comrades, and cops pulled their weapons; a massacre was only avoided when a Teamster drove a truck into the middle of the police, dividing their forces. Employers caved in August, submitting a proposal to a federal mediator that incorporated most of the union's demands, and the strike ended in a victory for the workers.[19] That victory led to strikes across Minnesota, including women garment workers who walked off the job at Strutwear Hosiery in 1935, an action supported by members of Local 574, who blocked the removal of goods from the plant. In April 1936, Strutwear gave in and the workers won. Solidarity was the order of the day in Minnesota.[20]

Finally, two hundred thousand textile mill workers struck in New England and the South. As early as 1894, Alabama had repealed its child labor law to attract New England textile mill owners seeking cheap, nonunion labor in the South.[21] After 1910, this trickle of capital mobility became a flood. Northern businesses targeted the South because of its lack of immigrants bringing socialist ideas with them, the traditions of paternalism that led to an easily controlled labor force, and a lack of unions. But poverty led to major strikes, first in 1929 and then in 1934. In 1929, workers had been fighting the "stretch-out," which forced workers to produce more by speeding up the machines. Workers faced murderous violence from their owners and from the National Guard. In 1934, the story was much the same. When the northern-based United Textile Workers attempted to organize southern mills to save its last remaining strongholds in New England from moving south, employer violence again ruled the day. Armed guards killed six workers at a South Carolina mill. Several governors, both in the South and in Rhode Island, mobilized the National Guard to end the strike and the union had to call it off after three weeks. Despite Roosevelt personally urging owners to rehire the workers, 75,000 throughout the South were blacklisted.[22]

These radical actions by everyday workers moved Roosevelt to greater support for worker rights. In 1935, he signed the National Labor Relations Act (NLRA), guaranteeing workers the right not only to join a union but to force an employer to bargain a contract. The NLRA established the National Labor Relations Board

(NLRB), a government agency with power to oversee the nation's labor relations. Employers were furious. *Business Week* ran an editorial titled "No Obedience!"[23] It was a huge victory but also deeply compromised, excluding domestic servants and farmworkers because southern politicians would only pass the bill if it did not apply to black workers in the South. Unfortunately, the reality of American racism forced a choice between excluding the poorest workers and no bill at all, much as right-wing forces have forced compromises on every major piece of legislation that expanded economic rights for Americans to this day.[24]

Still, only mass organizing would force employers to recognize a union. The AFL still refused to organize workers on an industrial basis, holding on to its preference for skilled workers while opposing efforts to organize factories. However, John L. Lewis, president of the United Mine Workers of America (UMWA), and his allies created the Committee for Industrial Organization in 1935 to demand industrial organizing in the AFL. When the AFL refused, Lewis and the CIO split entirely from the federation in 1937.[25]

The CIO, now the Congress of Industrial Organizations, changed American history. It organized the biggest workforces in America, including steelworkers, autoworkers, rubber workers, and electrical workers, turning them into mighty unions that would stand for the transformation of the working class into the middle class. Lewis poured millions of dollars of UMWA money into organizing campaigns. Communists and socialists led these organizing campaigns, even though Lewis hated communism. The communists were skilled organizers, many of whom had spent the past several years organizing unemployed workers. This radical cadre of trained organizers would lead workers to some of the greatest victories in American history.[26]

The CIO critically differed from the AFL in terms of its relationship with the government. The AFL believed it could never trust the government to help workers, preferring the power of workers negotiating with employers to win contracts. The CIO knew better and worked to elect Democrats, knowing that only liberal Democratic governments would pass the laws it needed to win. Lewis, Amalgamated Clothing Workers of America president Sidney Hillman, and other industrial union leaders formed Labor's Non-Partisan League to rally labor support for Roosevelt's reelection in 1936, which was wholeheartedly endorsed by rank-and-file workers, who lionized Roosevelt for using the government to help them.[27] By becoming a critical part of the New Deal coalition after Roosevelt's overwhelming victory that fall, industrial unions demanded state support for their plans. The extent to which they could muster that support would go far to determine the potential and limitations of industrial unionism.

The Flint Sit-Down Strike

In the mid-1930s, Flint, Michigan, was a city of 150,000 people. Auto companies, mostly General Motors (GM), employed 80 percent of Flint's workers. Like other companies, in the 1920s GM introduced welfare capitalism, trying to undermine unionism by providing financial incentives and social programs to its workers. But its attempts to maintain workers' loyalty faltered in the face of the Great Depression, with workers facing layoffs and the repossession of the homes GM itself had sold to them. Small strikes popped up at GM factories beginning in 1933, but the company refused to recognize a union. Instead, it paid nearly $1 million between 1934 and 1936 to hire two hundred spies to report on union activity and then hired other spies to spy on the spies to make sure they were not sympathetic to the unionists.[28] As one worker told Wisconsin senator Robert La Follette, GM "so completely run this town and have it so well propagandized to their own good that one don't even dare talk here. You have no liberties at all. You couldn't belong to a union and breathe it to a soul. That soul would probably be as spy."[29] Those spies routinely reported on workers attending United Automobile Workers of America (UAW) organizing meetings, and the company would fire those people.

GM workers faced the same problems as other workers: a lack of respect from employers, too little pay, unemployment, and overwork when they could work. When GM sped up the assembly line, one Buick worker said, "If you had to . . . take a crap, if there wasn't anybody there to relieve you, you had to run away and tie the line up, and if you tied the line up you got hell for it."[30] Workers chafed against foremen who drove them like animals. They felt like machines and they wanted to be treated like people. GM drove them to exhaustion when they worked and then laid them off for long periods of time. Fifty-six percent of GM employees worked fewer than forty weeks in 1934.[31] The rest of the time, they made no money at all. Meanwhile, foremen chose who would get laid off, and favoritism ruled the day.

The AFL had tentatively begun to organize the autoworkers by 1935, but only halfheartedly. Nearly all industrial workers, including in the auto factories, remained unorganized. That year, the UAW formed, building on the demands of workers in the auto industry that they unite under one union. The UAW joined the CIO when the new federation formed. John L. Lewis knew how critical organizing auto factories would be for the CIO. An early win was crucial. Henry Ford, whose brutal private army was well known by his workers, set the tone for how to crush unions. Rather than take on Ford, the UAW focused on GM. It attempted to negotiate with GM president William Knudsen for a settlement without a strike. Knudsen flatly refused.

UAW organizers visited workers in their homes, talked to them as they entered and left work, and held mass meetings. Said one organizer, it was "days of slow plodding and painful preparation which only much later bore its fruit."[32] Slowly, the union made progress. It won some small strikes in November and December 1936. The La Follette Committee, a Senate committee investigating the corporate suppression of unions, announced it would hold hearings on GM.[33] The UAW made an agreement with a glassworkers' union that provided windshields to GM. Their own strikes slowed down GM's production. This slog of organizing work created momentum. Still, by December 1936, only about 14 percent of GM workers were dues-paying UAW members.[34]

Despite these small numbers, UAW organizers decided to shut GM down in January 1937. But union activists would not wait. Workers in the Cleveland factory that produced parts for Chevrolet's auto bodies sat down on the job on December 28, 1936. Two days later, fifty workers at GM's Fisher Body plant in Flint began their sit-down occupation when management transferred three inspectors who would not leave the union.[35] These spontaneous actions in solidarity with fellow workers changed history. The slow organizing of the previous months led to more members and many more workers—perhaps a majority—who wanted to join the union but feared they would be fired. Many GM workers knew little about unions, having recently migrated from the rural Midwest and Appalachia. Organizers taught unionism to workers at the same time that they battled the auto companies. The evening after the fifty workers sat down, other workers discovered GM transferring necessary materials to other plants. Outraged, the workers erupted in fury, and support for the strike grew instantly. One of the greatest battles in American labor history was on.

In the vast majority of strikes, the workers walk out of the factory. That inherently gives the employer an advantage. Once the workers are outside, the employer can scheme to bring strikebreakers into the factory. The sit-down turns the tables. It makes the employer tactic of antiworker violence much more difficult, as they would destroy their own machinery with it. Of course, employers also thought the tactic was illegal. They considered their factories private property that workers had no right to occupy. Courts backed them up on this position. The UAW defended the tactic by arguing that it was the only option workers had to make sure the company did not give their jobs to strikebreakers. They cited a legal theory that a job was a workers' private property, an idea that some legal scholars advanced at the time.[36] The UAW did not invent this tactic. It had been used periodically in Europe for years, and several other small strikes in the months before the Flint strike had deployed it as well. These were usually quickie strikes, perhaps lasting a few days, usually only a few hours. They were spontaneous actions by angry workers, often started without consulting the union leaders. In February 1936, workers at the Goodyear rubber plant sat down in Akron, Ohio.[37] But Flint workers made the sit-down famous.

The UAW kept the workers disciplined and as busy as possible. They sang songs, exercised, and read newspapers delivered by their friends and family. Workers slept on car seats and commandeered the factory cafeteria for their meals. A strike committee met daily to check on everyone's state of mind and to plan for the next day. They made sanitation the first priority and banned alcohol and weapons. The union evicted workers slacking from their duties. Organizers worked closely with the workers and community to stay on message, keep the pressure on GM, and not allow frustrations to boil over in counterproductive ways.

A women's auxiliary formed to support the workers, bringing them food, clean clothing, newspapers, and other items to help them spend the long days inside the plant. Its leader, Genora Johnson, a mother of two and the wife of one of the strike leaders, took the microphone and urged the women of Flint to stand up (or sit down!) to GM and fight for the men inside. She shouted, "We will form a line around the men, and if the police want to fire then they'll just have to fire into us."[38] They picketed outside the plants and collected money to support the strike. This gave energy and momentum to both the men and to their wives outside. As one woman wrote, "I'm living for the first time with a definite goal."[39] Women, including Johnson, played a critical role in the shaping of the UAW in its early years.[40]

On January 2, a local judge granted GM an injunction to force the workers out of the plant. But the UAW publicized that the judge was a GM stockholder, embarrassing the company and exposing how it controlled the local courts. On January 7, the police destroyed the UAW's sound equipment across the street from the plant. Four days later, when the low temperature reached minus sixteen degrees, the company shut off the heat and announced the end of food shipments. That evening, Flint's police attacked the occupiers. Police sprayed tear gas and buckshot at the windows of the plant. The workers responded by spraying fire hoses from the roof and hurling stones, bottles, and car parts onto the police below. The police fired into the plant. Victor Reuther, a rising UAW leader, shouted to the sit-down strikers through the rooftop speaker on his car: "We wanted peace! General Motors chose war. Give it to them!"[41] Fourteen strikers suffered gunshot wounds and a deputy sheriff was hit in the knee by the bullet of his own officer, but workers repelled the police's attempt to recapture the factory.[42] Reuther later wrote, "I am convinced that the police lost not only that night's battle but the whole Flint war by providing us with the finest audience we had ever had" because it "served to nudge thousands of Flint workers off dead center and into an open commitment to the UAW."[43]

GM wanted Michigan's governor to send in the National Guard or state police to retake the factory, as so many governors had done for decades. But Michigan had a new governor for a new day: Frank Murphy. A committed New Dealer with a deep passion for helping the poorest Americans, Murphy has previously served as the pro-worker mayor of Detroit. He believed that workers faced massive oppression and government should create a more equal society. He ran for governor on a pro-worker platform, assuring Detroit's workers' paper, *Labor News*, "I have yet to go contrary to the expressed wish of Organized Labor in matters that affect it."[44] He later became attorney general before Franklin Roosevelt named him to the Supreme Court. UAW leadership understood what a gift they had in Murphy. Following his election in November 1936, as the UAW organized the plants, it determined to conduct no work stoppages in Michigan until after January 1, 1937, when Murphy was to take over as governor.[45] Even though their workers took the initiative and sat down a few days before his administration began, the UAW was well-aware of the necessary connections between successful unionism and friendly officeholders.

Murphy refused to do GM's bidding. Instead, he sent the National Guard to Flint strictly to serve as a peacekeeping force, preventing another GM takeover attempt, and urged both sides to negotiate a settlement. Once again, the government played a critical role in determining Flint's outcome. Ten years earlier, with the stridently anti-union Calvin Coolidge as president, the outcome would likely have turned out very different, no matter what the Flint strikers did. Moreover, the UAW had allies in Washington. The La Follette Committee sent investigators to Flint to explore the reason for the strike and how GM had used intimidation tactics to scare workers away from the union, such as forcing them to sign loyalty pledges. This helped publicize the justness of the workers' cause. Secretary of Labor Frances Perkins attempted to mediate the conflict, but GM refused to negotiate with the union. Perkins replied to this rebuff harshly: "I still think that General Motors have made a great mistake, perhaps the greatest mistake in their lives. The American people do not expect them to sulk in their tents because they feel the sit-down strike is illegal."[46] Roosevelt himself told Perkins, "Why can't these fellows in General Motors meet with the committee of workers? Talk it all out. They would get a settlement. It wouldn't be so terrible."[47] The continued government support of a negotiated settlement would remain critical.

Not everyone in power supported the UAW. The Michigan legislature, with many rural members who distrusted unions, refused to investigate the UAW's complaints about GM. Flint's major newspaper, the *Journal*, was so in GM's pocket and so stridently antistrike that a La Follette Committee investigator called it out as a "purely General Motors Company organ."[48] But thanks to worker activism in Michigan and around the country, a new breed of politician had arrived in Lansing and in Washington.

The Flint workers were ready to defy not only GM and the government but UAW leadership. One striker told a reporter that he and his fellow workers would simply ignore union leaders' orders to leave the plant "unless 'we get what we want.'"[49] Strikes require tremendous sacrifice from people who usually have few resources. Workers had families at home with dwindling supplies of money and food. This was the middle of winter. Workers inside the factory and family members at home got sick. The sit-down strikers received letters from family members that pulled at their heartstrings. But for most, the sacrifice was worth it. Ultimately, the workers wanted the UAW to represent them. That was the real goal. More money and better working conditions could only happen with a union. That is what GM refused to grant and that is what the workers refused to live without.

GM obtained a second injunction on February 1 that ordered a $15 million penalty on the union if the factories were not evacuated by February 3. This threatened not only the strike but the UAW's existence. The UAW not only ignored it, but another set of workers occupied another plant. Taking control over the Chevrolet No. 4 plant in Flint, where motors were assembled, created a crucial bottleneck in GM production. Escalating the strike was a brilliant strategy. By the end of January, after a long month, the strikers were losing their momentum and their faith. The No. 4 plant had terrible working conditions and angry workers. But it also had few union members because they were still scared of the company. It was next door to GM's Flint headquarters, including the offices of its well-armed company police, making it both an appealing and risky target. The UAW used military strategy to plan a brief but loud diversion strike in a different Flint plant that would draw out GM's forces; then strikers would occupy Plant 4 before the company knew what happened. It worked to perfection when groups of workers, both from inside the plant and from other plants, evicted the remaining company police while UAW leaders and members from as far as Detroit and Toledo barricaded the entrances to protect the workers. Worried that GM violence would lead to their deaths, the Fisher Body workers wired Governor Murphy, saying, "We fully expect that if a violent effort is made to oust us many of us will be killed, and we take this means of making it known to our wives, to our children, to the people of the state of Michigan and the country that if this result follows from an attempt to eject us, you are the one who must be held responsible for our deaths."[50]

The workers raising the stakes pushed the strike to victory. But the UAW also knew this was only possible because Frank Murphy was the governor. Only through an ally in the state capitol could workers expect to win after taking such a militant action. Murphy stated in strong terms that in a modern society, the people had an interest in strikes and that the government should help settle them fairly. Murphy actually thought that the sit-down strike was illegal, but he believed that the spirit of justice mattered more than the technical reading of the law and that, moreover, because GM had refused to follow the National Labor Relations Act and negotiate fairly with the UAW, it had also violated the law. Murphy was under tremendous stress throughout this ordeal; as a governor, he could not simply ignore a court injunction. But he refused to allow the state militia to enforce it, saying, "If I sent those soldiers right in on the men there'd be no telling how many would be killed. It would be inconsistent with everything I have ever stood for in my whole political life."[51]

Murphy was crucial, but it was the workers who made this victory possible through their use of collective power. The day the injunction was supposed to go into effect, February 3, the UAW led a mass march that reminded observers of an army going to war. Up to seven hundred women paraded through the streets of Flint, singing and shouting. UAW members from around the region drove to Flint to support their brothers inside the plant. Probably ten thousand people gathered in front of the Fisher Body plant as the injunction deadline approached. Flint's city manager asked the National Guard to bust up the protest, but once again Murphy would not give his approval. The city manager then mobilized a citizen police reserve that unionists feared would become violent anti-union vigilantes. The sudden rise in the potential for violence turned several other city officials toward favoring a settlement with the UAW. The workers had turned the tide.[52]

Faced with unyielding workers, with a governor on their side for once, GM withered. As historian Nelson Lichtenstein wrote,

"The UAW victory was possible not so much because of the vast outpouring of union sentiment among autoworkers, but because General Motors was temporarily denied recourse to the police power of the state."[53] On February 11, GM agreed to its first union contract, a one-page agreement that announced it would only bargain with the UAW and would not interfere with workers wanting to join the union. The workers walked out of the plants in a state of jubilation. UAW organizer Roy Reuther remembered, "It was a seething sea of humanity—a joy—fears were no longer in the minds of workers."[54] That sea rushed into the UAW, which signed up one hundred thousand new workers at GM plants and nearly half a million members total by the end of 1937. The union and company hammered out an agreement for a significant pay raise, the first of many that would slowly turn a hard job into steady employment that would allow working people to live a middle-class lifestyle. The Flint strike helped create the modern American Dream.

The win in Flint gave workers around the country courage to sit down on the job. Between September 1936 and May 1937, sit-down strikes affected plants employing more than 1 million workers. Overall, 5 million workers walked off the job and nearly 3 million joined a union in 1937.[55] Women at a Detroit Woolworth's department store occupied their workplace in February 1937 to demand union recognition, a pay raise, and the eight-hour day, taking the sit-down to the site of women's work and into a whole new industry. Working with the Hotel Employees and Restaurant Employees, the sit-down spread through Detroit, and with the threat of the strike going national, Woolworth's agreed to a contract. Department store workers around the country followed their lead and organized dozens of stores.[56]

Moreover, the rise of the CIO didn't just mean a few extra dollars in the pocket after getting a union contract. Unionization also changed what citizenship meant for the working class. They were a legitimate part of the nation's decision-making apparatus for the first time. They now had real power. But the extent to which they could enact that power continued to depend on a combination of their own militancy and the willingness of the government to maintain a level playing field between workers and employers.

Organizing After Flint

When the Flint settlement was announced, one striker told his fellow workers, "All that piece of paper means is that we got a union. The rest depends on us. For God's sake, let's go back to work and keep up what we started here!"[57] He was right. GM would not give up the fight to limit union power. The UAW itself was riven with factionalism. It would split into rival organizations before the CIO version won control over renegades who had rejoined the AFL. Some companies saw the writing on the wall and settled with the new unions. The UAW quickly organized Chrysler, again with Frank Murphy mediating.

Ford still led the way for companies that refused to acquiesce to unions. The UAW knew that Henry Ford's workers were scared of his thugs. The UAW needed to take a strong stand against Ford's intimidation, whatever the risk, to show that the union would fight back. On May 26, 1937, Walter Reuther and other union leaders walked toward the River Rouge Complex in Dearborn to hand union leaflets to workers. He invited ministers, journalists, and staffers of the Senate Committee on Civil Liberties to join him as witnesses. As they crossed an overpass, Ford's private army, still led by the violent ex-boxer Harry Bennett, savagely beat them, then denied it, despite photographic evidence. The Battle of the Overpass galvanized national attention on the Ford campaign. Ford still controlled Dearborn, and the city council passed an ordinance making it illegal to pass out flyers within city limits in order to eliminate UAW organizing; in the first six weeks of its passage, police arrested over nine hundred people for violating the rule. Between 1937 and 1941, Ford fired more than four thousand workers for unionism. He only caved in 1941 because the company risked losing out on defense contracts as the United States entered World War II, as it defied the Roosevelt administration's labor policy that accepted unions as legitimate partners. Once again, the combination of worker organizing and government action made a critical difference.[58]

On the same day as the Battle of the Overpass, 25,000 steelworkers walked off the job to demand their own union. John L. Lewis made organizing steel his top priority. He believed that he could not guarantee the success of his UMWA if steel, which used much of the coal to fuel its furnaces and had significant investments in the coal industry, was nonunion. He created the Steel Workers Organizing Committee (SWOC) and placed his chief lieutenant, Philip Murray, in charge. SWOC went after U.S. Steel, the largest and most powerful of the steel companies and the successor of the company that in 1892 had sent a private army to attack strikers at Homestead. Seeing the writing on the wall, U.S. Steel signed a union contract with SWOC in March 1937. This contract standardized pay, granted the eight-hour day, and instituted overtime pay. It started the steelworkers on the road to a dignified life.[59]

The so-called Little Steel companies followed Henry Ford's murderous path. When their workers struck for union recognition, the companies responded with the most brutal antiworker violence of the era. By May 28, 80,000 steelworkers were on strike, 46,000 of whom worked for Republic Steel. That company, headed by anti-union diehard Tom Girdler, hired the Chicago police as a private army and spent $40,000 on weapons for them. Between 1933 and 1937, the Little Steel companies purchased more poison gas than the U.S. military in their preparation for worker uprisings. On Memorial Day, hundreds of workers and supporters gathered to picket in front of Republic's main gate. A line of policemen met them. The police opened fire on the strikers and threw gas bombs. Ten workers died. Another thirty suffered serious injuries, nine of whom were permanently disabled. No one was prosecuted for the Memorial Day Massacre, even though the entire event was filmed. The La Follette Committee viewed the film and concluded that the police were "loosed to shoot down citizens on the streets and highways."[60] Girdler and the Chicago police remained defiant in the face of public outrage. Captain James Mooney said the march was led by communists. Sergeant Lawrence Lyons, testifying before the La Follette Committee, when asked whether a policeman on the tape had drawn his gun, impudently replied, "I don't know. He may be drawing his handkerchief."[61]

Little Steel defeated SWOC. The bravery of strikers could only go so far without state intervention. Roosevelt wanted to level the playing field, not unionize the nation. He responded to the Memorial Day Massacre and the strike that had led to it by saying to the union and the companies "a plague on both your houses" to reporters. The unwillingness of Roosevelt to back the union devastated the strikers and infuriated John L. Lewis. At the barrel of a gun, whether from Republic Steel's private army or the National Guard, the strikers had to give up. Whereas state support made the difference in Flint, state indifference left Little Steel unorganized.[62]

Still, the future was the position of U.S. Steel, not Tom Girdler. The National Labor Relations Board found repeated violations of the National Labor Relations Act with Little Steel's violence, their denial of collective bargaining, and their blacklisting of strikers. The NLRB ruled over and over again against Little Steel, and even if the penalties were small, they wore down the companies, forcing them to rehire fired workers and pay them compensation. Much like Ford, with the rise of government defense contracts, Little Steel finally decided the union was worth the benefits.[63]

The CIO's success rested on more than the state. It welcomed African American workers into the labor movement, often in the face of its own racist members. But CIO leaders knew that AFL-style racial exclusion would only serve to hurt all workers. When the CIO created the Packinghouse Workers Organizing Committee (PWOC), it relied on a multiethnic set of organizers that included Mexicans, African Americans, and eastern Europeans. Many were communists, radicalized by the experience of Depression unemployment and the continued hard lives of their fellow workers. They organized through rank-and-file activists building an interracial alliance, prioritizing the needs of black workers, and bringing together a diverse workforce through their common interests as hard laborers. PWOC, later the United Packinghouse Workers of America, remained an important union with significant black leadership for the next two decades.[64]

The CIO's victories came at a moment when enormous change in the nation's labor relations was possible, thanks to Roosevelt's popularity. But this was a very brief window and was only possible through compromises that often excluded many black workers. Southern Democrats despised the liberals in the Roosevelt administration, distrusted unions, and, most important, feared the newly powerful state would transform not just labor relations but also their Jim Crow racial system. Already, black workers were leaving the South for industrial jobs in northern cities. After some New Deal programs helped African Americans, and after Roosevelt's overreach when he tried to add more Supreme Court justices in 1937, southern Democrats in Congress began uniting with Republicans to halt liberal legislation.[65] The New Deal came to a screeching halt. But workers would have one more major victory: the Fair Labor Standards Act (FLSA). Signed into law in 1938, this groundbreaking piece of legislation set the standards of labor that joined the NLRA in redefining American work. It banned the worst forms of child labor, set the workweek at forty hours, mandated overtime pay above forty hours, and created the first federal minimum wage, set at 25¢ an hour. Over one million workers in low-wage industries immediately saw wage gains.[66] Yet, like the NLRA, the FLSA was a tremendously compromised piece of legislation. The final bill only covered about 25 percent of the labor force at that time and excluded agricultural laborers, as many farmworkers were black. The South also won exceptions that allowed it to pay lower wages than the rest of the country in some cases. Other groups excluded include circus employees, babysitters, journalists, and personal aides.[67]

The exclusion of farm labor from the nation's new labor system reflected southern fears of mobilized black workers during the 1930s. When Ralph Gray, a sharecropper from Tallapoosa County, Alabama, read the Communist Party's newspaper for southern workers, he converted to communism and began to organize sharecroppers for their rights. The county police brutally murdered Gray after a shootout in July 1931.[68] The Southern Tenant Farmers' Union, organized in 1934, claimed 7,500 members in Oklahoma and demanded land redistribution, with land owned by banks given to small farmers. It attempted to join the CIO, but John L. Lewis largely dismissed the idea because sharecroppers lacked the financial resources to pay union dues.[69] Still, this organizing alarmed southern whites. Similar actions took place in the West. The Cannery and Agricultural Workers' Industrial Union organized white, Mexican, and Filipino farmworkers in a major strike in the summer of 1933 and then a cotton strike that fall, culminating in growers murdering two strikers. It was these efforts that led southern Democrats to demand the exclusion of farmwork if any bill was to pass at all.[70]

The success of the strikes won transformative gains for American workers. The Flint strikers triumphed for two reasons. First, it was due to the strikers' tremendous bravery, sitting in a factory and inspiring their scared fellow workers to stand up to General Motors. Second, the strike took place at a time when the U.S. government sought to even the playing field between workers and employers. The fear of radicalism and workplace action moved the government in that direction. But even at this moment of unprecedented government intervention to assist workers, the state had sharp limits on what it would tolerate. It soon sought to end the sit-down strikes and other direct action tactics. In 1939 the Supreme Court declared the sit-down strike illegal. The ability of workers to take the disruptive actions needed to gain power would be subsumed by the Roosevelt administration's need to integrate unions into Democratic Party governance. This would be a mixed blessing for workers, as both the possibilities and limitations of their new power would become clear during and after World War II.

7

The Oakland General Strike and Cold War America

Union power created unprecedented abundance for the American working class, but it also sowed the seeds of its own decline.

The 1930s were a decade of struggle and victory for the CIO and the American working class. The 1940s demonstrated both the strength of those newly empowered workers and the limitations of unions to influence American politics. This power took place in context of American participation in World War II, beginning with Pearl Harbor in December 1941 and ending with the dropping of two atomic bombs on Japan in August 1945, four years in which the American public engaged in tremendous sacrifice and the government committed to an unprecedented investment in the American economy and society to win the war. During these years, the Roosevelt administration gave unions remarkable privileges in economic planning and government influence in order to forestall labor strife that would undermine production. When white male American workers went overseas to fight, women and people of color not only jumped at the opportunity to replace them in the workforce, they demanded it, engaging in protest to open up factories to African Americans.

Under the surface of American patriotism during World War II were millions of workers desperate to flex their muscles. They worked as hard as they could to win the war, but they also expressed great frustration at the hostility of their employers to their unions and the rising prices that ate up their increased wages. Workers lashed out after the war in the greatest wave of strikes in American history. It seemed that a new day of worker power might result.

When the war ended, unions hoped to benefit from their newfound power. In many ways, they did. But a new political era dawned, dominated by fears of the Soviet Union and communist infiltration that led to the Cold War and demagogue politicians such as Joseph McCarthy and Richard Nixon looking to become powerful by attacking anyone they suspected was a communist. This had a severe impact on unions, frequent victims of right-wing attacks. The combination of anticommunism's rising tide and the failures of unions to organize the South or overcome the racism of the white working class showed the sharp limits of the labor movement's power. It soon became clear that unions might be a junior partner in the American economy, but they would never sit at the head of the table.

World War II

Despite its big wins in the late 1930s, the CIO was unstable, in debt, and facing internal divisions in 1941. John L. Lewis and his United Mine Workers of America left the CIO after it did not follow him in turning against Franklin Roosevelt's reelection in 1940. Steel Workers Organizing Committee head Philip Murray replaced Lewis. He led the CIO on a huge strike wave in 1941, with 4,288 strikes involving nearly 2.4 million workers, winning major wage increases and victories over some of the nation's most anti-union companies. Once again, the strike was labor's most powerful and effective weapon.[1]

When the United States entered World War II on December 7, 1941, the world changed for unions. The government mobilized the American economy for full production, ending the Great Depression. In 1939, the federal budget was $9 billion; by 1945, it was more than $100 billion. The gross national product grew from $91 billion to $166 billion during the war.[2] The Roosevelt administration brought unions into national economic planning to an unprecedented extent. The CIO tied its anchor to the Democratic Party to ensure that workers received their fair share of this rapidly expanding economy. Sidney Hillman, president of the Amalgamated Clothing Workers of America, became the CIO's liaison to the Roosevelt administration. Hillman's influence on the administration grew so great that in 1944, Republican presidential candidate Thomas Dewey falsely claimed that before Roosevelt chose a vice presidential candidate, he had to "clear it with Sidney."[3]

To mediate conflicts between workers and employers, Roosevelt created the National War Labor Board (NWLB) in 1942. The NWLB had twelve members—four representatives of business, four of organized labor, and four named by the federal government. It guaranteed that all workers would pay dues in unionized companies, called "maintenance of membership," which led to a 40 percent increase in union dues over the period of the war, stabilizing CIO finances for the first time.[4] Union membership peaked at 35.4 percent of the nation's workforce in 1945.[5] Corporations had to agree to mandatory arbitration of all labor disputes, while unions agreed not to strike during the war. As early as June 1941, CIO leaders had worked with the administration to shut down a communist-led UAW strike in California aviation plants. But after the German invasion of the Soviet Union late that month, communist-led unions became the biggest supporters of sacrificing strikes to defeat the Nazis.[6]

Corporations did not like the new agreement with unions, but most accepted it given the lucrative government contracts they received. Union leaders did not like giving up the strike, but they accepted the benefits unions received in return. The two major exceptions were Montgomery Ward's chairman Sewell Avery, who despised the New Deal as socialistic, and John L. Lewis, who had turned on Roosevelt. Avery refused to negotiate a new contract in 1944 and his employees voted to strike. Montgomery Ward had many government contracts, so this threatened the war effort. Roosevelt ordered Attorney General Francis Biddle to fly to Chicago to appeal to Avery. Biddle told him he was hurting the war effort. Avery responded by saying, "To hell with the government!"[7] Biddle ordered two soldiers to pick Avery up and carry him out of the building. Avery hurled the worst insult he could think of at Biddle, yelling, "You, you New Dealer!" The federal government ran the company off and on until September 1945. Lewis, on the other hand, did not need the maintenance-of-membership clause, as the mines were completely organized through the coal region. So, in the spring of 1943, he brought his five hundred thousand miners off the job in the middle of the war for a pay raise, forcing the closure of steel mills. Faced with a direct challenge, Roosevelt ordered the mines' seizure. For the duration of the war, the government set sharp limits on both corporate and union behavior.[8]

But workers had their own agenda. While the government implemented both price and wage controls for the war's duration, prices rose faster than wages, and workers became squeezed by inflation. Moreover, workers had to pay new taxes. In 1942, they lost 10 percent of their paychecks to a war bond purchase, and in 1943, they lost an additional 5 percent to a "victory tax."[9] While nearly all workers supported the war effort, they also revolted repeatedly in so-called wildcat strikes, in which workers walked off the job without the approval of their union. Usually such strikes happened because employers changed work rules or fired workers. With foremen resentful over the unions that usurped their power, the shop floor was a site of daily struggle for control, leading to wildcats. In 1942 alone, 840,000 workers participated in wildcat strikes. Twenty-four thousand Chrysler workers walked off the job for four days in Detroit to protest the company's violations of their contract.[10] Workers at another Detroit auto plant struck when the company would not let them play checkers during lunch and at a third when the boss banned smoking.[11]

These impassioned workers did not look the same as the workers before the war. With millions of white men joining the military, employers hired white women and African Americans at unprecedented rates. The number of women in the workplace nearly doubled shortly after the U.S. entered the war, but they faced significant income discrimination. Men working in a defense production factory averaged $54.65 a week, with women receiving only $31.50. Union rules placed women at the bottom of the seniority scale, ensuring they would be laid off after the war. Norman Rockwell's "Rosie the Riveter" portrait that graced the cover of the *Saturday Evening Post* on May 29, 1943, personified these women. He drew a husky female worker eating a sandwich on her break, proud of her work. This realistic view of a worker is different from what we think of as the Rosie the Riveter image: a young attractive woman showing her new muscles. The defense company Westinghouse produced that in 1943. The "We" in "We Can Do It" does not mean women. It means Westinghouse workers and management, without interference from unions. The poster was used for two weeks and then forgotten for decades before it became a feminist icon in the past thirty years.[12]

Black workers streamed out of the South during World War II, looking for economic opportunities in the factories around the nation. The percentage of African Americans in the Detroit workforce rose from 8 to 14.5 percent.[13] African Americans long mistrusted many unions that wanted to remain all white. But they also created their own unions that would lead in the struggles for civil rights and labor rights. The most prominent was the Brotherhood of Sleeping Car Porters (BSCP). Founded in 1925, it organized the porters who served whites on Pullman sleeping cars. Its president, A. Philip Randolph, became the key black labor and civil rights leader of the period, and the BSCP served an indispensable role in the growing civil rights movement in the 1930s. Southern states banned the *Chicago Defender*, the nation's most important African American newspaper, from the mails, but BSCP workers spread it through the South as they worked on the trains. The BSCP was a community civil and labor rights effort. When they struck, women took jobs to support their husbands, while gathering porters' dues, signing up new union members, organizing meetings, and fighting for women working as Pullman maids to be represented by the union.[14]

Randolph and other black leaders demanded that African Americans see their share of economic advancement during the war. But as the war approached, persistent discrimination from both employers and unions meant that defense work remained strictly segregated. For instance, the International Brotherhood of Boilermakers barred black members, which shut African Americans out of the rapidly growing shipbuilding industry. Randolph called for a March on Washington to protest discrimination in defense industry work. It was to take place on July 1, 1941, with estimates of up to one hundred thousand African Americans expected to attend. Roosevelt desperately wanted to avoid the embarrassment of a nation preparing to fight fascism having its own racial caste system publicized before the world.[15] On June 25, he issued Executive Order 8802, prohibiting racial discrimination in the defense industry. The order also established the Fair Employment Practice Committee to investigate and resolve discrimination on the job. Roosevelt also agreed to end official discrimination in federal employment, although implementation depended on the agency. African Americans held about 3 percent of defense jobs in 1942, mostly janitors. But by 1945, that number rose to 8 percent, including many craftsmen and industrial laborers. Black employees of the federal government tripled. By 1944, 1.25 million African Americans were union members.[16]

Many whites resented the arrival of black workers in the factories. Grassroots worker power develops when workers identify any issue that outrages them. That could include oppressing other workers to keep the factories lily-white. On June 3, 1943, 25,000 white workers went on strike at a Detroit Packard plant when the company promoted three black workers. Packard's personnel director, C.E. Weiss, had bragged about being the first executive to bring blacks north to bust unions when he worked for Chrysler in 1917. He used this old trick to divide the United Auto Workers. UAW leadership ordered its members back to work the next day, but thousands remained on the racist picket line. The government sent out the message that it would fire anyone who did not go back to work. Thirty of the strike ringleaders were suspended on June 6, and the strike ended the next day. Several similar incidents took place in Detroit and other cities during the war. Miners in Butte, Montana, refused to work when their employer tried to import black workers to make up for laborers lost to the military, even though the union, the International Union of Mine, Mill, and Smelter Workers, was a leader in fighting for racial equality. Race trumped class for many white workers.[17]

The Postwar Strike Wave

When World War II ended in August 1945, factories immediately laid off millions of workers. The United Electrical, Radio and Machine Workers of America represented 700,000 workers at the beginning of 1945 and only 475,000 by the end of the year.[18] Many unions and policymakers feared a return to the Great Depression without the war to stimulate the economy. However, growing consumer demand and government investment in the economy combined with the United States rebuilding Europe and Japan to spur the longest period of economic growth in American history, one that continued, with few blips, into the 1970s. In 1945, though, employers returned the remaining jobs to white men. Women still wanted to work. For example, more women than men applied for industrial jobs at the U.S. Employment Service's Detroit office in the first year after the war. But in that same year, 3.5 million women of all races lost their jobs nationally. Unions agreed with this policy, ignoring women's seniority rights to replace them with men.[19] Women did demand fair treatment, however. In September 1945, twenty-four women fired from a toy factory in Bridgeport, Connecticut, held a picket line to protest their treatment. African American and Mexican American men and women also lost their factory jobs as white men returned.[20]

Workers of all genders and races found themselves frustrated by an economy that had created large profits for companies during the war but few material gains for workers. Their delayed impulses to demand their fair share of the growing economic pie became uncontrollable. The wildcat strikes of the war became official strikes immediately after it ended. In 1945, nearly 3.5 million workers struck. The next year, 4.6 million workers went on strike throughout the United States, the greatest number for one year in American history. Workers wanted to bring pre-war militancy to the postwar world. UAW leader Walter Reuther called for a national strike against General Motors on November 21, 1945, worked to negotiate higher wages with other companies, and forced GM to accede to the new wage standards when the strike ended in March 1946.[21] Akron rubber workers went on strike for the thirty-hour week; Camden shipyard workers walked off the job to demand laid-off colleagues be rehired; Detroit workers engaged in ninety wildcat strikes in September and October 1945.[22]

Union leaders wanted to expand their power across the nation. Unions were concentrated in the Northeast and the Great Lakes region, with smaller numbers on the West Coast. The South, Southwest, and Great Plains states had only small union populations. Politicians in large swaths of the nation had no reason to care about organized labor because unions did not threaten their power. The CIO rightfully feared that if it did not organize the South, companies would start moving their operations there to escape unions. During World War II, unions made steady progress in organizing the southern tobacco and steel industries, while the South's core textile industry also showed increasing promise. CIO membership grew from 150,000 to 225,000 in the South during the war.[23] To consolidate its gains and expand its reach, the CIO started Operation Dixie in 1946 to organize the South. It had some early successes, especially in the tobacco factories of North Carolina, where it won twenty-two of twenty-four union elections and ten thousand new members.[24]

Unfortunately, the CIO's strategy to organize the South reflected the racial divide at the heart of American society. The CIO wanted to organize both black and white workers. However, CIO leaders also feared alienating white workers who supported segregation. It actively discouraged black organizers from applying for jobs in Operation Dixie, even though black workers were more likely than whites to find a leftist alternative to elite domination of the South appealing.[25] In the 1930s, communists had organized hundreds of impoverished African American workers and farmers in Alabama into a militant force fighting for their rights.[26] But like the Alabama communists, the CIO faced brutal, lawless violence from southern elites, who felt both their control over labor and over the region's racial hierarchy increasingly threatened. Southern employers and politicians race-baited anyone calling to organize the South, accusing Eleanor Roosevelt of having black lovers and using anti-Semitism to demonize "outsiders" trying to organize workers. South Carolina senator Burnet Maybank stated, "The leaders of the CIO mainly are against the things for which the southern people stand."[27] In Arkansas, an anti-union militant killed a striker; he did not serve jail time, but the picketers did. The Ku Klux Klan murdered black strikers in Georgia, and a textile union organizer was shot and killed in Tennessee. Meanwhile, the white workers the CIO hoped to win over did not unionize, even though organizers downplayed the connection between labor rights and civil rights. The editor of the industry journal *Textile Bulletin* ranted against the CIO, saying that "the cotton mill employees of the South have the purest Anglo-Saxon blood in the United States" and would not tolerate working with African Americans. This was largely true. One CIO campaign at a Rome, Georgia, textile mill ended with workers in the targeted mill rejecting the union 1,982 to 438 after a concerted employer campaign of race-baiting, red-baiting, and relying on the deference to employers that had attracted textile companies to the region in the first place.[28]

Operation Dixie soon crumbled. The CIO's fears came true: Unable to organize the South, it watched helplessly as northern employers moved south to avoid unions in the decades after World War II. Workers themselves feared joining CIO unions in the South because they knew companies moved there precisely because they were union-free and they worried about their own factories closing if they unionized.[29] Racial division continued to make organizing southern states tremendously difficult. After the 1954 Supreme Court decision in *Brown v. Board of Education* that ruled school segregation unconstitutional, union leaders who took a stand to support civil rights found themselves facing internal revolts from white members, attacks from the Ku Klux Klan, and the departure of union locals from state AFL membership.[30]

Despite these southern setbacks, union workers fought hard to expand union power. Workers in Stamford, Connecticut, conducted a general strike on January 3, 1946, in solidarity with striking manufacturing workers, with twenty thousand people attending a joint AFL and CIO rally.[31] Thus began a remarkable year in American history, with general strikes popping up around the country, where all the workers throughout a city went on strike in support of other workers. The most important general strike before 1946 took place in 1919, when workers in Seattle launched a five-day strike that shook the nation. The legendary 1934 longshoremen's strike in San Francisco also used the general strike as a tactic. The Seattle action had begun with longshoremen as well, as shipyard workers protested having gone without a raise for two years. Thirty-five thousand workers walked off their jobs on January 21. Over the next two weeks, business cut off strikers' credit at grocery stores and police raided a cooperative set up to get food to the strikers. The rest of Seattle labor saw this as the first battle in a planned war against organized labor in one of America's most militant cities. The Metal Trades Council suggested a general strike, which the city's Central Labor Council approved and set for February 6. On that day, an additional 25,000 workers went on strike, shutting down Seattle. The strikers fed tens of thousands of people, staffed hospitals, and ensured order in the streets. The city ran peacefully. Business, employers, and newspapers called for its suppression. Perhaps union solidarity might have stood up to this pressure, but AFL president Samuel Gompers feared that the Seattle action was run by extremists and withheld strike funds. Fearful of violence and dispirited by the lack of AFL support, a few workers started returning to work on February 8, and the strike was declared over on February 11.[32]

The story of 1946 reflected 1919. Workers in Lancaster, Pennsylvania, called a general strike when the Conestoga Transportation Company tried to crush its union; after three days, the company caved, granting a pay raise and increased retirement benefits. Even in conservative Houston, Texas, up to ten thousand city workers demonstrated in support of the city's striking maintenance workers, leading to a movement that elected a pro-labor mayor later in the year. In Rochester, New York, when the city fired 489 workers trying to organize, nonunionized truck drivers engaged in a one-day strike in solidarity. This led to a spiral of increasingly aggressive union actions that led to a general strike on May 28. Within twenty-four hours, the city caved completely, rehiring all the fired workers and recognizing the right of these workers to form a union.[33] Business leaders despaired and became determined to reverse this aggressive union tide.

Oakland General Strike

On December 3, 1946, over one hundred thousand workers in Oakland, California—all members of AFL-affiliated unions—walked off the job. They shut down the city for two days to win much needed wage gains and challenge the stridently antilabor local political machine. This almost-unprecedented demonstration of worker power exhibited the amazing potential of worker solidarity. But this strike also shined a harsh light on the limitations of the American labor movement, even at the very heights of its power in the United States. Weaknesses both in terms of its national political power and divisions between union leaders and rank-and-file workers quickly showed themselves. In the aftermath of Oakland, we can see the start of the downward trend in union power that plagues American workers today.

World War II utterly transformed the San Francisco Bay. Half a million Americans moved there during the war to work in defense industries. Manufacturing in Oakland exploded as the federal government spread war production around the country. The *San Francisco Chronicle* said in 1943 of this investment: "The Second Gold Rush Hits the West." In Oakland, manufacturing employment rose 166 percent between December 1941 and August 1943. New military bases in the area employed thousands of people. Unemployment in Oakland fell from 15 percent in March 1940 to less than 2 percent in April 1944. Many of these new workers were women or African Americans. Seven thousand women were employed in one Oakland shipyard in 1943. Union membership in Oakland grew thanks to the maintenance-of-membership clauses the Roosevelt administration had allowed in exchange for unions not striking. Unfortunately, many African Americans were forced into segregated locals. Although divisions between the AFL and CIO continued nationally during World War II, in Oakland, more aggressive leadership took over many AFL unions who wanted to copy CIO tactics and build a militant labor movement in their city.[34]

Most Oakland employers hated unions. The city's Retail Merchants Association (RMA) was a powerful and deeply anti-union business organization. The department store owners who ran the RMA employed mostly women, who they believed would accept low wages. The RMA had close ties to the Republican, antilabor political machine dominated by *Oakland Tribune* owner Joseph Knowland, father of California senator William Knowland. To fight against both the RMA and the Republican machine, in March 1945, unions throughout the city held an unprecedented meeting and formed the United for Oakland Committee, seeking to challenge the machine in upcoming city council elections and create a city run by workers.

As in the rest of the country, when World War II ended, Oakland workers' demands for more money and political power became almost impossible for employers to control. The Department and Specialty Store Employees Union Local 1265 organized the workers at the RMA members' downtown stores. Early in 1946, they won victories at smaller stores and decided to take on two large Oakland retailers, Kahn's and Hastings. In October, four hundred workers, mostly women, at these two stores walked off the job to strike. Union leaders recognized this strike as critical to establishing postwar labor relations with the city's employers as well as fighting against the political machine, especially with Knowland running for reelection that fall. The *East Bay Labor Journal* wrote, "We have or have not a labor movement in Alameda County. The Kahn's strike will be the test. If Kahn's management is successful, you and your union may be next."[35]

This seemingly small action turned into the biggest challenge to corporate domination of American workers in the postwar years. Workers throughout the city were ready to strike because of their precarious financial situation in the year after the war ended. Unemployment spiked in the Bay Area with jobs harder to come by after tens of thousands of veterans returned. Take-home pay declined for workers at the same time that corporations made record profits. Workers feared the return of the Great Depression and the terrible lives they had fought so hard to change.

On November 28, the retail workers' strike escalated when the stores' owners, the RMA, the publishers of the city's leading newspapers, the district attorney, the Oakland police chief, the county sheriff, and other local elites met to coordinate a plan to break the strike using nonunion trucks to deliver goods, with the Oakland police providing security. Unions may have succeeded in winning major legal victories during the 1930s, but a decade later, the collusion of business, politicians, and police meant that the thirst to roll back those gains remained unquenched.

Angry at the police serving as strikebreakers, the city's AFL locals acted quickly. Al Brown of the Carmen and Drivers' Union jumped on a streetcar and took it over. He and his fellow drivers stopped the city's transportation network, effectively opening the Oakland General Strike. The AFL's Alameda County Labor Council put out a call for a general strike to begin the next morning. Workers from 142 Oakland unions, all affiliated with the AFL, walked off their jobs—bus drivers, teamsters, sailors, machinists, cannery workers, railroad porters, waiters, waitresses, cooks. For two days, Oakland shut down. Despite the cold December rain, over 100,000 workers participated, with crowds of 10,000 to 30,000 at various rallies. Twenty thousand strikers crowded the Oakland Auditorium for a mass meeting, and despite the rain, thousands more stood outside to hear the meeting broadcast on loudspeakers. All businesses except for pharmacies and food markets, which the workers deemed essential for the city, closed. Bars could stay open but could only serve beer and had to put their jukeboxes outside and allow for their free use. Couples literally danced in the streets. One Teamster later stated, "Strangers met in the middle of the night on the picket line and you would think they'd known each other all their lives."[36] Workers allowed children to visit Santa in front of a department store to give him their Christmas wishes. Recently returned war veterans created squadrons to prepare for battle against the police.[37]

The strike leaders were veterans of more than a decade of hard labor struggles. Many had participated in the San Francisco longshoremen's strike in 1934, one of the key labor actions of that dramatic year that spurred the National Labor Relations Act. Knowing from experience that good public relations were crucial to maintaining support, they refused to allow Oakland's harshly anti-union newspapers to publish, although newspapers in neighboring San Francisco angrily decried the strike and called the city's labor leaders "berserk."[38] Although white male unionists had taken over what had begun as a strike of female retail clerks, during the strike, women and men, whites and African Americans all marched together, seemingly with a lack of racial or gendered tension—at least according to remembered accounts—partially because most of these AFL locals were all white, while CIO locals with large black membership had not yet joined the strike.[39]

On the strike's second day, the thousands of World War II veterans recently returned to Oakland formed into squadrons and marched to their enemies in the city, including to the mayor's office to demand his resignation. Contingents, largely made up of Hawaiians working in the Bay Area, formed to check on strikebreaking. Major labor speakers roused the strikers in public events. Although the challenges of running a city quickly appeared, with some markets forced to close to save food supplies, by the third day the strikers still held up well and the potential for this action to transform Oakland remained real.[40]

The Oakland strikers did not have radical demands. They wanted their city to be a unionized city. They wanted more money and they wanted jobs. They did not demand social or political revolution. They focused especially on Kahn's and Hastings, the department stores at the root of the struggle. However, the strike threatened established leadership, both in the government and in organized labor. After the two days out of work, a majority of workers wanted to continue striking. CIO unions scheduled a meeting to consider joining in support, which would have had widespread implications for unionism around the country. But herculean challenges quickly developed. The Oakland political class rightly believed they faced not only a strike but a challenge to their power over to the city. Their resistance was implacable. Even worse, Dave Beck, the powerful and corrupt head of the Teamsters and mentor to the notorious Jimmy Hoffa, hated these strikers. A man opposed to worker power or to widespread organizing, Beck stated, "I say this damn general strike is nothing but a revolution. It isn't labor tactics. It's revolutionary tactics."[41] He did not mean that as a compliment. He pulled his powerful union off the lines over the objections of the local Teamsters leaders.

Without the Teamsters, one of the most important unions in Oakland, the strike began to wobble. That immediately led the employers to stop negotiating with the striking unions. Beck endorsed a moderate settlement that did not address the department store workers' concerns at all. The unions had little choice but to settle. Beck effectively red-baited the strike into oblivion. International union leaders, concerned about maintaining the strike and worried about the challenge to their own leadership, ended the strike on December 5 with no input from the rank-and-file workers who had led it in the first place.

The female retail clerks remained on strike an additional five months, finally giving up and returning to work without winning most of their demands. Women started this massive action and yet men took it over immediately, relegating women workers to the sidelines, just as they did in the labor movement and on the shop floor every day. The unions tried to mobilize politically after the strike, running a slate of city council candidates to fight against the political machine and to end the low taxes that wealthy merchants paid. An insurgent slate won four council seats in 1947 but lost a critical fifth seat that would have given them the majority. The Knowland machine remained in control. The renegades found themselves increasingly unsuccessful in passing pro-worker ordinances and faced a recall campaign when they pushed for a strong public housing plan in 1950. The direct action of the strike slowly wilted and died. Ultimately, the Oakland General Strike led to nothing but fond memories, even as unionized workers around the nation did win greater pay and benefits throughout the next twenty years.

The Oakland General Strike clearly demonstrates the significant change in the types of demands workers were making after World War II. The strike had specific political goals: overturning a hated city political machine, making Oakland a union-friendly city, and ensuring better wages. These popular objectives had the potential to transform the American power structure. The power of workers on display in Oakland was a sea change from the desperation workers felt a mere decade earlier.

But the strike also shows us how divisions within organized labor place sharp limits on how much power unions can exercise. Even in a strike without an explicitly radical platform, rank-and-file power threatened a leader like Dave Beck, who could take his powerful union off the lines. The American labor movement's diversity continued to lead to discord, not only between the AFL and CIO, but between conservative and left-leaning unions and between local union activists and their national bosses. Many of labor's most powerful figures had great personal ambition but also deeply distrusted their own union members. Many unions were also politically conservative and often supported Republican candidates, such as the United Brotherhood of Carpenters, whose leadership voted for Republicans until 1964. Even if most rank-and-file Oakland workers wanted the Knowland machine gone and pro-union politicians to replace it, the opposition of powerful national union leaders made that proposition very difficult and doomed the strike. Throughout the nation in 1945 and 1946, labor leaders sought to control their members, not encourage their activism, most notoriously when International Longshoremen's Association president Joseph "King" Ryan used physical violence and red-baiting to destroy dissident strikers in his own union.[42]

The Oakland strike and the other strikes of 1945 and 1946 served as the first of many hard lessons the postwar American labor movement would learn about their tenuous position in American life. Employer opposition to unions remained powerful, and business led a concerted effort to roll back the New Deal after the war.[43] White workers' commitment to white supremacy remained at least as strong as their commitment to their unions. Moreover, the growing backlash against communism as the Cold War rapidly developed put unions on the defensive. Within two years after Oakland, communists would be evicted from organized labor and Congress would pass sweeping antilabor legislation. Corporate leaders who despised the New Deal and the CIO seemed ascendant.

Unions acquiesced to the end of political radicalism and communist organizing by committing to working with companies to promote smooth operations and tamp down rank-and-file activism. The sit-down strikes of a decade ago would be no more. But in return, unions, increasingly tied to the Democratic Party, would demand a greater share of the economic pie for their workers and had the political power to see many of those demands to fruition. Corporations had to negotiate union contracts that gave large raises and whole new benefits such as paid vacations, health care, and pensions. The following decades would be the peak period of American working-class economic and political power, albeit a period that largely excluded black and brown workers from sharing in many of these benefits and one that kept women in a clearly subservient position. American unionism in the Cold War, typified by the Oakland General Strike, would be a maelstrom of contradictions, political limits, and missed opportunities for widespread change.

Cold War Workers

The decline of union radicalism was not written when the Oakland General Strike ended. The union movement still had a lot of momentum. Overall, union membership rose from 10 million in 1941 to 15 million in 1947.[44] But the 1946 strike wave led to a massive political backlash. Despite the growing power of the American working class, unions had almost no presence in much of the nation. More than 50 percent of CIO members lived in Ohio, Michigan, Pennsylvania, and New York, while only 14 percent lived in the South and Southwest. In these parts of the country, politicians had no political reason to support unions with voters who found unions distant, vaguely foreign, and often threatening.[45] The hate the CIO felt in the South during Operation Dixie was reflected in the votes of southern politicians and in the actions of southern white workers who saw unions as northern Jewish institutions that promoted race mixing and integration. In the 1948 U.S. Senate election that launched Lyndon Johnson into the national spotlight, he lambasted his opponent Coke Stevenson for being in the pocket of unions, even as Johnson himself courted CIO support behind the scenes. It was the smart political move for a conservative Texas electorate. It was much the same in Arizona. Democrats controlled state politics in the 1940s, but they had more in common with Alabama Dixiecrats than northern liberals. They despised the New Deal and would support Barry Goldwater's radical right 1964 presidential candidacy. Said one CIO organizer, "There are two types of Democrats here. Both are controlled by the same interests"; that is, the state's business community.[46]

By the end of 1946, calls poured in from newspaper editors and politicians to purge the communists from organized labor and make sure workers could never again call a general strike. Unions faced growing political pressure against their leftist members. The Smith Act of 1940 mandated that all aliens register with federal authorities and allowed for the deportation of alien subversives. The first Smith Act trial was against Socialist Workers Party members, including members of Teamsters Local 574, which had led the 1934 Minneapolis truckers' strike. Eighteen people were found guilty of violating the law, laying the groundwork for the anticommunist crusades of the postwar period.[47]

All of this led to the Taft-Hartley Act in 1947. This law banned most of the actions the CIO had used to win their transformative victories, including wildcat strikes, secondary picketing, mass boycotts, and union donations to federal political campaigns. Labor called it the "Slave Labor Bill" and found their newfound power suddenly fleeting. The bill allowed states to pass so-called right-to-work laws that force unions to represent people in the workplace who refused to become members or pay dues. This meant that politically conservative states could make unionization much more difficult, undermining the potential for a revived Operation Dixie. In today's anti-union mania, several states have recently passed such laws, including the former union strongholds of Wisconsin and Michigan, as well as West Virginia and Kentucky. Taft-Hartley also allowed the government to end strikes through legal injunctions and gave companies permission to terminate anyone in a supervisory position who did not follow the company line on labor issues. Finally, it required union leaders to pledge they were not members of the Communist Party, a crippling blow to the left wing of the CIO and the communist organizers who had done so much to bring workers into unions. The steel companies led the lobbying for the bill, the same people who had resisted unions until forced to cave during World War II. Its passage was a huge victory for corporate power over workers.[48]

President Harry Truman supported some curbs on union activity and had seized oil refineries and ordered workers back on the job when they struck in 1945. But Taft-Hartley went too far. In his veto message, he castigated Congress, writing, "When the sponsors of the bill claim that by weakening unions, they are giving rights back to individual workingmen, they ignore the basic reason why unions are important in our democracy."[49] But Congress overrode Truman's veto by a 68–25 margin in the Senate and in the House by 331–83 vote, a symbol of how, even after a decade of successful organizing, worker power faced overwhelming political opposition in the United States.

Both the AFL and CIO made repealing Taft-Hartley their top priority. But the CIO evicted eleven communist-led unions from the federation, representing over one million workers. The CIO's third-largest union, the United Electrical, Radio and Machine Workers of America (UE), left the CIO rather than fire their communist organizers. UE had organized major companies like General Electric, RCA, and Westinghouse and had created a democratic organization where rank-and-file workers had real say in how their union operated. This red-baiting began a new era in organized labor that prioritized Cold War politics over worker organizing, including assisting the CIA in overthrowing democratic governments in nations such as Guatemala and Chile.[50] The obsession with destroying communism among union leaders such as George Meany, who became AFL president in 1952, undermined the organizing that won the gains of the 1930s and 1940s. However, many rank-and-file members of the UE and other unions hated the communists in their own unions; some wrote to Congress asking for help to get rid of them. More conservative unions such as the International Brotherhood of Electrical Workers (IBEW) used anticommunist rhetoric to raid the UE, decimating that once strong and radical union.[51]

Those communists kept organizing. In 1950, miners in Grant County, New Mexico, went on strike against the Empire Zinc Company. The International Union of Mine, Mill, and Smelter

Workers—Mine, Mill for short—led these workers. Mine, Mill was a communist-led union, the direct descendant of the Western Federation of Miners, whose radical members had played a key role in founding the Industrial Workers of the World in 1905. Having spent decades organizing the largely Mexican American miners in southern New Mexico who faced enormous racial and class discrimination, union organizers and members had encountered tremendous repression in these remote places, as well as in cities such as El Paso, where it had organized smelter workers. A union with many communist organizers committed to racial equality, like other left-wing unions who fought for racial justice, Mine, Mill was kicked out of the CIO in 1950.

The Mexican American miners in Grant County who worked for Empire Zinc faced racism on the job and in their pay rates compared to whites. They struck for equality. Employers used their new Taft-Hartley weapon to win an injunction. Mine, Mill couldn't pay the fines for defying the order. Instead, the workers' wives took over. For the next seven months, women struck, despite police harassment and arrest. They dragged strikebreakers out of their cars, threw rocks at them, and even used knitting needles, rotten eggs, and chilies as weapons. Empire Zinc caved in January 1952, granting workers a major pay raise and installing indoor plumbing in the company houses of the Mexican American workers. After the victory, left-wing filmmakers came to New Mexico to make a movie about the strike, leading to the legendary *Salt of the Earth*, starring the workers and the union organizer who led the strike. But *Salt of the Earth* was blacklisted in the same anticommunist hysteria that led to Taft-Hartley and McCarthyism. Only thirteen American theaters showed it, and it was forgotten for a decade.[52]

Ejecting the communists from unions decimated labor's fight against racial and sexual discrimination. The United Packinghouse Workers of America was not communist-led but worked with communists to organize the black workers of the Chicago meatpacking plants and pushed African Americans into leadership roles. The UE had more female members than the other big CIO unions. Betty Friedan, later the author of the pioneering feminist book *The Feminine Mystique*, wrote for the UE newspaper. Unions such as the UE now had to use their scarce resources to fight off anticommunist unions stealing their members, instead of organizing workers and fighting for economic, racial, and gender justice. Soon, most disappeared or faded into irrelevance. With them went the radical edge that marked the labor movement's successes in the 1930s and could have reignited mass organizing and strikes in the future.[53]

With the communists gone and the AFL now organizing whole industries, rather than only craft unions, to compete with the CIO, there was little reason for the House of Labor to remain divided. The two federations merged into the AFL-CIO in 1955, with George Meany, AFL leader and staunch anticommunist, as president. Legislatively, unions continued to face setbacks, such as the 1959 Landrum-Griffin Act, which used the excuse of union corruption, a problem in some unions, to force onerous reporting requirements to the government and extended Taft-Hartley's anticommunist provisions. Workers would win their demands for higher wages but only in exchange for giving up the most effective tools for challenging corporate power. Yet the money workers won was completely unprecedented in American history. Their struggles led to blue-collar workers living lives of luxury they could not have imagined twenty years earlier, including home ownership, car ownership, and paid vacations. Even given the new restrictions, unions of the 1950s had power almost unbelievable to the observer of today's labor movement. By 1956, almost one-half of American manufacturing workers were union members. Most did not challenge capitalism in 1956, but they still stood up to corporations. In 1952, when the steel companies gave their workers a terrible offer with the hope of goading them to strike so that they could win a total victory against their labor enemy, President Truman nationalized the steel industry and kept the mills running with union members. Organized labor was ecstatic that the president would come down so decisively. When the Supreme Court ruled that action unconstitutional, the steelworkers again went on strike and Truman refused to enact Taft-Hartley provisions to make them go back to work. The industry caved to the demands of the United Steelworkers of America, including a large pay hike. This was real worker power.[54]

Despite the crushing of labor's radical edge, workers won enormous victories after World War II. Union power combined with the growing economy to allow workers unprecedented money.

The GI Bill, the Federal Housing Administration, the National Interstate and Defense Highway Act of 1956: All of these subsidized a new suburban life, at least for the white working class. Average unemployment in the 1950s was 4.6 percent, by 1969 it was 3.9 percent. It was night and day compared to the Great Depression.[55] Unions felt good about the future at the end of the 1950s. Many saw endless economic growth and growing benefits. For example, Al Hartung, president of the International Woodworkers of America, testified before Congress in 1958 to take Pacific Northwest timber out of production and save it as wilderness. He justified this, even though it might have cost his members work, by arguing that with the economy growing and the six-hour day seemingly inevitable, his members needed a place to spend their free time.[56] Hartung proved too optimistic, but his mind-set represents the state of labor in 1958.

Yet many workers were left out of this American Dream. African Americans, Native Americans, and Latinos could not move to the suburbs, often could not find work, and faced discrimination within unions determined to keep the best jobs for whites. Women of all races received far lower pay than men for the same work, if they could get it. Union leadership got fat and happy off the dues payments from their workers' contracts. Organizing decreased and coziness with employers grew. Young workers increasingly found the trade-off their Depression-era parents made—accepting a hard, mindless industrial job with little opportunity for advancement in exchange for steadily improving pay and benefits—unacceptable. The tinderbox of American society in the 1960s and 1970s would challenge both companies and the labor movement with new demands for worker power.

8

Lordstown and Workers in a Rebellious Age

Should work satisfy us, in addition to paying our bills?

By 1960, many workers had moved from poverty to a middle-class consumer lifestyle in twenty years. The American economy appeared to have a limitless horizon of consistent growth. The 1950s had not been as stable and bucolic as the media portrayed on television shows such as *Leave It to Beaver* or *Father Knows Best*, but an unprecedented series of rebellions shook American society in the 1960s and 1970s. The civil rights movement brought moral outrage into the streets of the South and the nation, while students demanded free speech on campuses nationwide. Martin Luther King Jr. and Malcolm X inspired or infuriated Americans. The heady, optimistic days of the Kennedy administration turned into the quagmire of Vietnam and cynicism of Watergate. Lyndon Johnson's Great Society fought the War on Poverty. Music and fashion transformed seemingly overnight during the late 1960s, with the use of marijuana and psychedelic drugs shocking an older generation. The Vietnam War divided the nation, killed 58,000

American soldiers, and led to some of the largest protests in American history. The massacre of students at Kent State and Jackson State Universities after Richard Nixon ordered the invasion of Cambodia roiled the nation once more. Nixon's self-destruction over Watergate solidified the transformation of the idealism of the sixties to the cynicism and disgust of the seventies.[1]

In the 1970s, the women's movement won the right to a legal abortion and rallied for the Equal Rights Amendment. The gay rights movement grew rapidly after the Stonewall riots, and with the election of Harvey Milk to public office in San Francisco announced it was flexing its nascent political power. Widespread environmental legislation cleaned up the rivers and the air, protected wilderness areas, and announced to corporations that their wanton pollution was no longer acceptable. African American, Native American, and Latino movements continued fighting for gains in housing, employment, and civil rights. Yet the growth of white backlash, especially over housing desegregation and busing as a solution to school segregation, roiled cities from Atlanta to Boston. Americans also questioned their place in the world, after the nation's failure in the Vietnam War, the combination of the oil crisis and recession that rocked the nation in 1973 marked the end of the postwar economic boom, and continued instability in the Middle East. The malaise Americans felt by the late 1970s helped bring down the Carter administration and elect Ronald Reagan.[2]

Workers were at the center of this turmoil, often divided between those who wanted to protect the privileged rights of white men and those who demanded unions be at the forefront of a society that fought for all Americans. The civil rights movement fought for racial equality in the workplace, while white workers often wanted segregation on the job. Working-class people of all races fought in Vietnam. Some workers led antiwar protests and others beat up antiwar protestors. The violence that marked America in these years led to the assassinations of labor leaders. A new generation of workers stood up to powerful institutions, including their own union leaders, and demanded a new era of freedom on the job. They had a different set of expectations about life than their parents had. This led to rebellions that would shake the union movement to its core. The most important of these was at Lordstown, Ohio, a strike the young workers in a General

Motors plant started in 1972 in defiance of their own union leaders. More than any other labor action, Lordstown represents the upheaval of the era. Yet the rank-and-file rebellions could not transform the union movement in the face of massive economic and political shifts remaking the nation and beginning the modern corporate and political war on the working class that continues today.

An Era of Anger, Change, and Hope

For organized labor, the 1960s were a decade of both comfort and disappointment. AFL-CIO head George Meany presided over a fat and happy union movement that had given up on its goals of transformative social change from the 1930s and 1940s. It won slightly larger pieces of the economic pie while supporting Democratic candidates who would fund the military-industrial complex that employed so many union members. Meany's hawkish Cold War foreign policy tied the union movement to American intervention overseas, a goal that occupied more of Meany's time than organizing the millions of unorganized American workers. Lyndon Johnson's 1964 election on a liberal agenda brought hope for better labor law. His Great Society pushed for a more equal nation with programs such as Medicare, Head Start, and an expanded food stamp program developed to fight poverty. But labor could not win its goal of repealing the right-to-work clause in the Taft-Hartley Act of 1947, which allowed states to pass laws mandating that workers did not have to be union members to work in union workplaces. Democrats dominated Congress, but conservative southern Democrats combined with Republicans to block a House bill that would have overturned the offensive law, similar to what they had been doing for years to limit union power.[3]

While the civil rights movement had been building success since the 1930s, it became a national story in 1954 when the Supreme Court ruled segregated schools unconstitutional in *Brown v. Board of Education*. The labor movement responded to civil rights in contradictory ways. While employment in the federal government was a step toward the middle class for some African Americans, most black workers labored for very low wages. The civil rights movement always focused on economic rights. The United Packinghouse Workers of America, which had a large black membership, was a major funder of the Student Nonviolent Coordinating Committee, which organized the Freedom Rides and voter registration drives to challenge white supremacy in the South.[4]

The 1963 March on Washington is known for Martin Luther King Jr.'s "I Have a Dream" speech, or at least the three lines of it that get played on television. But its full name was the March on Washington for Jobs and Freedom. It built on A. Philip Randolph's March on Washington movement in 1941 that opened jobs for African Americans in the defense industry. The 1963 march's demands included the passage of civil rights legislation, a $2-an-hour minimum wage (equal to $16.26 in 2018 dollars), federal law banning discrimination in hiring, and the expansion of the Fair Labor Standards Act to include agricultural workers, domestic workers, and other low-wage workforces that employed many African Americans.[5] Randolph led off the March by saying, "We are the advanced guard of a massive moral revolution for jobs and freedom" and that "the sanctity of private property takes second place to the sanctity of a human personality" in arguing for housing reform.[6] United Auto Workers president Walter Reuther spoke in favor of economic justice, the day's only white speaker. The AFL-CIO paid for the buses to get people to Washington, the United Packinghouse Workers subsidized transportation to the march for unemployed workers, and the UAW paid for the sound system that would blast King's speech into history.[7] Throughout America during the 1960s and 1970s, black workers fought to desegregate their workplaces and their unions, earn equal pay for equal work, and demand respect from their employers and their co-workers.[8]

On the other hand, many unions and union members were racist. Reuther supported the March on Washington, but UAW members often resisted the integration of their workplaces. In 1960, the UAW had 150,000 craft workers as members. Only 2 percent were African American.[9] The building trades fought hard to keep their jobsites lily-white, while black workers increasingly demanded equality on the job. The United Steelworkers of America gave lip service to black equality, but did not endorse the March on Washington and found itself under attack from the NAACP and other civil rights organizations over segregation in its locals and in its union leadership.[10] The success of the Memphis sanitation workers' strike in 1968, despite the assassination of Martin Luther

King Jr. while supporting it (discussed in chapter 9), and the rise of Black Power meant a growing militancy among black unionists.

However, for large numbers of the white working class, racial identity mattered more than class identity. White working-class families in South Boston violently resisted the integration of their neighborhoods and their schools in the 1970s, using the street tactics of strikes to attack African Americans. Black steelworkers struggled to fight racism within their locals, often with the union's leadership showing indifference. The Supreme Court ruled in *United Steelworkers of America v. Weber* in 1979 that employers could give minorities special preferences in hiring, and a 1974 decree between the steel companies and the United Steelworkers of America settled several discrimination cases and created a framework to hire blacks and women in the steel industry. These decisions angered white male workers, who saw their status as elite workers as under attack.[11] Richard Nixon's Philadelphia Plan to desegregate that city's all-white construction unions inflamed white workers even more, a cynical ploy from the president who believed doing so would undermine labor support for the Democratic Party and hoped it would draw black voters to the Republicans. Union members' support for the segregationist Alabama governor George Wallace's presidential campaigns of 1968 and 1972 demonstrated the power of racism on large sectors of the white working class.[12]

As Black Power rose in response to continued violence, poverty, and discrimination, unions found themselves unsure of where to step. They preferred liberal racial progress to black militancy, while Black Power activists saw union liberalism as hopelessly corrupted.[13] In 1968, black activists, concerned over the lack of black history and black studies in public schools, took control of the public schools in the Ocean Hill–Brownsville neighborhood of Brooklyn, fired white United Federation of Teachers (UFT) members, and replaced them with African Americans. The UFT then went on strike, shuttering the school system for thirty-six days. It accused the black community members of anti-Semitism (many of the fired teachers were Jewish); black leaders responded that the white teachers were racist. A. Philip Randolph spoke in favor of the UFT, arguing, "If due process is not won in Ocean Hill–Brownsville, what will prevent white community groups from firing black teachers or white teachers with liberal views?"[14]

The white teachers were reinstated, but this ugly incident once again demonstrated how strikes could spawn from racial tensions.[15]

The anti-Vietnam protests also split the labor movement. Unions played critical roles in the development of the New Left, the young, mostly white and college-educated radicals that led the anti-Vietnam movement. The major New Left organization, Students for a Democratic Society (SDS), began in 1962 at the UAW retreat in Port Huron, Michigan, where it wrote its founding *Port Huron Statement*. Unions provided important financial and organizational support to many SDS projects through the mid-1960s.[16] Despite common media portrayals of the time of the antiwar movement consisting of rich students and the working class supporting the war, many working-class people, especially African Americans, Native Americans, and Latinos, strongly protested the war.[17]

On the other hand, AFL-CIO president George Meany was perhaps the Vietnam War's greatest supporter. He worked with the CIA to create antisocialist labor movements and promote pro-American governments in Asia, Africa, and Latin America, destroying leftist unions that truly represented the poor workers of nations from Bolivia to Indonesia. In addition, many union leaders, including Meany himself, found the growing counterculture of the 1960s personally revolting. Peter Brennan, president of the Building and Construction Trades Council of Greater New York, agreed. On May 8, 1970, Brennan coordinated two hundred unionized construction workers to attack an antiwar march outside of Federal Hall in downtown New York City. In what became known as the Hard Hat Riot, the workers, carrying American flags, singled out the men with the longest hair for beatings. About seventy people went to the hospital as a result. Brennan claimed it was a spontaneous demonstration by workers sick of hippies desecrating the American flag. This was a lie. Nixon repaid Brennan by naming him secretary of labor.[18]

When the Democrats nominated antiwar candidate George McGovern for the presidency in 1972, Meany refused to endorse him. He hated McGovern for two reasons. First was McGovern's war stance. Second, that McGovern won because of rule changes after the riotous 1968 Democratic National Convention, which lessened the power of party bosses such as Meany, made him resent the candidate even more. Despite McGovern's pro-labor record in the Senate, Meany savaged the candidate's supporters as homosexuals, hippies, and long-haired freaks. He lied about McGovern's labor record to cleave unionists from the nominee. Nonetheless, thirty-three unions, representing a majority of unionized workers, rejected Meany and officially endorsed McGovern. McGovern even considered UAW president Leonard Woodcock for vice president. Nixon crushed McGovern that November. Meany's obstinacy was the last straw for many on the left, a number of whom saw the union movement as a dinosaur unwilling to make alliances with freedom movements, a perception that remains today.

Union Rebellions

The upheaval shaking American society led young workers to demand a real voice in how their unions operated. They criticized their union leaders as corrupt and out of touch, including George Meany. The feminist movement strongly challenged sexism in the workplace and in unions. Women held no high-ranking positions in the AFL-CIO or most other unions, and those unions ignored women's anger over sexual harassment, wage disparities, and the jobs closed to them. In response, the Coalition of Labor Union Women (CLUW) formed in June 1973 under the leadership of Olga Madar of the United Auto Workers and Addie Wyatt of the Amalgamated Meat Cutters. Madar had worked for the UAW since 1941, playing a key role in turning the UAW into one of the nation's strongest organizations fighting for women's equality. In 1944, the UAW held a national women's conference, and in 1955 it was the first union to establish a women's department.[19] She spearheaded the fight to desegregate the nation's largest bowling organizations in 1952 and led the UAW's conservation department in the 1960s, lining up union support for environmental legislation and land protection. Wyatt was the first African American woman to hold an executive position within an American union, as vice president of the Amalgamated Meat Cutters. Wyatt was a major player in labor's support for the civil rights movement. She was named as one of *Time* magazine's Women of the Year in 1975.[20]

In March 1974, 3,200 women met in Chicago for the CLUW's foundational meeting. Myra Wolfgang of the Hotel and Restaurant Employees and Bartenders Union said, "You can call Mr. Meany and you can tell him there are 3,000 women in Chicago and they didn't come here to swap recipes!"[21] The CLUW helped isolated women unionists around the country realize many others faced the same predicament, giving them collective power as women and as unionists. Women's movement leader Gloria Steinem attended as a representative of American Federation of Television and Radio Artists. Since then, women have increasingly flexed their muscles within organized labor. In the 1990s and 2000s, Linda Chavez-Thompson served as AFL-CIO executive vice president, and in 2009, Elizabeth Shuler became the federation's first secretary-treasurer. Randi Weingarten was named president of the American Federation of Teachers in 2008, making her one of the most important union leaders in the nation.[22]

As more industrial jobs opened to women, they had to fight against new forms of discrimination. When the government forced the Bunker Hill Mining Company to hire women in its Idaho smelter, the company required those women to be sterilized before they could work the jobs where they faced lead exposure. Concerned about lawsuits but unwilling to clean up its operations, it chose discrimination instead.[23] Grassroots groups formed to fight against this and other forms of sexism at work. The 9to5 movement began in 1973, dedicated to tackling issues that affected female office workers. It fought for the 1978 Pregnancy Discrimination Act and, much later, for the 2009 Lilly Ledbetter Fair Pay Act, allowing women more time to file equal-pay lawsuits against discriminatory employers.[24] Women also led the dramatic J.P. Stevens textile mill strike in North Carolina. Immortalized in the film *Norma Rae*, starring Sally Field and based on strike leader Crystal Lee Sutton, the Amalgamated Clothing Workers of America (ACW) organized textile mills in the deeply anti-union state of North Carolina against a company willing to close the factory. Thanks to Sutton's incredible bravery—when she was fired for her union work, she responded by standing on a workbench and holding up a sign that read UNION until she was physically removed—the workers overcame their fears and the ACW won the right to represent seven thousand mostly female workers.[25]

The labor movement and gay rights movement also began crafting alliances in this era. Gay, lesbian, and transgender workers have faced the same harassment and violence at work that they have in society at large. For decades, queer union organizers remained in the closet while campaigning. But by demanding respect within their unions, the gay rights and labor rights movements have expressed growing solidarity. By the early 1970s, they made real strides in unions in gay-friendly cities such as San Francisco and New York. Gay unionists often played roles in the union-reform movements of the 1970s. When unions began their boycott of Coors beer in 1973 for that company's antilabor practices, gay activists in San Francisco supported the boycott, despite its popularity in their community. Public sector unions such as the American Federation of Teachers and the National Education Association became national leaders in fighting for protection of gay members from firings for their sexual orientation. The California AFL-CIO played an important role in defeating the state's 1978 antigay ordinance, and Service Employees International Union Local 503 was a top ally in fighting a series of antigay ballot measures in Oregon during the 1990s that would have discriminated against openly gay unionized teachers. An attack on gay unionists meant an attack on the fundamental idea of a union contract and thus forged stronger bonds among these allies in the progressive struggles of the past three decades. In 1997, the AFL-CIO announced Pride at Work, a national organization of lesbian, gay, bisexual, and transgender unionists, as a constituency organization within the federation. Gay rights now had official union approval.[26]

The late 1960s and 1970s witnessed new environmental legislation. Earth Day in 1970 rocked the nation, as people organized to force industry to clean up their pollution. This included workplace safety as well, as Richard Nixon signed the Occupational Safety and Health Act, creating an agency to oversee workplace safety and health that would begin operation on April 28, 1971. Workers challenged their unions to fight harder on environmental issues, including the workplace environment, during the 1970s. Said United Auto Workers Local 1112 president Gary Bryner: "I wouldn't want to see all the automobiles banned because they pollute the air. Yet I realize what the hell good is my livelihood if the air's gonna kill me anyway."[27] The fight for clean air had gone back to the Donora smog event of 1948, when a U.S. Steel plant in Donora, Pennsylvania, belching poison in the air interacted with a weather inversion to trap the pollutants in the air, killing twenty workers. This incident inspired a series of legislative efforts, including the Clean Air Act of 1970.[28]

Workers faced significant toxic exposure both outside and

inside the workplace. Unsafe workplaces contributed to the deaths of thousands of workers per year, and occupational poisoning from the thousands of new chemicals created each year, exposure to asbestos and radioactive materials, and the inability of unions to obtain information about the toxic materials their members worked with led to growing calls for reform.[29] Tony Mazzocchi of the Oil, Chemical and Atomic Workers (OCAW) led on these issues. He dedicated himself to vigorous workplace safety programs in union contracts, empowering union members to become activists on the shop floor for workplace health and building bridges between the labor and environmental movements to make the workplace environment an important agenda item for both. Mazzocchi became the national leader in pressing the Occupational Safety and Health Administration to issue stronger asbestos standards to protect both workers and consumers. Mazzocchi's work with environmentalists paid off for his union. In 1973, the OCAW went on strike against Shell Oil because of health and safety fears. Environmental organizations urged their members to return their Shell credit cards and boycott the company's stations in solidarity with the OCAW.[30]

The involvement of unions in the era's larger social issues belied tensions within unions as well, reflecting the larger rejection of authority that helps define the era. Beginning in the late 1960s, rank-and-file rebellions began within many unions. This started in the coal mines. John L. Lewis had run the United Mine Workers of America (UMWA) from 1919 to 1960. He was a dictator in his own union, tolerating no dissent. In 1963, Tony Boyle took over the UMWA. Boyle combined Lewis's authoritarianism with indifference toward his own members' safety. In 1968, seventy-eight miners died in a Farmington, West Virginia, mine explosion. In front of grieving families, Boyle stated, "I share the grief. But as long as we mine coal, there is always the inherent danger of explosions."[31] Workers were furious and disgusted at words that sounded like they came from the mouths of mine owners.

In response, workers started Black Lung Associations (BLA), grassroots efforts to fight for help with the deadly lung disease called pneumoconiosis that coated their lungs with coal dust. They wanted Congress to pass a mine safety law. And they did it in defiance of Boyle. Led by young miners returned from Vietnam or coming from cities where they had witnessed the tactics of the civil rights movement, they held public actions such as shutting down the West Virginia statehouse. They demanded that West Virginia allow for greater black lung testing, for agreements to fund health and pension programs even when workers lost their jobs, and for expanded workers' compensation. The protest succeeded, and West Virginia gave them most of their demands in 1969. This led to federal legislation with the Federal Coal Mine Health and Safety Act that passed with near unanimous congressional support before Richard Nixon reluctantly signed it late in the same year.[32]

The success of the miners' actions led to Miners for Democracy, a movement to retake the union from Boyle. Joseph "Jock" Yablonski was a longtime UMWA official until Boyle fired him in 1965. Yablonski challenged Boyle for the presidency in 1969. Boyle "won" by a two-to-one margin in the official count, but Yablonski called for a federal investigation over widespread voter fraud. On December 31, 1969, three men hired by Boyle murdered Yablonski, his wife, and his daughter while they slept at home. The UMWA executive council embezzled $20,000 from union funds to pay the murderers. In 1971, the federal government threw out the 1969 election. Miners for Democracy ran a reform slate led by Arnold Miller, a leader of the black lung movement. Miller defeated Boyle in 1972, not long before Boyle was convicted of multiple crimes. Miller's victory was a great moment for union democracy. The 1973 UMWA convention went on for eleven days and gave all members who wanted to speak a chance at the microphone. It also granted miners the chance to vote on their contracts for the first time in the union's history.[33]

The miners' spirit reverberated through organized labor. Edward Sadlowski led the rebellion among the Steelworkers. An antiracist environmentalist and peace activist, in addition to a third-generation steelworker, Sadlowski had a vision of a union movement fighting for social justice, one reminiscent of the CIO's early leftist years. He ran for head of his district council on a reform platform in 1973. The United Steelworkers of America leadership rigged the election against him. Sadlowski appealed and the Department of Labor mandated a new election, which he won in a landslide. A new, more democratic day seemed to have arrived in that union.[34] Rebels in the United Brotherhood of Teamsters created Teamsters for a Democratic Union to fight against their union's notorious corruption, personified by its president, Jimmy Hoffa.[35] By the mid-1970s, it seemed that the youthful rebellions transforming the United States would also radically change its unions in their image.

Lordstown

The anger of the sixties generation over both their jobs and their unions bubbled over most famously at the General Motors plant in Lordstown, Ohio, outside of Youngstown. This factory manufactured the Chevrolet Vega, a low-cost small automobile GM hoped would compete with Japanese imports such as Honda and Toyota. The workers had wages and benefits their fathers who organized GM could barely have dreamed of in 1937. But by 1972, the Flint sit-down strike was a long time ago. The world had changed a lot. The UAW had grown up. It bargained good contracts. Wages were better and hours shorter. Workers had health care plans, pensions, and paid vacations. Their fathers could not complain much, given their youths of poverty and privation.

But the new generation of autoworkers, at Lordstown and elsewhere, were angry: at their lives, at their union, and at society. Working the assembly line day after day, year after year, provided no satisfaction in an age that valued personal liberation. The Lordstown workers averaged only twenty-four years of age. Commenters frequently mentioned the long hair and beards of white workers, the Afros of black workers. It was not just Lordstown. More than one-third of all UAW members in all Chrysler plants were under the age of thirty, half had worked there less than five years, and African Americans had come to dominate the workforce at many Michigan auto plants.[36] The rebellious spirit of the 1960s reverberated throughout American workplaces at this time, but in particular at auto factories such as Lordstown where the workers were unusually young. Many had fought in Vietnam. Lordstown workers looked at their fathers, who had worked in the Youngstown steel mills for decades, and they saw an endless future of working the assembly line.

GM managers saw workers as profit-generating machines, not living, breathing humans. Rather than ask workers what they wanted or how they thought they could contribute to making a better vehicle, GM and many other American companies saw unions as an enemy that had no right to participate in production decisions or to give suggestions on how to make the job more fulfilling. With companies feeling this way about unions, workers held the similar anger toward their bosses. Tensions between foremen and workers were high in Lordstown, as they were throughout the auto industry. Trying to get their living machines to work faster, GM sped up work at Lordstown, making fewer workers do more. This only made the young and volatile workforce more dissatisfied. Said a union official, "If you were 22 and had a job where you were treated like a machine and knew you had about 30 years to go, how would you feel?"[37] Neither the UAW or GM had a good answer for that question.

By 1972, UAW leadership was made up of old men who had come of age in the great struggles of the past. They had little in common with many of the union's members. In 1950, Walter Reuther and GM had agreed to what became known as the Treaty of Detroit. This was a long-term contract that provided great wages and benefits to UAW members, but with the union giving up any right to bargain over production decisions or broader national industrial policy. These contracts put a lot of money into workers' pocketbooks but also meant the end of unions challenging the fundamental precepts of capitalism in the United States. After 1950, unions focused on material benefits and largely accepted as inevitable changes in production that might make the work less satisfying or throw workers off the job, such as speeding up production or automation. When the Lordstown management instituted the speedup, UAW leadership had no useful response.[38]

That doesn't mean the UAW was clueless about the need for democracy on the job. Walter Reuther, who died in a 1970 plane crash, fought against racism in his union and in his nation. Although Reuther's record on dealing with racism in UAW plants was mixed, he pushed for civil rights and personally opposed both the Vietnam War and the AFL-CIO's support of it. In 1968, he pulled the UAW out of the federation, complaining of George Meany's politics and his refusal to commit to organizing, and worried that Meany's stodgy leadership was undermining labor's future. Reuther had planned to take his union on strike against GM in 1970, hoping for a revival of the social movement unionism the UAW pioneered. Reuther's replacement as UAW president, Leonard Woodcock, implemented Reuther's plan, but the strike nearly bankrupted the union and won little, even as it cost GM $1 billion in profits. Moreover, the contract that ended the strike allowed the company to automate the production line, combine two divisions in the Lordstown plant, and eliminate jobs.[39]

The 1970s were tough on American manufacturers, especially the car companies. For generations, the American companies had faced little foreign competition. They made large cars with low gas mileage. These defined the suburban, commuter, mall-going, car-centric culture of the postwar period. Big cars fit a period of abundance and consumption. But the 1970s shook the core assumptions of the automakers. They started facing unprecedented competition from foreign manufacturers, particularly in the form of small cars from Japan with high gas mileage. Americans began buying these cars, especially as the long period of economic growth slowed and the nation's relationship with the oil-producing nations of the Middle East soured. In response, GM created the Chevrolet Vega at its retooled and automated Lordstown plant. Claimed a GM official, "The concept is based on making it easier for the guy on the line. We feel by giving him less to do he will do it better."[40]

Lordstown workers hated it. By "giving him less to do," GM really meant speeding up the line and laying workers off. The job was *hard.* The factory had previously made the Chevrolet Impala at a rate of sixty an hour. The Vega sped off the line at 101 an hour. This gave workers thirty-six seconds to perform eight separate operations. GM, still committed to the high profits it made off larger cars, felt the Vega would never make money. So it hired managers for the plant with the explicit goal of squeezing as much profit out of the workers as possible. One young woman complained, "I don't even have time to get a drink of water" because she was worked so hard.[41] Said another, "Every day I come out of there I feel ripped off. I'm gettin' the shit kicked out of me and I'm helpless to stop it. A good day's work is being tired but not exhausted. Out there all I feel is glad when it's over."[42]

Workers fought back against the boredom and drudgery of the job and the capriciousness and dictatorial manner of their foremen and managers in a number of ways. First, they "worked to rule," refusing to do anything outside of what was specifically stated in the contract. This is a strike in its own way, with workers collectively resisting their bosses and deciding how hard they would work and what they would or would not do on the job. This included filing grievances over everything not explicitly listed in the contract. By February 1972, five thousand grievances clogged up the system, while workers demanded the rehiring of laid-off workers and slowed down production.[43] GM responded by firing many of the militant workers, angering the rest of the workforce even more. Workers also doubled up the work in teams without managers' approval, allowing one worker to work twice as hard for thirty minutes while his partner rested and then switching after that half hour.

The workers also protested by sabotaging their own work. They smoked marijuana and drank on the job. They frequently did not show up to work on Monday. The let cars go by without finishing them. They took days off or quit.[44] Three hundred women worked at Lordstown, and the problems they faced added to the general discontent. One twenty-year-old woman complained off the constant sexual harassment she faced from foremen, saying, "They can be real nasty."[45] Ten percent of the workforce was African American and around 5 percent was Puerto Rican. The workers at least claimed that racial solidarity was more frequent than racial tension. Local 1112 president Gary Bryner, age twenty-nine, said, "The young black and white workers dig each other. There's an understanding. The guy with the Afro, the guy with the beads, the guy with the goatee, he doesn't care if he's black, white, green or yellow. . . . They just wanted to be treated with dignity. That's not asking a hell of a lot."[46] Bryner himself had gone to work at Republic Steel in Youngstown when he graduated from high school in 1959, just like his father. He became involved with the United Steelworkers of America until he was laid off in 1963. When he got hired at Lordstown in 1966, he had union experience and, given his age, was the perfect representative for this youthful workforce. He understood the other Lordstown workers and the generational divide between them and their fathers. He talked of how men used to brag about how manly it was to work as hard as possible, but noted that his generation said, "I'm man enough to stand up and fight for what I say I have to do. It isn't being manly to do more than you should." Instead, workers wanted to "open up a book, he might want to smoke a cigarette, or he might want to walk two or three steps away to get a drink of water." He, and increasingly she, wanted to be treated with dignity.[47]

But GM had no interest in treating workers with dignity.

Instead, it sent doctors to workers' home to check up when they claimed to be ill and created compulsory overtime when the factory switched to the new yearly model. Workers were simply fed up. These attitudes not only infuriated GM but also UAW leadership. The UAW did not know what to do with these rebellious workers who often ignored the international. The companies wanted the UAW to control their workers and make them obey orders and live up to the contract. That was part of the idea behind the Treaty of Detroit. But the aging UAW officers in Detroit did not have that kind of control over a rebellious plant of young workers. Fewer jobs and sped-up work was something the leadership saw as unavoidable. UAW officers did not think the Lordstown workers had it so bad.

The workers disagreed. So they went on strike, against the will of the UAW. Said Bryner, "We demanded the reinstitution of our work pace as it was prior to the onslaught" of the speedup.[48] Tensions had begun to rise in late 1971, when GM sent workers home early several times without pay. By the middle of January 1972, the local leaders planned for a wildcat strike. That happened on March 5. Ninety-seven percent of the Lordstown workers voted to go on strike. They claimed they had reasonable demands. They wanted the line slowed down, they wanted 350 laid-off workers rehired, and they wanted, as Bryner noted, some kind of a plan to "change the boring, repetitive nature of assembly line work."[49] Both UAW leadership and GM decided that a short strike might help the workers blow off steam, so they worked together to manage the rebellion. GM, dealing with unfinished and even sabotaged cars being sent to dealerships, hoped a quick agreement with UAW leadership would show that wildcat strikes were ineffective and that collective bargaining through established employer-union partnerships was workers' best route to improving their lives.

UAW leadership immediately took over the negotiations and brought it back to traditional collective bargaining. Both GM and the UAW wanted this strike to end fast. It lasted eighteen days. GM agreed to restore almost all the jobs eliminated in the 1970 contract and dropped fourteen hundred disciplinary layoffs against current workers. On the other hand, nothing really changed for the workers. They still could not question their bosses about production decisions or make suggestions to improve workplace culture. They were still frustrated, with their lives and with the UAW. Their own elected leader, Gary Bryner, became their target, saying in the aftermath, "They're angry with the union, When I go through the plant, I get catcalls."[50] Black workers claimed the union leadership did not support their needs, and racial tensions increased on the shop floor.

The three-week strike received national attention for the generational rebellion it represented. Both employers and union leaders feared the "Lordstown syndrome" taking over American workplaces as young workers wanted more for their lives than a lifetime on the assembly line.[51] Activists saw what they wanted to in Lordstown. The consumer crusader Ralph Nader thought this would do for workers "what the Berkeley situation of 1964 did for student awareness," while leftist publications believed it was a "trial run of the class struggle of the '70s."[52] George McGovern visited Lordstown during his presidential campaign, trying to tap into the energy of that strike. The blue-collar rebellion became a major media and political phenomenon of the period, with newspaper articles, TV reports, Senate hearings, and a special task force in the Department of Health, Education, and Welfare to study the issue of dissatisfaction at the workplace. The commission issued a report titled *Work in America*. It saw that the heart of the problem was that workers simply expected better lives than their parents: "A general increase in their educational and economic status has placed many American workers in a position where having an interesting job is now as important as having a job that pays well."[53] Or as J.D. Smith, treasurer of the Lordstown local, said, "They're just not going to swallow the same kind of treatment their fathers did. They're not afraid of management. That's a lot of what the strike was about. They want more than just a job for 30 years."[54]

The Lordstown strike did not lead to a victory for workers, or a rollback of automation transforming workplaces. Lordstown workers themselves had no answer to how to create more satisfying factory jobs. It does however represent a titanic period of upheaval in the history of American labor, with new groups demanding respect and rights on the job, widespread workplace militancy, and an overall atmosphere of rebellion that can still inspire activists today.

Deindustrialization

Lordstown workers were disappointed that their strike did not fix most of the problems they faced. In fact, most of the movements for union democracy foundered badly. First, these union dissidents often did not represent the position of many workers. When they did take power, they often struggled to use it. When Edward Sadlowski ran for president of the United Steelworkers of America in 1976, his opponents accused him of radicalism and being closer to Harvard professors than steelworkers. Sadlowski said in an interview that he wanted fewer steel jobs in a society that found workers more fulfilling work. This mirrored the dissatisfaction with boring jobs held by the Lordstown strikers. But other workers read this as saying Sadlowski wanted to destroy steel jobs in an economy then in economic stagnation. Sadlowski was crushed in the election. Meanwhile, Arnold Miller was completely overwhelmed by leading the United Mine Workers. He turned out to have the same authoritarian characteristics as Tony Boyle. Everyday miners were still angry, but their reformist union leader proved a disaster. He retired in 1979, but the moment had passed and little changed in the UMWA. Teamsters for a Democratic Union reformers kept fighting for democracy in their union. They finally won the Teamsters presidency with Ron Carey in 1992, but his own illegal kickback scheme to fund his 1996 reelection campaign brought him down as well. The spirit of Lordstown went unfulfilled.[55]

But maybe those workers never really had a chance to articulate what union democracy would look like or how to find fulfilling jobs for working-class people. Even the best union leader in American history probably could not have defeated the widespread structural changes in the American economy that began in the 1970s. The postwar economic boom came to a screeching halt. A stagnant economy and high inflation racked the country beginning in 1973. The same year witnessed the Arab oil embargo, when Middle Eastern nations refused to sell to the United States because of the nation's support of Israel in the Yom Kippur War. This made the United States subject to international energy-supply problems for the first time, leading to gas shortages and skyrocketing prices, as well as creating new markets for fuel-efficient cars like those made at Lordstown. In 1969, the United States had 3.5 percent unemployment. By 1975, it was 8.5 percent. In 1974, the nation had an 11 percent inflation rate. Fears about inflation rather than concern for workers led the administrations of Jimmy Carter and Ronald Reagan to abandon America's industrial base in return for upper-class tax cuts and an economy based on high finance instead of middle-class jobs.[56] Lordstown workers quickly learned that their jobs might be boring, but with factories closing around them, they just became grateful for a job that paid the bills.

When Carter entered the Oval Office in 1977, labor hoped the White House would put the working class back on the right track. But Carter's fears about inflation combined with a growing conservative backlash to the liberal policies of the mid-twentieth century to make him wary of supporting unions. Carter also governed to the right of a Congress with sizable Democratic majorities in both houses, meaning that he could have crafted a liberal legacy that expanded the safety net and oriented the economy to help working Americans, but he did not. Nowhere did Carter fail worse than in his actions on the Full Employment and Balanced Growth Act of 1978 (aka the Humphrey-Hawkins Act). Sponsored by legendary pro-union senator Hubert Humphrey and Congressional Black Caucus co-founder Augustus Hawkins, this bill would have committed the government to provide full employment at prevailing wages for anyone who wanted a job. They hoped this law would overcome the racial divisiveness over jobs in the period of white backlash to civil rights. But Carter's advisers hated it. They worried about inflation. Sadly, the AFL-CIO also worried that full employment with the right to sue the government for a job would undermine union abilities to negotiate high wages for its members. It represented the interest of its members, but not of all workers. By March 1977, the new administration decided to oppose the bill as written and pressured its sponsors to take away all its enforcement mechanisms and government commitments. Carter managed to water the bill down to the point of meaninglessness when he signed it in 1978. Full employment in government economic planning would never happen in the United States. Carter refused to expend any political capital on organized labor, and by the 1980 election, disgust with the president within labor was profound. When a reporter asked International Association of Machinists' president William "Wimpy" Winpisinger what Carter could do to recover his reputation with labor, the angry union leader said, "Die."[57]

The punch in the chest of the economic downturn was followed by the right hook of deindustrialization. Companies began closing unionized factories and sending jobs to the nonunion southern states, to Mexico, and to Asia. Millions of union jobs simply disappeared beginning in the 1970s, shipped overseas, automated, or lost to foreign competition. This devastated union communities. On September 19, 1977, the Youngstown Sheet and Tube Company shut down its operations, laying off approximately 4,100 workers. Known as Black Monday, it embodied the deindustrialization decimating America's industrial core, dooming cities such as Youngstown to long-term decline and entrenched poverty. In 1977 alone, twenty-one steel mills closed in eight states, throwing nearly 22,000 workers off the job.[58] If this was the only factory to close, Youngstown might have recovered. In 1979, the Brier Hill Works closed. In 1980, U.S. Steel closed its Ohio Works and McDonald Mills. In 1985, Republic Steel shuttered its Youngstown mill. Fifty thousand Youngstown workers lost their jobs during these years, in steel, other industries, and the stores and shops that relied upon steel wages for an economically healthy community. By 1992, only about 1,000 people worked in Youngstown steel mills, compared to 40,000 after World War II. Between 1970 and 2000, the population of Youngstown fell from 141,000 to 82,000. In 2018, it had about 64,000 people. By the mid-1980s, Youngstown had the nation's highest arson rate. Enormous stretches of the city are abandoned. The steel companies never took responsibility for the long-term pollution they inflicted upon the city. General Motors' Lordstown factory nearby is still open, but workers there no longer have to wonder what life would be like without their mind-numbing assembly line jobs. They can see it in their neighborhoods and in their families.[59]

Deindustrialization became standard corporate policy during the 1970s. Growing trade deficits with Japan and cheaper labor overseas combined with American foreign policy to incentivize companies to move production overseas and to import goods without the tariffs that had protected American jobs. Companies invested in new factories overseas rather than modernize factories at home, meaning that U.S. production was outdated and inefficient compared to its competitors. In 1965, Mexico instituted the Border Industrialization Program to attract U.S. companies to new factories along the Mexican border. In the 1970s, companies began to find this cheap labor attractive, and by the 1980s, it was a rush to close American factories and move them over the border. In 1970, Bendix closed its York, Pennsylvania, factory to open a new plant in Mexico, Warwick Electronics threw sixteen hundred Illinois workers out of a job to open factories in Mexico and Japan, General Instrument kept its Taiwan plants open while shutting down two New England factories, and RCA closed a Cincinnati factory that employed two thousand workers and sent the jobs to Belgium and Taiwan. The Lordstown factory stayed open, but the UAW started giving back their hard-won gains in wages and benefits in contracts by the early 1980s in order to incentivize GM and other auto companies to stay in the United States. Despite this, hundreds of auto and auto-supply plants have closed in the past forty years.[60]

This is where the workplace activism of Lordstown, of the Black Lung Associations, and of the Steelworkers' revolt went. The 1960s and 1970s seemed like a time when the potential to re-create the United States was possible. In some ways it did happen, both in society and at the workplace. Women and African Americans demanding their voices be heard in unions, the growth of democratic unionism, and the creation of new demands on employers did not go away. Neither did the gay rights movement, the African American freedom struggle, or the feminist movement. But much as those movements also had to face a cultural backlash that included the defeat of the Equal Rights Amendment and the rise of conservativism that sought to limit black influence in politics, the workplace rebellions also floundered in the face of larger transformations. The decline of unions, of factory jobs, and of industrial communities decimated the base of workers who felt economically secure enough to make radical demands of their employers. Globalization and the threat of factory closures made worker uprisings hard to sustain. By 1980, the workplace uprisings defined by Lordstown were not dead, but strikes became more defensive last stands than attempts to demand greater dignity for workers. As the historian George Lipsitz wrote about the dissident Teamsters he knew in the 1970s, "The intelligent and militant young workers that I knew didn't rise to positions of influence within the trade-union movement; most could not even hold on to the jobs they had when economic restructuring crippled the industrial infrastructure of their cities."[61] With millions of factory jobs lost, the union movement declined. The dissatisfaction of American workers could have led to widespread changes in the American workplace and within the unions themselves. Instead, by 1981, government and corporations decided to crush unions entirely, starting a process that continues today.

9

Air Traffic Controllers and the New Assault on Unions

When government opposes unions, workers suffer.

The spirit of the 1970s could have transformed American unions. But like so much about the liberating and democratic spirit of the 1970s, the 1980s saw those hopes dashed against the rocks. A reinvigorated corporate lobby began organizing against the labor unions, consumer advocates, and environmentalists who had fought for the reforms that made the United States a much fairer, cleaner, and safer nation for everyday people. Corporate support of Ronald Reagan would have cataclysmic results for American workers. Reagan led a new era of union busting, which combined with corporations shutting factories in the United States and reopening them in Latin America and Asia to devastate the heart of the American labor movement. The rapid decline of the most progressive labor unions, such as the United Auto Workers, severely impacted the ability of working Americans to influence the political system. All of this created a whole new and hostile world for labor unions by the late 1980s, and they still have not recovered. The pivotal strike of this moment was that of the nation's air traffic controllers in 1981.

The Professional Air Traffic Controllers Organization (PATCO) was one of the most democratic unions in the country. They were militant for their rights, and when they went on strike in 1981, they expected to hold the nation's air traffic hostage until they won their demands. This was a sign of the growing power of public sector unions—government workers who had brought a new face to the labor movement in the previous decade. Reagan's decision to fire all the striking air traffic controllers not only ended the existence of PATCO but also launched a new era of union busting throughout the United States. This began what I call the New Gilded Age, an era, like that of a century ago, in which increasing income inequality and an employer-government alliance ensure workers once again have no power. Not many strikes sum up a period in American history more than that of the air traffic controllers.

Public Sector Unionism

Government workers make up a very different sector of labor in America than private workers. For most of the nation's history, especially before the New Deal, the government at all levels was small enough that federal, state, and municipal employees made up a small percentage of the workforce. There was still an open question about their work status: Were they workers or were they primarily public servants? Could they strike, and if they could, was this attack on the people themselves?

These first became central questions for Americans in 1919, when the Boston police went on strike. They had very good reasons for striking. Boston police had not received a pay raise since 1854. The starting salary for new officers was exactly the same as it had been sixty-five years earlier. Cops made only about half an average worker's salary in 1919 and had to pay for their own uniforms. They decided to form a union and petitioned to join the American Federation of Labor. The AFL first accepted police officers in June 1919, and cops around the nation immediately signed up. Soon, there were thirty-seven police locals around the nation. The Boston police commissioner and chamber of commerce argued that police could not be unionists because it would create "divided loyalty," a phrase demonstrating their fear that the cops would no longer be a force dedicated to defending the interests of capitalists. After the police commissioner suspended nineteen men for union activity, the police responded by voting to go out on strike by a vote of 1,134 to 2. Massachusetts governor Calvin Coolidge called out the state militia to repress the strike and fired all the Boston police. Coolidge rode his popularity as union-busting governor into the Republican vice presidential nomination in 1920 and then the Oval Office after Warren Harding died in 1923. Public sector workers were not granted collective bargaining rights under the National Labor Relations Act of 1935 and remained unaffected by most New Deal labor legislation.[1]

That was an inauspicious start for public sector unionism. However, the growth of the government during the New Deal and the postwar liberal state that followed required a lot more government workers. With the acceptance of unions into the mainstream of American society during the postwar era came a new movement to unionize government employees. In the 1950s, the mayors of Philadelphia and New York created bargaining for municipal employees, and Wisconsin instituted the first collective bargaining for state employees in 1959. On January 17, 1962, President John F. Kennedy signed Executive Order 10988, granting federal employees the right to collective bargaining for the first time. Federal workers still lacked the legal authority to bargain over wages and did not have the right to strike. But it was a start.[2]

Many of these government workers were African Americans, thousands of whom found employment in agencies like the U.S. Postal Service, where they fought against Jim Crow postal facilities, while many thousands more worked, often in low-paid jobs, for state and local governments.[3] During the 1960s, that meant the fate of these workers became a major part of the civil rights movement. The American Federation of State, County, and Municipal Employees (AFSCME) fought to win union contracts for public sector employees around the nation. This union had grown from one hundred thousand members in 1955 to two hundred thousand in 1963.[4] Their effort came to a dramatic, tragic, and ultimately successful head in Memphis. On February 1, 1968, two Memphis sanitation workers, Echol Cole and Robert Walker, were crushed to death by a garbage truck after its compressor shorted out and started working uncontrollably, catching the two unfortunate workers unawares. These deaths outraged workers angry at their lack of labor rights and civil rights. They demanded union recognition, better safety standards, and higher wages. The notoriously racist Memphis mayor, Henry Loeb, blew off the campaign. Frustrated by the city's continued discrimination against them, the all-black sanitation workforce walked off the job on February 12. The city's black community united behind them. National civil rights leaders, including Martin Luther King Jr., came in support. King was canvassing the nation preparing for the Poor People's Campaign he planned for Washington, D.C., in the summer of 1968, hoping to unite the poor of all races to demand policies that fought economic inequality and poverty. King told workers, "You are demonstrating that we can stick together and you are demonstrating that we are all tied in a single garment of destiny, and that if one black person suffers, if one black person is down, we are all down." On March 28, King returned to lead a mass march. Police shot and killed a sixteen-year-old protestor that day. Loeb declared martial law, but the next day, two hundred workers continued to protest with their iconic signs reading I AM A MAN. King returned to Memphis once more, on April 3; the following day, he was tragically murdered by an assassin named James Earl Ray. In the aftermath, with King's martyrdom and the sanitation workers' cause intertwined in the public imagination, the city finally agreed to a contract.[5] The Poor People's Campaign took place that spring, but without King's vision and leadership, it foundered in the face of an indifferent public.[6]

Public sector workers in the 1970s reflected the militancy of the Memphis workers. The postal workers set the tone. By the late 1960s, postal workers had a union but lacked collective bargaining rights, as did other public workers. Many worked second jobs because the pay was so low, especially in New York City, with its high cost of living. That is also where postal workers' militancy was concentrated. Many of the post offices were old, overheated or freezing cold depending on the season, dusty, and dank. When Congress voted itself a raise of 50 percent while refusing to do anything for postal workers and President Nixon's budget did not call for a pay raise, it lit the match of fury at the government. New York postal workers called for a strike. When Congress suggested a 5.4 percent pay raise in response, workers rejected it after comparing it to the congressional pay raise and went on strike on

March 18, 1970. Within a few days, two hundred thousand workers struck from New York to Los Angeles. They did so against the orders of their own union leaders, making this the nation's largest ever wildcat strike.[7]

To strike, postal workers had to break the law. Writing to AFL-CIO president George Meany, Brooklyn postal clerk Steve Parise argued that the illegality of a strike was irrelevant: "Our union and our rank and file feel that the Government has forfeited its immunity to a strike, not only because its open disdain for these men, but also the humility of financial hardships they have forced upon our families, such as seeking welfare to survive."[8] By March 25, the nation's entire postal system had ground to a halt. Nixon responded by creating Operation Graphic Hand, sending 25,000 National Guard members to New York to operate as scabs and deliver the mail. They failed miserably. Some of the postal workers were also National Guard members. They convinced their fellow troops not to move the mail. Nixon had no choice but to negotiate. The final agreement, settled on March 25, gave the postal workers a 14 percent pay increase and collective bargaining rights on wages and working conditions, although not the right to strike. The workers were not punished for having engaged in an illegal walkout. This was a landmark moment in the history of public sector unionism, ushering in a decade of enormous advances for these workers.[9]

It seemed that public sector workers would achieve ever greater victories. Government worker unions grew dramatically. By 1980, 40 percent of the nation's public workers were union members, and the number of public worker strikes skyrocketed from 36 in 1960 to 536 in 1980.[10] However, by the late 1970s, increasingly hostile governments had begun to push back, partially because of the same economic problems that undermined the radical democratic movements of the industrial unions in that decade. Greater raises and benefits for public workers became politically unpopular as other workers suffered. Governments also began to side with business over workers. After its success in Memphis, AFSCME expanded through the South. This coincided with the rise of black political power in southern cities as the civil rights movement consolidated its gains. The establishment of black voting and desegregated schools led to rapid white flight into suburbs. This meant southern cities became dominated by African Americans who could vote their own leaders into office. Many cities elected their first black mayors in the 1970s. AFSCME became heavily involved in southern urban politics, seeking to elect African Americans to power who would, presumably, use that power to increase the wages and working conditions of black workers.[11]

One of those cities was Atlanta. The campaign of Maynard Jackson was an extension of the idea of labor rights as civil rights. Jackson was a young civil rights activist seeking to challenge white political power in Atlanta. He was also the first black attorney to work for the National Labor Relations Board office in Atlanta. As vice mayor, Jackson had supported organized labor, breaking with mayor Sam Massell over a 1970 sanitation strike. Jackson's win in the 1973 mayoral election was a moment of rejoicing for African Americans across the United States, as the rise of black political power seemed a confirmation of the civil rights movement. But Jackson's desire to be reelected in difficult economic times won out over alleviating low wages for city workers.[12] In Jackson's first three years as mayor, the sanitation workers received no raises and salaries remained stuck at an average of $7,500 a year. This placed a full-time worker supporting a family of four below the poverty line. Jackson placed the corporate leaders' concerns about inflation over the dignity of the workers who had elected him. The workers demanded a 50¢-an-hour raise. Jackson refused to negotiate. By 1975, he wouldn't even return AFSCME's phone calls. Over the next two years, workers slowly engaged in increasingly assertive labor actions, such as a one-day strike in July 1976 and a wildcat strike in February 1977. Finally, on March 28, 1977, workers marched to City Hall to demand a meeting with Jackson. While Jackson did come out, he completely dismissed their concerns, infuriating them. The next morning, thirteen hundred workers went on strike. Jackson claimed the strike was an attack on black political power. He fired all the striking workers on April 2. The civil rights establishment favored Jackson over the workers. Jackson and his corporate allies completely crushed the strike.[13]

That supposedly progressive mayors could defeat public sector unions gave newly emboldened conservatives taking over the Republican Party, such as Ronald Reagan, confidence that they could do more to repeal organized labor's power. Reagan aligned himself closely with employers in his successful 1980 presidential election campaign, complaining about the regulations that helped keep the environment clean and workers safe on the job. Reagan, the former head of the Screen Actors Guild, was the first union leader ever to occupy the White House. But in the 1950s, he turned staunchly conservative and became the public face of General Electric's campaign to spread pro-business propaganda; he won the California gubernatorial election in 1966 on an unwaveringly antiprotest and law-and-order agenda. From the first day of his presidency in 1981, Reagan sought to repeal many of the gains workers had made in the 1970s. He gutted agencies like the Occupational Safety and Health Administration (OSHA) that helped workers stay safe on the job. Penalties for OSHA violations declined from an average of $558.86 between 1973 and 1976 to $192.63 between 1981 and 1984.[14] This was not an auspicious time for public sector workers to challenge the government.

The Air Traffic Controllers Strike

Air traffic controllers worked a stressful job. Hundreds of lives were in their hands at all times. As one controller in Newark noted, "a rotten employer will create a union every time," and the Federal Aviation Administration (FAA) was a rotten employer, dominated by former military officers who saw the controllers as former enlisted men—as many were Vietnam War veterans.[15] Despite the nation's rapidly growing air fleet, the FAA did not hire enough controllers. Workers were stressed and overwhelmed, waking up with nightmares about crashing planes. There were an average of twelve fatal crashes a year between 1962 and 1966, with ten more in the first eight months of 1967.[16] The work was incredibly intense. New York congressman Guy Molinari said of watching a controller at work: "I plugged in a headset and watched him take care of an awful lot of traffic, and his knees were drumming constantly; and you could see the type of tension and pressure he's operating under. The man had been there eighteen years. . . . You can see the pressure cooker there."[17] Moreover, American controllers worked longer hours with less vacation and sick time than controllers in every other industrialized nation.[18]

The FAA had ignored its own regulations manual for years. In August 1966, Chicago controllers decided to slow down air traffic by doing exactly what the FAA manual instructed and no more. They made sure that planes had landed and turned before allowing the next plane to land. By following FAA rules to a T, the controllers demonstrated their power, made flying safer, and massively backed up air traffic. Such slowdowns would become standard operating procedure for angry controllers over the next fifteen years. Los Angeles controllers engaged in similar actions, forcing the FAA to grant the workers pay raises and provide them with comfortable chairs. Building on this victory, and with the assistance of famed attorney F. Lee Bailey, an amateur flier himself who had gotten to know New York flight controllers, activists from around the country met inside LaGuardia Airport and created the Professional Air Traffic Controllers Association (PATCO) in 1968.[19]

The new union soon showed its power. Later that year, PATCO organized Operation Air Safety, a national program that again slowed down air traffic by strictly following FAA rules. Delayed fliers deluged Congress with angry calls. It worked. PATCO won automatic union dues deducted from paychecks and convinced President Johnson to sign a bill exempting controllers from restrictions on overtime pay.[20] In June 1969 and March 1970, controllers engaged in sickouts, with hundreds calling in sick to protest hostile supervisors, again slowing the airways to fight for dignity on the job.[21] The second sickout nearly destroyed the union. FAA supervisors fired eighty union leaders, embittering union activists. However, Richard Nixon agreed to rehire the fired air traffic controllers except for one sickout leader, because he wanted to court union support. He also signed a bill allowing controllers to retire with full benefits after twenty years if they were over fifty years old, or after twenty-five years otherwise. For controllers, the lesson was that their aggressive strikes against the government would cause it to cave. Eighty-four percent of the air traffic controllers voted in September 1972 to grant PATCO their exclusive bargaining rights.[22]

PATCO grew rapidly after these victories. Joseph McCartin, whose book *Collision Course* is the most important book written on the union, stated, "Between 1972 and 1977, PATCO emerged as the most militant, most densely organized union in any bargaining unit of the nation's largest employer, the U.S. government."[23] PATCO's actions infuriated the government and irritated the American public. But with public sector strikes illegal, the air traffic controllers had limited options to achieve their aims. PATCO also developed an increasingly acrimonious relationship with the FAA. Supervisors bitterly opposed the union contract and tried to escape it at every opportunity. Workers had to carry copies of the contract with them to enforce it on the job. They used their newfound power to file grievances on everything from parking and wearing jeans on the job to using a sick day to care for a family member and speaking freely in the workplace without facing discipline. The veterans who had become air traffic controllers rejected the military hierarchy mind-set of their bosses. They had enough of that in Vietnam.[24] The overwhelmingly white and male membership, often racist and sexist toward co-workers, used union rules to press for the loosening of personal conduct rules that reflected an angry and irreverent post-Vietnam generation.[25]

As the 1970s went on, PATCO's rank-and-file militancy grew and controllers' patience with the government shrunk. PATCO won raises for members at the busiest airports in 1977. In doing so, it used the leverage it had over the nation's travel to win its demands. Threatening a strike around Thanksgiving 1977, PATCO president John Leyden said the fact that Christmas was coming "has not escaped our board of directors."[26] But only winning raises for the big airports deeply angered members at the smaller facilities and fed a growing discontent that PATCO leadership went too easy on the government, while also infuriating the general public worried about their holiday plans.[27] PATCO endorsed Jimmy Carter for president in 1976, believing he would sign a bill allowing all federal workers to negotiate their pay. But with growing inflation and tight budgets, the Carter administration refused to negotiate in good faith. Militants thought the leadership had sold out by signing a new contract that did not address their demands, and the members only ratified it by a slim margin. The union forced a work slowdown over the airlines refusing to grant free international flights to the controllers, but internal support for this tangential issue was low and a judge fined PATCO $100,000. Carter now hit PATCO with blow after blow. First, the FAA downplayed a report showing the high rates of hypertension and stress among controllers, ignoring their needs for greater staffing and less-intensive work. Second, Carter ended the program that allowed early retirement for controllers. Third, after a 1978 crash blamed on pilot error, controllers lost legal immunity for crashes.

These failures infuriated PATCO militants, and they took it out on their president, John Leyden. A movement called Fifth Column, made up of young and angry controllers, challenged Leyden, demanding an aggressive stance with the government and the FAA. This led to Leyden approving the planning of a strike for 1981; even though government workers' striking was illegal, teachers in St. Louis had recently won raises because of nearly unanimous strike support. Leyden agreed to a strike if at least 80 percent of the membership favored it. Yet this could not stop the attacks on his leadership. In 1980, his vice president, Robert Poli, took on Leyden for PATCO president. When he realized he had lost the confidence of his fellow board members, Leyden resigned. With Poli's election, the radicals ruled the union. This was a democratic union, but would union democracy lead to good choices?[28]

With their relationship with Carter strained beyond repair, in 1980, PATCO took the fateful step of endorsing Ronald Reagan for the presidency. Reagan had dealt with most unions fairly as governor of California and signed the 1968 law that gave California public sector employees collective bargaining rights, despite his conservative record as governor of California and his status as a right-wing hero. Public sector unions had struck illegally in California more than one hundred times between 1970 and 1974, and Reagan had taken no harsh action against them. Given that many of the white men who made up the core of PATCO were not politically or socially liberal, the choice to endorse Reagan made sense to them. PATCO had endorsed Republicans before, including Richard Nixon in 1972. PATCO presented Reagan with a list of points they wanted him to agree to in exchange for an endorsement, including collective bargaining rights for pay and the right to strike in some circumstances, as well as better working conditions and shorter working hours for the exhausted controllers. Reagan agreed after some hesitation, and PATCO endorsed him, noting that Reagan would provide the "best leadership for federal workers."[29] Reagan blew out Carter that November.[30]

PATCO leaders believed Reagan would negotiate with them, but only if they struck, which they knew was illegal. The union demanded improved working conditions and a thirty-two-hour workweek. It also wanted a $10,000 pay raise and fully funded retirement after twenty years on the job. These demands were not unreasonable; between 1970 and 1977, the consumer price index rose by 65 percent, but federal workers' wages rose by only 47 percent. Their standard of living had declined despite negotiating better contracts.[31] PATCO was dreadfully wrong about how Reagan would respond. The union should have seen the writing on the wall. When he took office, Reagan immediately slashed the budget for the Occupational Safety and Health Administration and appointed anti-union members to the National Labor Relations Board. PATCO and the Reagan administration bargained for the first half of 1981, with the union threatening to strike. The administration offered a 5 percent raise, exemptions from federal caps on overtime pay, a 20 percent bonus for working nights, paid lunch breaks, and significant severance pay. This was far beyond what the U.S. government had ever offered a union. PATCO leaders reluctantly agreed. But then the members overwhelming rejected the contract. The president of the Pittsburgh local called it a "Band-Aid for a cancer."[32] The strike that followed would transform the American labor movement.[33]

In 1955, Congress had passed and President Eisenhower had signed into law a bill that made strikes by government workers punishable by a year in prison. But the government had caved to PATCO in the past and the union had endorsed Reagan. They had a strong bargaining chip: how could the president fire the nation's air traffic controllers? It would make air travel unsafe, as inexperienced or incompetent replacement controllers would have to keep planes from flying into each other. However, the FAA had been preparing for this strike since 1978. FAA administrator Langhorne Bond gave speeches about how the controllers were overpaid and underworked.[34] Union radicals were not intimidated. Neither was Ronald Reagan. When word of the contract terms came out, conservatives in the government were angry at the concessions, and Reagan's team got the message not to negotiate further. The rejected contract was the final offer.

National union officials were not happy with PATCO. AFL-CIO president Lane Kirkland certainly did not like Reagan, but he saw the PATCO position as weak. Kirkland, other union leaders, and congressional Democrats told Poli that PATCO could not win this strike. They certainly did not have support from the public. As early as 1978, a *Washington Post* editorial called PATCO "one of the most arrogant federal unions around" for slowing down all flights going into Washington for free international flights, one of the controllers' demands and a cause the paper called "doubly offensive."[35] But the controllers were not to be dissuaded. Said PATCO regional vice president Michael Fermon, "Why would a group of people, with all of the threats and rhetoric being made against them, with everybody in government saying what they're going to do to them, go out and break the law? If we do that, don't you think it means we have serious problems in our occupation? You think we just decided, all of a sudden, to take a chance and just throw everything away?"[36] On the morning of April 3, 1981, the controllers set up a picket line instead of going to work.[37]

Reagan, who represented invigorated conservative activists who believed in the free market and hated unions, saw this as an opportunity to prove his tough leadership style would work. He would repay PATCO for its support by destroying the union. Reagan held a press conference in which he gave the controllers forty-eight hours to return to work or face termination. David Gergen, a Reagan adviser, wrote that the president said, "Dammit, the law is the law and the law says they cannot strike. Having struck, they have quit their jobs, and they will not be rehired."[38] Reagan's threats just made the strikers more determined. Said striker James Stakem, "When I was a marine in Vietnam, I was sure of what I was doing, I believed in being there. I wouldn't have listened to Ho Chi Minh then, and I won't listen to Ronald Reagan now."[39] Controllers remembered the threats they faced down in 1970 and believed Reagan would not follow through. In the words of Minneapolis controller Ray Carver, "Fuck the president. We've done it. Let's stand by it. Let's see what the outcome is. If they can make her float, let her float."[40]

The AFL-CIO quickly distanced itself from PATCO. Said UAW president Doug Fraser, "This could do massive damage to the labor movement."[41] Possibly, if the other unions who worked on airlines had gone out on strike, illegal though it would have been, the unions could have won. But neither the International Association of Machinists and Aerospace Workers nor the Air Line Pilots Association (ALPA) had any stomach for this, in part because PATCO showed little interest in working with them and in part because a militant PATCO thumbing its nose at the government threatened the entire labor movement. ALPA members viewed the shutdown of the air as a threat to their own livelihood.

In fact, when ALPA president J.J. O'Donnell later called for the government to rehire the fired strikers, the pilots were so angry that they voted him out of office.[42] Publicly, the AFL-CIO said it supported the strikers. Privately, it sent out letters to its unions banning them from engaging in any secondary strikes or more radical actions to support the controllers. AFL-CIO president Lane Kirkland told Reagan he opposed "anything that would represent punishing, injuring or inconveniencing the public at large for the sins or transgressions of the Reagan administration."[43] Publicly he stated, "It is all very well to be a midnight gin militant to stand up and call for general strikes, but member unions will have to make their own decisions. I am not going to make the appraisal."[44] Many local union activists helped out the strikers and were angry at the federation for not doing more, but just as many other union members wrote angry letters denouncing the strikers. There was no stomach among rank-and-file unionists for a massive action to defend the controllers.

PATCO aimed to cripple the nation's flight capacity, but between the automation already transforming the airline industry and the government deploying all available personnel with any experience in air traffic control, flights fell by only about 50 percent. The airlines lost $35 million a day, but they supported Reagan and were willing to take short-term losses to tame the workers they felt held them hostage. The general public felt little sympathy for the strikers. In a period of high inflation and declining fortunes for the working class, PATCO's demands angered more Americans than they inspired. PATCO was openly indifferent to public opinion, feeling its power resided in the ability to shut down the runways. Not only did they overstate that power, but Americans were tired of being delayed in the air through PATCO strikes and slowdowns. Workers who made lower salaries than air traffic controllers wanted to take their jobs. In the weeks after the strike began, 45,000 people applied to become controllers.

The law did not require Reagan to fire the 11,345 people who did not return to work. But he wanted to make a point. About 10 percent of the strikers returned after Reagan threatened their jobs. Others filed for retirement. But most were left with nothing. Seventy-eight were arrested for defying court orders to stop the strike and return to work. A court ordered PATCO to pay the airlines $28.8 million to make up for lost profits. In October 1981, the Federal Labor Relations Authority decertified the union as the official bargaining agent of the air traffic controllers. PATCO was dead. Reagan then banned the strikers from government employment for life. President Bill Clinton rescinded that ban in 1993, but only about eight hundred controllers returned to a federal job.

The strident actions of public sector workers that began with the postal workers in 1970 decisively concluded with the controllers' firing. Between 1981 and 1982, teachers' strikes fell 42 percent, while state worker strikes in New York fell 90 percent between 1981 and 1988.[45] Government workers became public symbols of bloat for conservatives to attack, not workers who were seeking a better life. This attitude has continued to the present, with Republicans attacking public sector unions wherever they take power, such as has happened in Wisconsin and Iowa since 2010.

The Corporate War on Unions

The PATCO strike was the greatest disaster in American labor history. It launched a new era of union busting in the United States that continues to this day and allowed the Republican Party to stop pretending they thought unions were employers' partner in American capitalism. It was the first shot in the now nearly four-decade-long open warfare on the working class by the Republican Party, a position that became so politically mainstream by the 1990s as to be embraced by large sections of the Democratic Party, including by President Bill Clinton when he signed the North American Free Trade Agreement and the welfare reform bill, both of which doomed millions of Americans to poverty and bad jobs, or no jobs at all.

For private employers, the PATCO strike and the firing of the air traffic controllers marked the beginning of the modern corporate war on organized labor. Reagan's attack on PATCO empowered employers to declare open warfare on their own unions. It gave them confidence that they could treat their workers like Reagan had treated the air traffic controllers and the government would not intervene. Once again, the government would play a critical role in the success of labor unions. As the government, starting in the Oval Office, began to end the decades of serving as a relatively neutral arbiter between employers and unions, employers anticipated winning back the gains they had reluctantly given to unions since the New Deal.

For instance, in 1983, copper giant Phelps Dodge goaded its workers in Arizona to go on strike in order to eliminate all its unions. The copper industry was in deep trouble in the early 1980s. Pressure from abroad, especially from the giant mines of Chile, led to a reduction in copper prices. U.S. mining corporations responded both by investing overseas and by laying off American workers. Phelps Dodge closed its Arizona mine for five months in 1982. When it reopened, the company wanted it union-free. It offered its unions a terrible contract in which workers' wages would be tied to the worldwide price of copper, forcing them to bear the direct brunt of fluctuations of commodity prices. The United Steelworkers of America, the largest of the thirteen unions at the mine, was flexible in its negotiations. It agreed to a wage freeze for the entirety of the three-year deal. But it would not change its cost-of-living requests. The other mining companies had agreed to this very reasonable request. Instead, Phelps Dodge announced a $2-an-hour wage cut for new workers and major changes in grievance procedures, disciplinary actions, and other basic union rights. They also began the unprecedented step of forcing a medical co-pay on workers, something that we see as inevitable today but which was outrageous to many workers three decades ago.[46]

The workers struck, surrounding the mine so strikebreakers could not enter. Phelps Dodge and the state of Arizona coordinated a devastating response that was reminiscent of the brutality unions faced a century earlier. They created the Arizona Criminal Intelligence Systems Agency (ACISA), a state-funded undercover police force developed only for this strike. Using tactics from the violent days of the early twentieth century, ACISA agents infiltrated the unions, wiretapping about half of the union meetings. The agency shared intelligence information directly with Phelps Dodge officials. Phelps Dodge began smuggling arms into the mine to prepare for an armed struggle. Divisions rose within the workforce. George Mungia, an aging copper worker, could strike and potentially lose his pension. Or he could scab for two months and qualify for the pension his union fought to give him. He went for his own self-interest, knowing that Phelps Dodge would never give up. About 400 of the 1,480 workers did the same. Overall, though, the workers' solidarity was stronger than the company imagined. On August 8, about one thousand strikers and supporters surrounded the mine entrance, chasing away the strikebreakers and forcing others to remain inside the mill. In response, the state provided an army to end strikers' resistance. In what was referred to as Operation Copper Nugget, 426 state troopers and 325 National Guard members, assisted by helicopters, tanks, and military vehicles, retook the entrance to the mines. Eight days later, ten strikers were charged with rioting. The strike collapsed quickly after this overwhelming display of corporate, military, and legal power. In September 1984, the workers voted on whether to work without a union or maintain their union without a job. They voted out the union. In 1986, the National Labor Relations Board rejected the last union appeals. It was a complete victory for Phelps Dodge. The company became entirely union-free in Arizona. The ACISA was disbanded in 1984 after it had served its purpose to assist Phelps Dodge.[47]

A similar attack decimated the meatpacking unions. In 1985, Hormel decided to bust the United Food and Commercial Workers (UFCW) local in its Austin, Minnesota, plant. Average wages in meatpacking had plummeted in the early 1980s as the industry sought to close union plants and move them to nonunion states. In 1982, the average hourly wage for a meatpacker was $9.19. By January 1985, that had fallen to $7.93. Hormel demanded a 23 percent pay cut for the workers in Austin, to $8.25, even though the company had made a $29 million profit in 1984. The Austin plant was a new, state-of-the-art facility that could have been a model for a new day of labor in the industry, but Hormel sped up the work and endangered workers' lives even before it demanded the wage decrease. This was nothing but greed operating in a new atmosphere where the compromises with workers made in the aftermath of the New Deal no longer had to be honored.[48]

By the mid-1980s, in the wake of PATCO and Phelps Dodge, the UFCW acquiesced to Hormel's pay-cut demands to save any jobs it could. But the Austin local erupted in anger over Hormel's greed and their union's fear. Local P-9 defied international leadership, preferring to go down fighting than give up everything they had fought for over the previous decades. Fifteen hundred workers walked off the job in August 1985, a strike that would last ten months. P-9 proved quite resourceful. It began what today is called a "corporate campaign," hiring a public relations representative to embarrass Hormel nationally, publicizing the campaign to put pressure on the company to settle fairly. P-9 ran national newspaper ads targeting the company's poor labor practices, picketed at the company's national headquarters, and turned a local campaign in a Minnesota town into a national event in order to gain public attention for their cause.[49]

Nationalizing the cause was effective and brought Hormel unwanted publicity. Workers' wives organized fund-raisers, clothing drives, and other activities to sustain the strike. But the UFCW leadership opposed its striking local because it feared the meatpackers would do to them what Reagan had done to PATCO and Phelps Dodge had done to the Steelworkers. When P-9 members protested Hormel at other plants, UFCW leaders were hostile. One shift of workers in Algona, Iowa, crossed the picket line on orders from the union to ignore the strikers. At Hormel's Fremont, Nebraska, plant, the union told workers that if they honored the picket line, they would be violating their own contract. Only 65 of 850 did so. Workers at a Dallas factory did respect the lines and briefly shut down their facility, but without support from the international, this proved very hard to maintain. When 750 workers in Ottumwa, Iowa, honored the pickets, Hormel fired 500 because of their violation of the contract's no-strike pledge.

The campaign annoyed Hormel executives, but it made no difference to corporate strategy. Hormel brought in strikebreakers, and once again, the government stepped in on the side of the company when the Minnesota National Guard allowed them into the plant. This undermined the strike. Four hundred sixty members crossed the picket line to retain their jobs. UFCW leaders ordered P-9 to end the strike. An overwhelming majority of the workers voted against their leadership once again, wanting to continue. At that point, the UFCW took over the local against the workers' wishes. By September, the UFCW had negotiated a new four-year contract with lower wages and the elimination of both the guaranteed annual wage and a one-year layoff notice that the workers had originally won in 1940. Of the remaining 850 workers who had not crossed the picket line, fewer than one hundred ever received their jobs back. A year later, Hormel demanded further concessions. When the union refused, the company outsourced most of the jobs.[50]

This was a different era from the four decades prior to 1981. The rise of Reagan and the growth of open union busting after PATCO removed the façade that corporations had ever accepted unions in their workplace. They started using private union busting firms again to break strikes and intimidate workers from joining unions.[51] While the UFCW international leadership looked bad for selling out their local, it is hard to see how P-9 could have won. Hormel had all the momentum and all the ability to simply close factories and move.

Unions themselves deserve a good bit of the blame for their poor performance in dealing with these problems. After the big organizing campaigns of the 1930s and 1940s, many unions barely attempted to continue organizing and instead turned to consolidating their power. When many workers said "the union" they meant the elected officers, not themselves. They saw the union almost like they saw their bosses. Union leadership became lazy and self-satisfied. Unions assumed their contracts with companies were stable and focused on raises and benefits for members instead of challenging corporate power. Maybe that made sense at the time given the power of unions in the 1950s and 1960s. But by the 1980s, union leadership simply had no ability to respond to the overwhelming attacks on their power. AFL-CIO leadership was staid. The era of George Meany gave way to the even more tepid presidency of Lane Kirkland—a man who did not come from a working-class background and had trained for a career in diplomacy before working for the labor movement.[52] He was an anticommunist technocrat more concerned with promoting anticommunist unions overseas—especially supporting the Polish Solidarity movement—than with fighting for unionism in the United States. When Kirkland became AFL-CIO president in 1979, 21 percent of the U.S. workforce was in a union. By the time John Sweeney defeated Kirkland's preferred successor in 1995, that number had shrunk to 13 percent.[53]

Some unions made herculean efforts to save their jobs, including workers at the A.E. Staley Manufacturing Company corn-processing plant in Decatur, Illinois. Staley decided to crush its union, the Allied Industrial Workers of America (AIW) in the early 1990s, hiring a union-busting firm, tearing up the long-standing contract, and demanding back nearly everything the union had won over the past half century. AIW was a small union with few resources. Staley locked out the workers who refused to surrender. The workers responded by engaging in innovative protests, successfully pressuring Staley's clients to end their contracts with the company, going on speaking tours to raise funds and build solidarity, and working with students, clergy, community members, and national activists to continue their fight. The lockout lasted for more than two years. But once again, a union could not stand up to a determined corporation and AIW finally gave into company demands.[54]

Occasionally, the resistance did succeed. In 1989, the Pittston Coal Company refused to renew its contract with the United Mine Workers of America, leaving fifteen hundred people without health care. Two thousand Pittston workers went on strike in April 1989. In September, ninety-eight workers and one minister engaged in a four-day takeover of a mine to publicize their struggle. Wildcat strikes popped up the coal fields of southern Appalachia, with up to 37,000 nonunion members striking to protest their own terrible working conditions and health care. In February 1990 Pittston capitulated on most issues, including health care for retired miners. Aluminum workers in Ravenswood, West Virginia, won a nearly two-year battle with their employer after they were locked out in October 1990. A corporate campaign exposed illegal action conducted by the owners and worked with unionists around the world to protest company meetings in nations such as Switzerland to pressure the company, eventually forcing it to cave to a contract that provided security for union workers.[55]

But the Pittston and Ravenswood victories were rare exceptions that proved the norm of union losses. Most workers, fighting against huge corporations like Phelps Dodge, Hormel, and Staley, or against the U.S. government itself, could not win. The rapidly declining membership of American unions meant reduced political power for workers as well. By the 1990s, much of the Democratic Party became indifferent to the labor movement, even as Democrats continued to accept union money and get-out-the-vote efforts. No one personified this more than President Bill Clinton, an Arkansas centrist who embraced corporations and who owed nothing to organized labor. Clinton's push to pass the North American Free Trade Agreement (NAFTA) in 1993 was a catastrophic blow to American workers. NAFTA is a tripartite trade agreement between Canada, the United States, and

Mexico that eliminated most trade barriers between those nations. It incentivized American and Canadian employers to move their factories to Mexico by eliminating the tariffs that had previously made products from Mexico more expensive.[56]

NAFTA was the culmination of thirty years of American policy that began in 1965, when Mexico instituted the Border Industrialization Program. This plan attracted American industries to the Mexican side of the U.S.-Mexico border by offering them low wages and no strong unions. The U.S. government supported the effort as part of its attempt to improve relations with its southern neighbor. The apparel and electronics industries rushed to build Mexican factories. Their success led to an avalanche of fleeing American jobs. By 1986, when Ford and Mazda opened a factory in Hermosillo, Mexico, the construction cost of $500 million was half of what it would have cost in the United States, and the pay of $2 an hour for workers compared to about $30 in the United States when benefits were included. Unions had no answer to capital mobility and still do not today.[57] Since NAFTA's passage, the United States has lost 5 million manufacturing jobs. Companies threatened to move jobs to Mexico to force down wages. Fearful of losing their jobs, American workers accepted rollback after rollback, but the companies eventually closed their American plants anyway. Moreover, the unions most affected were the same big industrial unions that had turned the American labor movement into a force for social democracy in the first place: the United Auto Workers, the United Steelworkers of America, and other CIO unions. The best of the labor movement disappeared with the jobs.[58]

It is depressing to look at the labor movement of 2018 from the perspective of 1970. That era of public worker activism, union militancy, and working-class democracy ran headlong into a steamroller of aggressive corporate conservatism, capital mobility, and newly empowered government hostility. We will never know what would have happened to the labor movement had Ronald Reagan come to terms with PATCO instead of destroying the union. Reagan's actions gave corporations tacit permission to destroy the unions they always hated. While the labor movement's response to the setbacks it faced demonstrated a fat and happy leadership who forgot how to organize the working class, it's also far from clear that even the best leadership could have overcome such a merciless war from Washington and from multinational corporations. Once again, the fate of the labor movement had at least as much to do with government's willingness to accept it as a legitimate part of society as it did with any tactic or leadership structure unions did or did not have.

10

Justice for Janitors and Immigrant Unionism

Workers of color are the labor movement's future.

The corporate and government attack on unions that started in the 1980s has never stopped. Today, organized labor is at its weakest in a century. Brief moments of hope give way to tumults of despair. With Barack Obama's 2008 election to the presidency, unions hoped to revitalize the close relationship between labor and the government. Despite his indifference to labor in his first term, in his final four years, Obama's Department of Labor and the National Labor Relations Board crafted many policies and rulings that made it easier for workers to organize and expanded rights at the workplace. But the election of Donald Trump brought the corporate anti-union warriors back into power. His appointees have repealed rule after rule that helped workers. A politicized NLRB makes it impossible for workers to advance their rights.[1]

This is the continuation of the decades of anti-union extremism that Reagan began. As of 2017, only 10.7 percent of workers are union members. In 1983, when Phelps Dodge decided to crush its unions, that number stood at 20.1 percent. Private sector union density is only 6.4 percent, the lowest number in at least a century. More than half of all private sector union members live in five northern states. A much higher number of government workers are unionized—34.4 percent.[2] They are the latest victims of Republican attacks. Several states in recent years, including traditional union strongholds such as Wisconsin and Michigan, have passed so-called right-to-work laws that allow union members to opt out of their unions, even though the union must represent their interests.[3] This has decimated public sector unions in those states by significantly reducing union dues and in some cases disallowing bargaining over most issues.[4] The 2018 decision in *Janus v. AFSCME Council No. 31* ruled so-called "fair share" fees, which require nonmembers to pay union dues because the unions negotiate contracts that affect all workers and represent even nonunion members in grievances, an unconstitutional restriction on freedom of speech. This absurd decision, creating restrictions on union speech that simply do not exist for any other institution in the United States, is part of the same right-wing attempt to crush unions that spurred Reagan to destroy PATCO and Phelps Dodge to destroy its unions. With the Republican Party unwilling to tolerate unions' existence and many Democratic Party leaders lukewarm to unions, American workers have lost many of the gains of the entire past century.[5]

This has led to a significant increase in income inequality and social instability, leading to protest movements on both the left and the far right, as desperate people want change to an unjust system. Robotics threaten to take away many working-class jobs, whether self-service scanners in grocery stores, computer screens to order from at fast-food restaurants, or self-driving vehicles that make human workers antiquated.[6] The decline of hope in the working class has contributed to a rise in overt, aggressive racism and a desperation that leads white workers to vote for Donald Trump, who talks a populist game and gives voice to their fears about diversity, immigration, and changes in American culture while pursuing policies that destroy what is left of the nation's economic safety net.[7] While Trump and the Republicans eviscerate labor protections, white workers blame black and Latino fellow workers instead of employers and politicians. As we have seen throughout American history, race trumps class for enormous numbers of white workers.

Workers have lost a lot, and they will probably lose more before things get better. A service economy based around low-wage jobs without union protections or the hope of rising into the middle class has replaced the industrialized union economy. New forms of employment have developed, such as subcontracting and temp work that strip workers of stability and workplace power and a system of corporate outsourcing has allowed American companies to slash costs and raise profits by closing American plants and reopening them in Latin America or Asia, creating a global system of labor exploitation that has undermined unions in the United States.[8]

Despite all of this, workers continue to fight for justice. In fact, the very workers often demonized by the white working class have led the way in the new struggle for labor rights. Today's union movement does not look like the union movement of the past. It is increasingly African American and Latino workers, often immigrants and often undocumented, who are at the front of the movement. Many are women, many are LGBT. They often do not work in factories. Instead, today's struggles involve teachers, home health care workers, fast-food workers, farmworkers, and graduate students. These activists reflect the diversity of the nation and the diversity of the workforce.

This chapter focuses on one of the most iconic strikes of recent decades: the Justice for Janitors strikes organized by the Service Employees International Union in the late 1980s and early 1990s. The African American and Latino workforce, many recent immigrants from Mexico and Central America, not only combined demands for racial and economic justice but also brought the needs of immigrant workers to the center of the labor movement. This marked an epochal shift within the labor movement, away from the anti-immigrant and pro-white policies that have marked far too much of labor history and toward unions being on the front lines of the struggles of people of color, including in the fight against Donald Trump's racist immigration policies.

Immigration, Latinos, and the Labor Movement

The immigrant-centric labor movement stems from the Immigration and Nationality Act of 1965. The United States once had high immigration rates, but white workers often responded through racism. By 1924, anti-immigrant sentiment from the labor movement helped close most of America's borders to southern and eastern European immigrants, as well as Asian immigrants. From that time until 1965, the only large groups of immigrants that came to the United States originated in Mexico. The Immigration Act of 1924 had an exception for Latin Americans because southwestern farmers demanded them for cheap migrant labor.[9] California, Texas, and Arizona farmers had long sought the most exploitable labor possible, and that usually meant people of color, with the exception of during the Great Depression when white migrants from the South took those jobs and Mexicans faced deportation, even if they were American citizens.[10]

Latinos have long organized themselves for economic and racial justice. Their experience as farmworkers led to organizing in some of the most oppressive working conditions in the country. For example, the United Cannery, Agricultural, Packing, and Allied Workers of America (UCAPAWA) formed in 1937 and organized workers in the food industry from Missouri to California, mostly people of color. Leftist in orientation and close to the Communist Party, it and the many women in its leadership positions fought for racial and economic democracy among people struggling to survive, only to be crushed in the Red Scare of the 1950s.[11]

During World War II, to replace white laborers who had gone to work in defense industries or joined the military, farmers lobbied the government to help them acquire cheap Mexican labor. The Bracero Program began in 1942, bringing workers to the United States on short-term contracts that would end with their return to Mexico after the growing season. These workers faced heavy exploitation, terrible living conditions, life-threatening heat, and rampant discrimination. By 1945, 125,000 Mexicans had come to the United States as part of the program, but they faced such discrimination in Texas that the Mexican government refused to allow them into that state.[12] That program ended in 1965 when the United States passed the Immigration and Nationality Act. This transformed the nation's legal system, once again opening the borders to immigrants from across the world. It also capped legal immigration by nation of origin. As the American economy grew in the 1980s, low-wage jobs opened in agriculture, construction, landscaping, and restaurants. At the same time, the

Mexican economy collapsed in 1982, and the ensuing economic chaos drove millions of Mexicans across the U.S. border to work in the United States without documentation, creating an underclass of easily exploited workers without legal immigration status. Refugees fleeing U.S.-supported right-wing dictatorships in Guatemala and El Salvador added to their ranks. They would prove critical additions to the U.S. labor movement in coming decades.

In the same year that the 1965 Immigration Act passed, the United Farm Workers (UFW) brought the plight of Latino farmworkers to the public eye. Building on previous work by Filipino farmworkers in California, who began organizing in the 1930s, and Mexican American lettuce harvesters in that state's Imperial Valley in 1961, the UFW rose to represent the oppression faced by some of the nation's poorest and most forgotten workers. Community organizers Dolores Huerta and Cesar Chavez had started the National Farm Workers Association in 1962 to organize Mexican American workers. This turned into the UFW. Chavez's brilliance was in his ability to inspire people around the nation. He galvanized liberal whites, capitalizing on a major shift within the African American civil rights movement toward black power, which alienated white liberal supporters. Chavez happily picked up those supporters and used them toward his aims of his grape boycott, sending them around the nation to picket grocery stores carrying California grapes. Tapping into the idealism of the era, he presented himself as a martyr for his members through his famed hunger strikes. Ministers, students, journalists, and organizers descended on Delano, California, to help, to learn, to take the struggle back to their communities. The UFW won the grape boycott in 1970, with growers signing their first union contract. The UFW did not have long-term success as a labor movement, partly because of Chavez's own failings and discomfort with letting workers set the union's agenda, partly because of continued hostility from growers, and partly because Chavez himself demonized the undocumented immigrants competing with his members for jobs, even though they were often UFW members' relatives. By the mid-1980s, the UFW had lost most of the fields it had organized in the previous twenty years.[13]

Despite these problems, Chavez inspired farmworker movements to form around the country. The Coalition of Immokalee Workers in Florida fights for the rights of tomato pickers and has successfully fought to get fast-food chains to pay a higher price for that fruit.[14] The Farm Labor Organizing Committee, which began in Ohio in 1967, has won successful campaigns against the Campbell Soup Company in Ohio and the Mount Olive Pickle Company in North Carolina.[15] Pineros y Campesinos Unidos del Noroeste originated in 1977 in Oregon to resist raids to deport immigrants and has remained a critical force in fighting for Latino workers' rights in that state.[16] Even today, these workers face pesticide poisoning, heat stroke, thirst, dilapidated housing, and wages that are near slavery in places. Farmworkers often lack a day of rest. Farmwork is still dominated by Latinos, often undocumented immigrants from Mexico, Guatemala, Honduras, and El Salvador, or guest workers from nations such as Jamaica with no hope of staying in the United States legally. These workers are easily exploited and lack allies. Workers in New York's Hudson Valley report extreme isolation, desperately missing home and living without a community in the United States.[17]

The Rise of SEIU

When Americans think about immigrant workers, they often think of farmworkers. But after the Immigration Act of 1965, millions of immigrants moved to American cities from Miami to New York to Los Angeles. There they joined African Americans, Puerto Ricans, and other people of color making up the urban working class. Laboring as nurses, mechanics, waiters, cooks, and cannery workers, they began to change the face of not only the workplace but also the unions. The rise of this new workforce coincided with the rapid deindustrialization of the nation, the shipping of millions of jobs overseas, and the decimation of the industrial unions that had driven the union movement since the 1930s. Low-wage service workers, often immigrants and people of color, took on a larger role in the labor movement. The Service Employees International Union (SEIU) rose to organize these workforces and became the nation's largest labor organization. SEIU started as a janitors' union in Chicago in 1921 and remained focused on poorly paid, often immigrant workers. It built its organizing model not on the giant industrial factories already disappearing in the 1960s but on the small workplaces of one, two, ten, or one hundred workers that scattered service workers across the economy.

SEIU focuses heavily on organizing health care workers. This is hard, nasty labor, days filled with bodily fluids and the suffering and pain of the ill. It is also deeply intimate work, replete with enormous emotional costs on providers, families, and patients. While doctors are well paid, much health care labor pays very little. That women, especially women of color, do this work is not a coincidence, as these workers have historically made far less money than men. The United States had 2.5 million workers in health care by the late 1950s, more than steel and railroads combined. Yet health care workers found themselves ignored by the public and the media, who paid more attention to industrial work as the "real" union jobs as opposed to the more numerous service sector jobs.[18]

A New York union calling itself Local 1199 started organizing the city's pharmacy workers in 1932. In the 1950s, it began organizing African American and Puerto Rican health care workers, leading to a 1959 victory in the city's Montefiore Medical Center, which had fostered a culture of solidarity, thanks to many of the workers living on-site and the overall disgust at the poor wages and working conditions in the hospital. In the aftermath, in May 1959, workers in six hospitals voted to strike by a 2,258 to 95 vote. They received great support from New York's other unions, who told their members that they needed to support the strikers regardless of race. This was important for a white working class that often viewed people of color as their enemy. Said one local to its members, "These strikers are *human beings*, no matter what their color or country of origin." Nearly two hundred union locals provided active support for these workers, with donations pouring in that allowed these impoverished people to maintain their strike. On June 22, forty-six days into the strike, New York City mayor Robert Wagner intervened. He sat both sides down and hashed out an agreement that was only a partial victory for 1199. It did not grant them union recognition and instead created a committee to arbitrate future disagreements. But the organizing continued internally, and a year later, three thousand New York hospital workers were represented by collective bargaining agreements. Local 1199 constantly submitted demands to the arbitration committee while realizing that true victory would not be achieved until New York granted health care workers collective bargaining rights, which they did not have nationally because of the New Deal labor legislation compromises that excluded professions dominated by black workers. Local 1199 kept the pressure on the state and in 1962, its president, Leon Davis, served thirty days in jail during a strike to organize Beth-El Hospital, which led not only to a union victory but also to the state extending collective bargaining rights to nonprofit hospitals. In 1998, 1199 merged with the Service Employees International Union, helping to make SEIU the nation's most powerful and important union in the twenty-first century. Thanks to struggles such as 1199's, in 1974, hospital workers finally received collective bargaining rights nationally, giving them the basic rights of American employment like overtime after eight hours and the minimum wage.[19]

But not all health care workers labored in hospitals. Many worked in the homes of the sick and elderly. They remained classified as "domestic companions," like babysitters. Long hours, hard working conditions, and low pay were standard. They had their own fight for respect. The National Domestic Workers Union originated in Atlanta in 1968, and the National Committee on Household Employment helped Washington, D.C., home health care workers demand the right to form a union. By 1978, SEIU had a full-blown campaign to organize New York home health care workers, with the Trinidad-born Cecil Ward in charge and two of the four organizers being African American women. By connecting civil rights to labor rights in a workforce that was largely women of color, organizers slowly built these campaigns into powerful forces organizing some of the nation's most exploited workers. By the mid-1990s, SEIU had organized 74,000 workers in California alone and home workers became a central element of that union's growth to become the nation's largest.[20]

Justice for Janitors

SEIU also organized another critical part of the nation's low-wage service economy: janitors. Janitors work everywhere, but they are hidden in the shadows, laboring in offices and classrooms while office workers and students are at home. Their work is low wage and low skilled, making them highly replaceable. Given how people of color are relegated to the lowest paying jobs, even today, African Americans and Latinos often work as janitors. Janitors do the work of scrubbing toilets, and, in the absence of unions, are forced to work faster with fewer co-workers, leading to exhaustion and occupational injuries. Exposure to toxic chemicals is common; EGBE, or ethylene glycol monobutyl ether, a suspected carcinogenic substance, was used in 22 percent of cleaning products according to a 1997 study.[21]

SEIU began organizing janitors in Los Angeles in 1946, focusing on the biggest companies and winning large-scale contracts. SEIU helped make labor rights and civil rights synonymous for thousands of workers. Local 399 in Los Angeles fought against nonunion firms and ultimately represented five thousand Los Angeles janitors. Between 1976 and 1983, wages rose by an average of 50¢ an hour each year. This also led companies to seek out nonunion firms through subcontracting the work.[22]

Commercial real estate values crashed in the 1980s and a small number of building conglomerates took ownership of many of the nation's office buildings. Instead of employing their own janitors, these conglomerates contracted the work to outside cleaning companies that put enormous downward pressure on wages and working conditions. This was part of the larger move toward outsourcing that plagues the economy to the present, creating greater divides between the have and have-nots, with contractors making profits by keeping wages as low as possible. These companies hired many undocumented workers, especially from Central America, whom they believed had little power to resist exploitation. In 1983, the average wage for a janitor in Los Angeles surpassed $12 including benefits. By 1986, with companies having escaped most of the union contracts, janitors' wages had plummeted to $4.50 an hour, and their benefits had disappeared.[23] The percentage of janitors in major cities represented by SEIU fell from 62 percent to 52 percent between 1977 and 1981.[24]

The Los Angeles story repeated itself around the country. In 1985, Pittsburgh's Mellon Bank broke its SEIU contract by firing its janitorial staff and replacing them with a nonunion contractor. SEIU struck and Mellon claimed the dispute was between the contractor and the union, avoiding all responsibility for the cleaning staff. Two years later, the National Labor Relations Board ruled Mellon had engaged in an unfair labor practice and the janitors returned to their jobs with back pay. In fighting Mellon, SEIU had built upon community support through a public relations campaign. It saw this victory as a model to rebuild its janitorial contracts.[25]

Thus SEIU inaugurated the Justice for Janitors campaign. The plan targeted building owners rather than janitorial contractor firms. SEIU started organizing the janitors in Denver and specifically targeted Latino immigrants as the future leaders of the union. The big-building corporations held the real power and could roll the higher costs of treating workers decently into the contract. Even if SEIU organized a single contractor, if the building owner gave the contract to another company, the building would once again lack a unionized staff. The contractor could not raise wages at will without destroying its own profits, as it did not set the price. They had to pressure the building conglomerates.[26]

SEIU hired large numbers of experienced Spanish-speaking organizers, many of whom had gotten their start with the United Farm Workers, to sign up and motivate the Latino workforce. It focused on high-publicity tactics directed at corporations who rented in buildings where owners exploited janitors, using street theater to grab attention. In Philadelphia, it paraded a giant toothbrush in front of a company that forced janitors to clean toilets with toothbrushes.[27] The SEIU moved city by city, establishing each as a union stronghold. That was a key tactic, because the difference between a unionized city and nonunionized city was huge. In 1988, New York janitor and SEIU member Omar Vasconez made $11.29 plus benefits, while in nonunion Atlanta, Mary Jenkins made $3.40 with no benefits. He had job protection and she could be fired at will.[28]

This was hard organizing. Many workers, often undocumented, feared marching in front of their workplaces because they worried they could be fired or even deported.[29] Yet SEIU convinced thousands of janitors to sign union cards, and the campaign had early successes in Denver and Atlanta before moving on to the tougher, larger cities of Los Angeles and Washington, D.C. In Atlanta, SEIU targeted thirteen hundred janitors, mostly African American women, and got nine hundred to sign union cards. They engaged in highly public one-day strikes at major corporate headquarters in the city such as Coca-Cola, Georgia-Pacific, and CNN. When one major building owner resisted the campaign, SEIU started a national boycott against his buildings.[30]

Local 399 in Los Angeles became the center of the national campaign in 1990. The outsourcing and subcontracting of the buildings led to a rapid collapse in the local's membership, from five thousand in 1978 to eighteen hundred in 1985.[31] Many of the Los Angeles janitors were refugees from the U.S.-supported right-wing dictatorships that had terrorized their populations in Guatemala and El Salvador. In the 1980s, the Central American population tripled in Los Angeles, to more than 150,000. By 1990, more than 60 percent of janitors in Los Angeles were Latino, more than double a decade earlier.[32] These refugees already understood social and political struggle. They were, as a whole, less scared of civil disobedience than native-born workers or immigrants from some other nations. One organizer noted the Salvadoran immigrants weren't scared because "there [if] you were in a union they killed you. Here . . . you lost a job at $4.25."[33] In fact, undocumented migrants often worked as janitors because it was relatively safe from immigration authorities, as they were uninterested in catching only two or five undocumented workers in a single raid. Despite their legal status, these workers and SEIU organizers began following building owners to their nice restaurants and country clubs to heckle them, while using leaflets and demonstrations to get the buildings' tenants to place pressure on the owners to settle the issue. They wanted the contractors to accept unionization without an election. This strategy sidestepped the National Labor Relations Board, and a process that by the 1990s was being gamed by the employers to make it extremely difficult and slow for workers to win a contract. This is both because employers could force workers to sit through anti-union presentations and flood the workplace with anti-union propaganda and because employers could delay an election for years, replacing much of the workforce in the meantime. SEIU strategy instead built community support for the workers and placed public pressure on the companies to do the right thing, borrowing many of the tactics of the civil rights movement and United Farm Workers to build public sympathy.

Perhaps the most aggressively anti-union building owners and contractors in Los Angeles were at Century City, in a sizable office complex where International Service Systems (ISS), a Danish-based multinational corporation, had the janitorial contract. This was in a wealthy part of the city, right next to Beverly Hills, with rich and powerful tenants. SEIU slowly built a campaign there through 1989, organizing workers and placing public pressure on Century City and its clients. Organizers visited workers in their homes and convinced them that they could achieve victory. SEIU brought Danish union activists to Los Angeles to learn about the struggle and put pressure on ISS in its home country.[34] With the building owner and ISS unwilling to deal, the union led the janitors on a strike in April 1990. SEIU knew workers had a great deal of power. The wealthy companies inside the office complex did not want to see their janitors, and they did not want to see trash in their wastebaskets and dirty bathrooms when business opened in the morning. The renters might have nothing against the janitors per se; they just did not want to think about them. The loud protests and striking completely disrupted the tenants of these buildings, who had very little at stake if their janitors unionized. Those tenants began pressuring ISS to come to a deal.

ISS had different ideas. In the new anti-union era, police once again could be deployed by corporations to attack strikers. On June 15, 1990, as four hundred striking janitors attempted to cross a street, the Los Angeles police began beating them. They did so after shouting orders to disperse only in English to a group of workers who were largely monolingual in Spanish or spoke indigenous languages. As office workers from these buildings looked on in horror from their windows, the police attacked the strikers for two hours. They used their riot batons to beat the workers at the front of the line and then engaged in a flanking action that trapped the strikers in a parking garage. When the workers tried to flee, they were arrested for failure to disperse. Ninety workers were injured, nineteen seriously. One suffered a fractured skull. A pregnant worker named Ana Veliz miscarried her baby. Thirty-eight workers were arrested.[35]

This action, reminiscent of Henry Ford's and Little Steel's murderous attacks on workers in the 1930s, backfired badly. Public sympathy overwhelmingly supported the janitors after the violence. Tom Bradley, the mayor of Los Angeles, had mostly stayed out of the strike until this point, but after the beatings, he spoke out for the janitors. It seemed to many that the police wanted to teach these immigrants a lesson for causing problems. SEIU sued the Los Angeles Police Department for civil rights violations, leading to a $2.35 million settlement in 1993. ISS finally caved after SEIU Local 32B-32J president Gus Bevona, a powerful New York local head who had previously been indifferent to the Justice for Janitors campaign, told the company's president that if he did not settle with the Los Angeles workers, Bevona would take the workplace actions to New York. ISS signed the next day. This led to the establishment of a master contract in Los Angeles in 1991, covering all the buildings SEIU represented with the same salaries and benefits. SEIU's janitorial membership in Los Angeles skyrocketed to 8,000 from 1,800 five years earlier.[36]

A union contract did not transform the lives of janitors overnight. There was much work to be done if the Justice for Janitors campaign was to see sustained success. Other cities, especially Washington D.C., saw even more intransigent building owner resistance than Los Angeles. These complex campaigns required organizing thousands of workers dispersed across buildings around a city, including a sophisticated media strategy, and the building of community alliances forced a centralized leadership to run the campaign instead of local union officers. This was a big change for a union that had traditionally allowed locals to run their own operations with little oversight. The success of Justice for Janitors and SEIU's rapid growth in the 1990s led to greater centralization. The international union took over locals in cities from San Diego to Atlanta that refused to participate in the Justice for Janitors campaign and that even tried to resist the new organizing model because entrenched local leadership found the new SEIU threatening. No union has more effectively organized low-wage workers in the past fifty years than SEIU, largely because of these centralized campaigns.[37]

The Justice for Janitors campaign, one of organized labor's greatest victories of the past three decades, announced SEIU's arrival on the national labor scene. A new campaign in 1995 led to a citywide contract in Los Angeles that standardized wages and benefits in the city by 2000.[38] By 2000, the Justice for Janitors campaign had organized janitors around the country, with companies seeking to sign new contracts in order to stave off the bad publicity SEIU had successfully used in Los Angeles and elsewhere. By 2005, SEIU represented 70 percent of janitors in twenty-three of the nation's fifty largest cities. In the twenty-first century, with its newly invigorated attacks on unions and worker power, that's impressive.[39]

A New Era of Organizing

The success of Justice for Janitors helped reshape the national labor movement. The AFL-CIO had only two leaders in the forty years since the two labor federations merged in 1955—George Meany and Lane Kirkland. Meany was more dedicated to helping the CIA fight the Cold War by attacking leftist unions in Guatemala and Chile and supporting the Vietnam War than he was in organizing the nation's unorganized workers.[40] Kirkland was an uninspiring leader, comfortable in the boardrooms talking to employers but with no vision for rebuilding the labor movement at a time when a union-busting federal government and employers had significantly reduced the overall number of union members.[41] By 1995, in the aftermath of NAFTA's passage and the Republican wave in the 1994 elections, neither of which Kirkland had any answer for, leaders of the unions most dedicated to organizing combined to find a new AFL-CIO president. Led by SEIU president John Sweeney and leaders from the United Auto Workers, United Steelworkers, International Brotherhood of Teamsters, and American Federation of State, County, and Municipal Employees, among other organizing-first unions, reform-oriented unions pushed Kirkland into retirement.[42]

The campaign to replace Kirkland revolved in part around Justice for Janitors tactics, with establishment candidate Thomas Donahue saying that unions should not be blocking bridges, as Washington SEIU janitors had done in their campaign.[43] This fear of mass action reflected the established labor movement's inability to adjust to the anti-union realities of the day. Sweeney's slate reflected the hopes for an invigorated labor movement, with Linda Chavez-Thompson as vice president, the first person of color to serve in the AFL-CIO's leadership. United Mine Workers of America president Richard Trumka, who had gained notoriety for leading his union to a victory in the Pittston coal strike of 1989–90 that had used mass disobedience tactics reminiscent of the Flint sit-down strike, became secretary-treasurer; he would eventually take over for Sweeney in 2009.[44] The Sweeney campaign, called the New Voice, promised a resurgence in organizing using Justice for Janitors as a model. They defeated Donahue and the potential for a new day in the labor movement was on the horizon.[45]

To organize the millions of workers needing a union meant

reaching out to the new working class, the people of color and women who labored in restaurants, hotels, and hospitals. To accomplish this, the new AFL-CIO leadership sought to reenergize organizing for the first time in nearly a half century. Organized labor tapped into campus activism, trying to rebuild the trust it lost with the college left during the Vietnam War. It started Union Summer in 1996 to connect young activists with the labor movement, hoping to build future union organizers and leaders.[46] Today, this is a nine-week internship for college students to get their feet wet in the union movement, fighting on campaigns to help bring economic and social justice to American workers.

Several of the first Union Summer veterans took the labor struggle back to their campuses, creating organizations such as United Students Against Sweatshops (USAS). The anti-sweatshop movement developed out the exploitation of foreign labor in sweatshops where American apparel companies had moved their operations since the 1960s. This movement swept college campuses around the nation between 1998 and 2001 and sought to hold universities responsible for the conditions of production of school apparel, requiring administrations to sign agreements to affiliate with the Worker Rights Consortium, a monitoring organization that inspects overseas sweatshops to ensure their products are made under humane standards. Many USAS activists entered the labor movement after graduation, providing skilled young organizers to rebuild unions.[47]

One of Sweeney's greatest successes was reshaping the labor movement's position on immigration. SEIU and other service unions, such as the Hotel Employees and Restaurant Employees (HERE and today UNITE-HERE), fought to integrate immigrants into the labor movement. This led to a drastic transformation of the American labor movement from the leading opponent of immigration it had been for most of its history to one of the nation's greatest supporters of a fair and just immigration policy.[48] Today, unions are on the front lines fighting Donald Trump's anti-immigration platform. Not every union member supports this. Much of the white working class remains committed to a racist view of how the nation should look and which workers should benefit. But the union movement cannot survive without organizing immigrants. Fighting for the rights of immigrants is both the morally correct and politically savvy position.

The rise of immigrant-based unionism created a new center of American labor organizing in Las Vegas, where explosive growth in the entertainment industry after World War II created thousands of service industry jobs. Culinary Union Local 226 established itself as the city's most powerful union, organizing entire restaurant staffs, from valets to cocktail waitresses, and had the power to shut down entire resorts, as it did with a six-day strike in 1967 that led to employers caving on wages, and again in 1970, costing thousands of angry tourists their vacations. By the late 1960s, the Culinary Union played a critical role in promoting civil rights and the integration of casino work in Las Vegas and had many African American shop stewards and other union officials. Between 1998 and 2008, Culinary Union membership doubled to more than forty thousand while union numbers were declining nationwide, with higher wages for service workers in Las Vegas than in other American tourist destinations. Today, the Culinary Union holds almost unmatched political power in urban and state politics, mobilizing a diverse membership that is 56 percent Latino and nearly 20 percent Asian American for policies that help all working people.[49]

Immigrant restaurant workers continue to start their own campaigns to fight for dignity. In the aftermath of September 11, 2001, when seventy-three low-wage workers died at the Windows on the World restaurant in the World Trade Center, a Moroccan immigrant restaurant worker named Fekkak Mamdouh and a young organizer, Saru Jayaraman, founded the Restaurant Opportunities Center (ROC). In the nearly two decades since, ROC has organized thousands of workers; exposed the low wages and terrible working conditions the largely immigrant and unseen restaurant workers experience behind the kitchen door; revealed the racism, segregation, and sexism that defines jobs in the restaurant industry; and played a key role in fighting to end the tipped minimum wage, which in most states allows restaurant workers to make far less than the standard minimum wage, as low as $2.13 an hour, under the idea that tips make up the difference. In reality, the tipped minimum wage dooms most restaurant workers to lives of instability and poverty. ROC has been at the forefront of the nation's economic justice movement, playing a role in campaigns to end the tipped minimum wage in eight states and several cities, including both the state of Maine and the city of Flagstaff, Arizona, in November 2016.[50]

The Challenges We Face

The new emphasis on both organizing and integrating immigrants and racial minorities into the front lines of the labor movement that came about from John Sweeney's election as head of the AFL-CIO was long overdue and very welcome. It energized the labor movement. However, by 1995, the deck was stacked so heavily against organized labor that even a reinvigorated movement found itself overwhelmed by both corporate and state opposition. Take, for example, another campaign to organize Latino immigrant workers by the Laborers' International Union of North America (LIUNA). LIUNA won a years-long battle to represent largely Mayan immigrants from Guatemala who demanded a union in their North Carolina meatpacking plant. Meatpackers have recruited Latino laborers since the 1980s, in part because many are undocumented and thus have little ability to protest their dangerous working conditions and low pay. But in Morganton, North Carolina, workers started walking off the job in protest of their wages and working conditions as early as 1991. As a LIUNA official stated, "We didn't organize anybody. There was union there before the union got there." Workers in the plant fought against a lack of bathroom breaks, low wages, unpaid hours, and the company deducting the cost of their supplies from their wages. Like the Justice for Janitors strikers, many of these workers had survived Guatemala's civil war and understood the need for solidarity to fight against mutual oppression. In 1995, the Morganton workers walked off the job and voted to join LIUNA a few months later.[51]

But strikes are just a single dramatic tactic in the labor movement. They show worker power but today are all too often, as they were a century ago, constrained by the enormous legal and structural impediments to building upon that burst of workplace action to create long-term change. In this case of the North Carolina workers, Case Farms engaged in a multiyear set of delaying tactics, using the system of labor law against the workers. It challenged the results of the union election, appealing it all the way to the Supreme Court. Even though it lost the case, the bosses refused to meet with union representatives and bargain until 1998. Even then, it refused to give in on any issue and pulled out after the mandated year of bargaining. It also promoted several union leaders to supervisory roles, taking them out of the union and undermining union support in the plant. The effort to unionize finally collapsed in December 2001.[52] The system of labor law that developed during the New Deal is now so captured by the corporations that many union activists believe it is not worth trying to win National Labor Relations Board–supervised elections, precisely for the reasons demonstrated by the North Carolina meatpackers. Despite the Justice for Janitors beatings, the state rarely uses direct violence against workers today. It just makes it impossible for their unions to survive or thrive.

Most unions have been pummeled in recent years. When the government bailed out General Motors and Chrysler during the recession in 2008, the companies forced the United Auto Workers into two-tiered contracts, meaning that new workers would never get the level of wages and benefits of established workers. While the UAW has pushed back against this to some success in the decade since, even after a generation of compromising with employers, the UAW could not stop further attacks, nor would companies see it as a partner.[53] Modern union rebels, still influenced by Lordstown strike, continued to demand greater union democracy and a more aggressive strategy, good things in principle, although it is hard to see how they would be more effective, particularly when even the Obama administration did not bother to protect the UAW in the auto bailout.[54] The UAW's weakness reflects what has happened to the nation's industrial communities, destroyed by outsourcing and deindustrialization. The factories where the Flint workers sat down and established the UAW are long gone, and the city is devastated by outsourcing and capital mobility. The Fisher Body plant in Flint, where the sit-down strike took place, closed in 1987. Today, Flint is one of the nation's poorest cities, now notorious for Michigan's Republican-dominated government poisoning it with lead in the city's water.[55]

Republican state governments not only poison the working class, they also destroy their remaining unions. After the 2010 Republican election wave wept Democrats out of power in the Congress and Senate and turned state legislations and governorships to the Republicans, the corporate lobby sought to eliminate the union threat. The front line was Wisconsin, where Governor Scott Walker, a man bought by the billionaire Koch brothers, and a right-wing radicalized state legislature pushed a bill through that not only allowed nonunion public workers to opt out of their unions but severely restricted what those unions could bargain over, giving workers no reason to be a union member. Seemingly out of nowhere, a union stronghold had turned hard right. Despite enormous protests at the Wisconsin state capitol that gave commenters hope that this conservative revolution would be turned around and a new dawn of protest was upon us, Wisconsin voters reelected Walker twice, and states such as Iowa, Michigan, and Missouri have copied his model of destroying unions. As throughout American history, the fate of labor unions largely rests on the ability to elect politicians that will allow them to succeed.[56]

There are many reasons to feel pessimistic. The decline of union membership means unions have less money to influence politics. This has contributed to skyrocketing income inequality. Yet there is reason for hope. Millions of Americans are disgusted by developments in the nation over the past decade. While some working people have fallen into the black hole of blaming immigrants and people of color for their problems, thanks in part to the emphasis on unions organizing low-wage workers in recent decades, many others have sought to create grassroots campaigns to demand change to help workers. Occupy Wall Street began in September 2011, changing the conversation about income inequality. While these protests that began in New York and spread around the country fell apart in the face of disorganization, a lack of clear goals, and a consensus decision-making model that privileged those willing and able to sit through seemingly endless meetings, Occupy activists have become critical players in a variety of protest movements in the years since. Ballot measures to raise the minimum wage have passed not only in liberal states but even in traditionally conservative states such as Nebraska and Arkansas. Americans everywhere feel disempowered by the new economy and Occupy gave voice to those fears, setting off sparks of activism across the nation.[57]

We have seen that organizing spark in many places. The fast-food workers' struggle, particularly in the Fight for $15 movement, has had a significant impact on American politics despite the fast-food industry still paying some of the lowest wages in the nation. SEIU has funded this movement, even though they stand to gain no union dues from fast-food workers unless they win a union contract, which is even more challenging than winning higher wages. The United Food and Commercial Workers International Union created the Our Walmart campaign to pressure the nation's largest private employer to raise its wages. Neither movement has won major victories, and both unions have had to pull out resources because of the incredible expense of funding campaigns that will not lead to union dues. But both have also contributed to the larger transformation in the conversation about income inequality in recent years. And as Sarah Jaffe has discussed in her brilliant recent summary of the explosion in grassroots activism, *Necessary Trouble*, there is plenty of reason to have hope about the future if we keep fighting for our rights.[58]

One final strike will demonstrate what is still possible for American workers and what drastic challenges they face. When Verizon demanded huge givebacks from the company's phone line workers in 2016, as well as outsourcing more jobs overseas, the company's two unions—the Communications Workers of America (CWA) and the International Brotherhood of Electrical Workers (IBEW)—struck. The Department of Labor mediated the strike, and the final agreement was sharply pro-union. It not only included language against outsourcing jobs but also allowed Verizon stores to be part of the unions' bargaining unit. Since Verizon has sought to dump its old landline phone operations for years, the future could be bright for the unions if the workers in Verizon's new mobile-focused working model can now be unionized. With service workers as the new working class, figuring out ways to channel those workers' discontent into labor victories must be central to labor strategies in the present and future. Moreover, the use of direct action tactics harks back to dramatic tactics of the past. Verizon strikers harassed strikebreakers staying in hotels, waking them up at five a.m. with cowbells and whistles and forcing the police to intervene, and the use of mobile pickets in front of Verizon cell phone stores caused the company to lose up to 30 percent of their business during the strike.[59] At the same time, this only happened because it was Obama's Department of Labor that mediated. The strongly pro-employer Trump Department of Labor would surely have acted differently.

Workers won a 10.9 percent raise, no pension cuts, and other demands. Mike Tisei, chief steward at one of one of the nation's two unionized Verizon wireless stores, said that the agreement "means a better quality of life and meaningful economic security for our families. Today [May 30] is a great day for my family and working families along the East Coast, and it's only possible because we stood together."[60] It is this sort of service worker, low paid and often short-lived in the job, that is the future of unionism. Can unions like the IBEW and CWA turn those low-paid jobs into high-paid jobs? Can SEIU turn the Guatemalan American janitorial workers into the next autoworkers, with pensions and vacation pay? There was nothing special about industrial work in the 1930s. Working in a Ford plant in 1932 was not more prestigious than working at McDonald's or Walmart today. The key to a dignified future is making those jobs good jobs for the working class. The Verizon strike helped move that goal one step forward. So did Justice for Janitors and so does every single campaign that fights for the rights of workers. In that we have to take hope. Despite all the terrible things happening to workers and unions today, the American labor movement will never end so long as we demand justice and equality, not just for workers who look like us or who share our same religion or who share our same national origins, but for all workers.

Conclusion: Take Back Power

We live in what I call the New Gilded Age. Today, we are re-creating the terrible income inequality and economic divides that dominated the late nineteenth century and created the violent responses that included the Haymarket bombing and the assassination of President William McKinley. Once again, we have a society where our politicians engage in open corruption, where unregulated corporate capitalism leads to boom-and-bust economies that devastate working people, where the Supreme Court limits legislation and regulations meant to create a more equal society, and where unions are barely tolerated. Life has become more unpleasant and difficult for most Americans in our lifetimes.[1]

This has already had a profound impact on American politics. The 2016 election witnessed the rise of an angry populism that took two forms. The groundswell of support for Bernie Sanders should energize us. Despite the bitterness felt among some of his supporters that Hillary Clinton defeated him in the primary, remember that Sanders was a last-second candidate with no infrastructure in place to win the primaries. Had he started his campaign in 2013, as Clinton effectively had done, the final result might have looked different. That he came close at all was due to the work of thousands of volunteers and the feeling of millions of Americans that mainstream candidates did not represent them. His run brought issues of economic justice to the forefront of the election year and created the most left-leaning Democratic party platform in U.S. history. The only flaw in how we think about the Sanders run is that we forget that presidential campaigns are not social movements. Rather, social movements should pressure politicians, moving them in the direction we want them to go. No politician can solve our problems. We have to solve them by making politicians do what we want. That single-payer health care and a significantly increased minimum wage now are positions anyone serious about winning the 2020 Democratic nomination must hold to win the primary is a sign of this.

Unfortunately, many people, including large swaths of the white working class, found their populist candidate in Donald Trump. Running on rhetoric about keeping factory jobs in the United States and demonizing immigrants and Muslims as our enemies, his campaign brought back the worst tendencies of white workers to choose racism over inclusivity. Trump had the best performance by a Republican among union voters since Ronald Reagan's blowout win over Walter Mondale in 1984. Trump's rhetoric about populism has conflicted with his actions, which have included a huge tax cut to benefit the wealthy and the decimation of polices that protect workers, perhaps beginning to make some of his voters realize they were fooled. But the appeal of racism will likely remain strong for many white workers.

What the 2016 election and its aftermath should reiterate to all of us is the deep connection between who controls the government and the success of the labor movement. As the historian Jefferson Cowie has written, there has only been one major period in American history when the power of workers coincided with the power of government to help unions—from the 1930s to the 1970s or early 1980s. Other than this "Great Exception," we have struggled against a corporate dominated government.[2]

We need to reorient American society in order to make it pro-worker again. First, workers have to take control over their own destiny in order to give themselves power. No government is going to do anything for workers if workers do not demand it first. A militant worker movement may not be enough to win victories. The strikes for the eight-hour day, the Industrial Workers of the World's radical actions, Homestead strike, the Great Railroad Strike of 1877, these and so many other actions challenged power and forced it to respond. Too often, it responded by crushing workers' movements. But each and every one of these movements laid the groundwork for what workers gained in the twentieth century. We may not win our struggles today, but each fight—Justice for Janitors, Occupy Wall Street, the Fight for $15, the Bernie Sanders campaign—is helping to prepare for the next time workers can take power in this country.

Second, we can only succeed by welcoming all workers into our movement. This book has centered on the ways race has divided the working class throughout American history. It often continues to do so today. It is too easy to blame employers for this. Yes, at times employers have intentionally divided workers by race, by bringing in black strikebreakers to antagonize white strikers or hiring immigrant workers who spoke a variety of languages to keep the workforce from organizing. But more often than not, white workers have prioritized their racial identity over their class identity without any help from their bosses. This is one of the major reasons why the American working class has struggled to express its power. "Making America Great Again" cannot mean "Making America White Again." Doing so will allow employers to divide us and presidents such as Trump to run on populist slogans while granting unprecedented powers to bosses to rule our lives. We have to embrace all workers, regardless of race, gender, immigration status, disability, or sexuality. There can be no compromise on this point.

Third, nearly all of us are workers. Too often today, the media equates *worker* with *blue-collar factory employee.* With these jobs increasingly gone, our lives are more defined by service work or office work than by factory labor. Nearly all of us are workers, whether you are an Uber driver (a company that makes money by refusing to classify its drivers as employees, putting the onus of employment on their backs while the company profits), a graduate student, a McDonald's worker, or a bank teller, in addition to those of us who still have jobs in steel mills and auto factories. As in late nineteenth-century movements such as the Knights of Labor, we need a broad definition of *worker,* building class consciousness among the 99 percent of us against the 1 percent who control us.

Too often we identify with our bosses and our companies instead of with our fellow workers. Your boss is not your friend. Without a union, your boss can fire you at will. And while you might be the best worker the company has ever seen, you have no power to control your own destiny without a union.

Finally, our movements need to take power by understanding how to leverage the American system of government for our benefit. The critical moment for workers finally winning their demands was organizing and fighting to place politicians in office who would support their goals, and then pressing those politicians to do what they wanted them to do. The leftward march of the New Deal happened because workers in 1934 went on a series of huge strikes. Working-class Americans voted for Franklin Roosevelt's reelection in 1936 by an enormous margin, while in Michigan, those same voters put Frank Murphy into the governor's office. These moves paid off when Murphy finally made the government a neutral arbitrator of the Flint strike and Roosevelt pushed for progressive legislation such as the National Labor Relations Act and Fair Labor Standards Act. While Democrats in recent decades have often taken unions for granted or even disliked them, that has happened in no small part because unions do not have the power they used to have. If we are to win back our rights, we have to win in the political realm. That means dealing with one of the two major parties. There is nothing in American history that suggests third parties can succeed electorally, nor is there evidence that third-party runs to the left move the Democratic Party to the left. One of the major parties has to become the workers' party in order for us to win our rights. Someday that might be the Republican Party, but only if it gives up its focus on corporate domination. The Democratic Party may be flawed, but today it is our best chance at turning a political party into an instrument of workers' rights. It happened once before and it can happen again, but only if we make it happen by organizing both inside and outside the political parties.

American history is a story of freedom and oppression, often at the same time. True freedom cannot come without economic emancipation. We came very far to gain that freedom through the struggles of workers in the two centuries before today. In the past four decades, we have given back much of our freedom. Only through our combined struggle to demand the fruits of our labor can we regain our lost freedoms and expand those freedoms into a better life for all Americans. I hope this book helps us understand the paths taken and the paths ahead.

Acknowledgments

I would like to very much thank the staff at The New Press for their support of this project from its inception. That is especially true of my editor, Jed Bickman, who always had solid ideas on how to improve the book and didn't get too cranky when this manuscript was a little later than he would have liked. I would also like to thank my co-bloggers at *Lawyers, Guns, and Money*, where this book originated with my "This Day in Labor History" posts: Scott Lemieux, Robert Farley, David Watkins, Simon Balto, Melissa Byrnes, Dave Noon, David Brockington, Shakezula, Vacuum Slayer, Christa Blackmon, Paul Campos, Dan Nexon, and Steven Attewell. Thanks as well to Joseph Slater for teaching me so much about public sector labor over the last several years. Virginia Scharff continues to deserve more credit than anyone else for turning me into a writer and for demonstrating that a historian should write whatever they feel like writing; my debt to her cannot be fully paid. Many thanks to my colleagues at the University of Rhode Island for their support, as well as my own union director, Jay Walsh, for his leadership in our continued fight for faculty power on campus.

My parents remain the greatest supporters any child could ever hope for. I certainly wouldn't be where I am today without that support. And then there is my wife, Katie McIntyre, the best person I have ever known. Endless love to you.

Appendix: 150 Major Events in U.S. Labor History

1. **August 20, 1619**—First African slaves imported to Jamestown, Virginia, starting the history of slaves as the core workforce of southern plantations and creating a racialized system of work in what would become the United States.
2. **October 26, 1676**—Nathaniel Bacon dies, effectively ending Bacon's Rebellion, a revolt of largely poor whites, including former indentured servants, that helps lead Virginia planters to invest more heavily in African slaves.
3. **September 9, 1739**—Stono Rebellion begins. In the largest slave rebellion before the American Revolution, recently imported slave warriors from Africa kill between forty and fifty whites in South Carolina before being captured and killed.
4. **May 30, 1741**—Two slaves killed as part of New York Slave Conspiracy, a possible plan among slaves and some poor whites to burn rich people's property in Manhattan. Although proof was sketchy, at least thirty slaves and four

whites were killed over the next weeks by a white population scared of slave revolts.

5. **December 10, 1789—**Moses Brown hires Samuel Slater to build the nation's first modern textile mill in Pawtucket, Rhode Island, beginning the Industrial Revolution in the United States.
6. **October 28, 1793—**Eli Whitney applies for a patent for the cotton gin. This technology would greatly expand slave labor in the South and provide the raw cotton for industrialization in northern states.
7. **January 8, 1811—**German Coast uprising begins in Louisiana, a slave revolt that panicked whites and led to the brutal death of around ninety-five slaves.
8. **October 26, 1825—**Erie Canal opens after over one thousand workers die building it, continuing the nation's transformation during the Industrial Revolution and the indifference to the lives of workers.
9. **August 21, 1831—**Nat Turner's Rebellion begins in Virginia. It would result in the deaths of approximately sixty whites and nearly two hundred slaves.
10. **February 13, 1837—**Political rally in New York City leads to the Flour Riot, an early expression of discontent over developing capitalist economy and its unfairness to working class.
11. **May 10, 1837—**Panic of 1837 begins, leading to widespread unemployment among the northern working classes.
12. **October 30, 1837—**Nicholas Farwell's hand crushed in a railroad accident, leads to Massachusetts court ruling in 1842 that workers took on responsibility for dangerous working conditions by agreeing to work for an employer, which creates a doctrine that shelters employers from most responsibility for their unsafe workplaces.
13. **February 13, 1845—**Lowell Female Labor Reform Association forces Massachusetts to investigate conditions in city's mills.

14. **March 20, 1854**—Republican Party is founded, emphasizing the idea of "free labor" as the natural state of labor in the United States. This ideology that prioritized white men working for themselves in an economy that spread wealth around fairly equally formed its core opposition to the slave economy, but it left little room for African Americans.
15. **June 23, 1855**—Celia, a slave in Missouri, kills her master who used her for sexual labor, a common fate for female slaves.
16. **May 23, 1861**—Escaped slaves arrive at Fort Monroe, Virginia, fleeing to Union troops at beginning of the Civil War. General Benjamin Butler classifies them as contraband and does not return them to their masters. The beginning of the slave self-emancipation that ended American chattel slavery.
17. **November 7, 1861**—U.S. Army occupies Sea Islands in South Carolina and begins the Port Royal Experiment to have former slaves work cotton plantations as free labor.
18. **September 22, 1862**—President Abraham Lincoln issues preliminary Emancipation Proclamation, abolishing slavery in lands under rebellion from the United States.
19. **February 23, 1864**—Collar Laundry Union, led by Kate Mullaney, goes on strike, leading to a rare victory for women workers in this era.
20. **January 16, 1865**—General William Tecumseh Sherman issues Special Field Order No. 15, granting land to former slaves. President Andrew Johnson overturns it shortly after he enters the Oval Office, undermining the demands of freed slaves for land and economic emancipation.
21. **February 13, 1865**—Sons of Vulcan, a union of iron puddlers, win the nation's first union contract.
22. **April 9, 1865**—Robert E. Lee surrenders his forces, effectively ending the Civil War with a total defeat for the South and its slave labor system.

23. **November 25, 1865**—Mississippi institutes its Black Code, attempting to reinstitute slavery in all but name.
24. **December 6, 1865**—Ratification of the Thirteenth Amendment, outlawing slavery in the United States.
25. **August 20, 1866**—National Labor Union, an early federation of workers, demands Congress pass an eight-hour-day law.
26. **September 18, 1873**—Panic of 1873 begins due to railroad speculation, leading to widespread unemployment in northern cities. This is emblematic of the boom-and-bust economy caused by unregulated capitalism in the post–Civil War era that doomed workers to poverty.
27. **January 13, 1874**—Police crack down on workers protesting unemployment in Tompkins Square in New York.
28. **June 21, 1877**—Ten alleged members of the Molly Maguires, an Irish secret society blamed for labor radicalism in the anthracite country of Pennsylvania, are executed.
29. **July 14, 1877**—Great Railroad Strike begins, leading to large-scale protests against economic exploitation. President Rutherford B. Hayes orders the military to crush the strike, creating a precedent for the government to use the military to attack workers.
30. **May 6, 1882**—Chinese Exclusion Act becomes law after California workers organize to eliminate competition from Chinese laborers.
31. **March 1, 1886**—Great Southwest Railroad Strike begins, as the Knights of Labor, the nation's first broad-based labor organization, expands its reach across the nation. The ability of the railroad capitalist Jay Gould to put down the strike marked the beginning of the Knights' decline.
32. **May 4, 1886**—An anarchist throws a bomb into a group of police at Haymarket Square in Chicago, leading to the execution of innocent anarchists and marking the end of the eight-hour-day strikes roiling the United States that spring.
33. **December 8, 1886**—American Federation of Labor forms

in Columbus, Ohio, a union federation dedicated to promoting worker power but avoiding most electoral politics or attacking the fundamentals of capitalism. It comes to dominate the labor movement.

34. **August 13, 1887**—Newark leathermakers lock out employees to destroy the Knights of Labor in their city, a sign of how American employers will organize to keep their shops union-free.

35. **November 22, 1887**—Whites commit the Thibodaux Massacre in Louisiana, murdering striking black sugar workers, part of the broader post–Civil War campaign by white elites to keep black workers subjugated to employers.

36. **January 14, 1888**—Edward Bellamy publishes *Looking Backward.* This becomes the era's most popular book as people look for an alternative model to replace exploitative capitalism.

37. **January 23, 1890**—United Mine Workers of America founded, becomes the nation's first powerful industrial union.

38. **July 6, 1892**—Workers of the Pinkerton Detective Agency, frequently used as strikebreakers, are attacked as they attempt to land in Homestead, Pennsylvania, where steelworkers are striking against Andrew Carnegie's Carnegie Steel.

39. **July 23, 1892**—Alexander Berkman, an anarchist, attempts to assassinate Henry Clay Frick, who had brought the Pinkertons in Homestead. This action, done without worker approval, turns public opinion against the strike.

40. **July 11, 1892**—Striking miners blow up the Frisco Mill near Coeur d'Alene, Idaho, as violence becomes a more common response of increasingly desperate workers.

41. **February 7, 1894**—Gold miners at Cripple Creek, Colorado, go on strike. They won because the Colorado governor used troops to support them instead of the mine owners, demonstrating the central role of the state in determining the outcome of strikes.

42. **April 30 1894**—Coxey's Army, a ragtag group of unemployed Americans, march into Washington, D.C., to demand federal jobs for the unemployed.

43. **June 26, 1894**—American Railway Union, led by Eugene Debs, calls a boycott in solidarity with striking workers in the company town of Pullman, just outside of Chicago, Illinois. The government responds to the shutdown of the rail system by using the military to destroy the ARU and imprison Debs. He converts to socialism in prison.

44. **December 5, 1894**—Alabama repeals its child labor law to attract New England textile mills, an early sign of how northern manufacturers would move to the South to find easily exploitable labor.

45. **June 22, 1896**—Mine owners in Leadville, Colorado, agree to lock out their employees and, unlike at Cripple Creek, a new governor uses the state militia to assist employers.

46. **September 10, 1897**—Sheriff deputies in Lattimer, Pennsylvania, massacre nineteen striking miners.

47. **May 1, 1899**—Florence Kelley begins work with National Consumers League, a middle-class organization dedicated to eliminating child labor, making labor feminism part of the larger women's rights movement.

48. **May 12, 1902**—Coal miners in Pennsylvania strike. With a coal shortage looming, President Theodore Roosevelt intervenes, creating a new precedent of the federal government mediating strikes rather than serving as the private army of employers.

49. **February 11, 1903**—Japanese-Mexican Labor Association forms, an unprecedented cross-racial organization to fight for the rights of all farmworkers. The unwillingness of California unions to accept Japanese workers leads them to reject the JMLA, dooming it.

50. **November 23, 1903**—Colorado governor sends the state militia to crush Western Federation of Miners strike at

Cripple Creek, leading to the WFM turning to reject capitalism.

51. **April 17, 1905**—*Lochner v. New York* decided by the Supreme Court, overturning a state law that limited bakers to working sixty hours a week. The court effectively ruled that companies could name whatever conditions of employment they chose.
52. **June 27, 1905**—Industrial Workers of the World founded. This radical alternative to the American Federation of Labor would organize the nation's most exploited workers for the next fifteen years, providing a sharp challenge to capitalism before it faced a violent crackdown from employers and the state.
53. **February 15, 1907**—In response to California workers demanding the end of immigration from Japan, Theodore Roosevelt and the Japanese government agree to halt most immigration from that nation.
54. **December 4, 1907**—Theodore Roosevelt agrees to use the military to end an IWW-led strike in Goldfield, Nevada.
55. **February 24, 1908**—*Muller v. Oregon* decided by the Supreme Court, which justifies a law limiting the hours women could work by claiming women had special status that men did not.
56. **November 2, 1909**—Spokane free speech fight begins, one of many IWW-led struggles to spread its doctrine freely in western cities.
57. **October 1, 1910**—Two leaders of the International Association of Bridge and Structural Iron Workers bomb the *Los Angeles Times* building because of its hatred of unions, killing twenty-one employees.
58. **March 25, 1911**—Triangle Fire kills 146 workers in New York, leading to widespread reforms in building safety and workplace safety and galvanizing the nation's attention on American working conditions.

59. **May 3, 1911**—Wisconsin passes nation's first workers' compensation bill, providing small amounts of money to injured workers.

60. **February 24, 1912**—Police beat women and children during the Bread and Roses strike in Lawrence, Massachusetts, an IWW-led effort to organize the city's mills worked by impoverished immigrant laborers.

61. **August 23, 1912**—United States Commission on Industrial Relations is formed to investigate the conditions of work in the nation and the violence of strikes and labor actions. For the first time, employers are forced to testify about the labor conditions of their workplaces.

62. **June 7, 1913**—Madison Square Garden hosts Paterson Strike Pageant, an IWW-attempt to build support for a textile worker strike in Paterson, New Jersey. The pageant is reviewed favorably but divides the workers and helps undermine the strike.

63. **August 3, 1913**—Police attack farmworker strike led by IWW in Wheatland, California, leading to deaths of two workers, a deputy sheriff, and a district attorney.

64. **April 20, 1914**—Colorado National Guard and company police attack a tent camp of striking miners near Ludlow, Colorado, killing at least nineteen, mostly women and children. The Ludlow Massacre leads to John D. Rockefeller Jr. being hauled before the United States Commission on Industrial Relations and forced to testify about his knowledge of the strike. In the aftermath, he helps craft company welfare programs to undermine labor action by improving conditions of work.

65. **October 15, 1914**—Woodrow Wilson signs the Clayton Antitrust Act, which alleviates the use of court injunctions against labor strikes. AFL head Samuel Gompers calls it "labor's Magna Carta" but courts limit its effectiveness.

66. **November 5, 1916**—Vigilantes in Everett, Washington, open fire on a boat filled with IWW members attempting to organize the city, killing at least five radicals.

67. **July 12, 1917**—Mine owners in Bisbee, Arizona, round up strikers and IWW sympathizers, load them onto railcars, and dump them in the New Mexico desert. The Bisbee Deportation attracts national outrage, but the companies suffer no consequences.

68. **August 1, 1917**—IWW organizer Frank Little lynched in Butte, Montana, where he had gone to organize miners.

69. **June 16, 1918**—Socialist leader Eugene Debs gives speech criticizing American involvement in World War I. Shortly after, he is arrested for violating Espionage Act as part of the federal government's crackdown on radical labor .

70. **February 6, 1919**—Seattle General Strike begins. Workers shut down entire city for five days in solidarity with striking shipbuilders.

71. **September 9, 1919**—Boston police go on strike to demand the right to a union. Governor Calvin Coolidge fires them all. The popularity of his action makes him the Republican candidate for the vice presidency in 1920 and he rises to the Oval Office when Warren Harding dies in 1923.

72. **November 11, 1919**—American Legion attacks the IWW union hall in Centralia, Washington. The IWW shoots back and kills four Legion members. One IWW member is lynched that night and the Centralia Massacre leads to long prison sentences for the union members.

73. **December 21, 1919**—The radical Emma Goldman is deported to the Soviet Union as part of the larger Red Scare, a government-led purge of the nation's radicals, a campaign that included massive civil liberties violations.

74. **August 25, 1921**—Battle of Blair Mountain ensues when ten thousand West Virginia miners take up arms against their employers in the largest civil insurrection since the Civil War. It is put down by mine owners, law enforcement, and the U.S. military using airpower against its own citizens for the first time.

75. **April 9, 1923**—Supreme Court decides *Adkins v. Children's*

Hospital, striking down federally mandated minimum wage for women in Washington, D.C., and delivering a devastating blow to advocates of labor rights.

76. **May 26, 1924**—President Coolidge signs the Immigration Act, cutting off most immigration from southern and eastern Europe, closing the door to the immigrants who had made up much of the American working class in the previous forty years.

77. **June 2, 1924**—U.S. Senate passes a constitutional amendment to ban child labor, but the states reject it.

78. **August 25, 1925**—Brotherhood of Sleeping Car Porters is founded. This union of African American porters combines labor rights with civil rights, and its leader, A. Philip Randolph, would become the greatest civil rights leader of his generation.

79. **August 23, 1927**—Massachusetts executes the Italian immigrant anarchists Nicola Sacco and Bartolomeo Vanzetti after their conviction for murder in an unfair trial and with shoddy evidence. Despite national and international outrage, their execution demonstrates the continued power of antiradicalism.

80. **April 1, 1929**—Loray Mill strike in Gastonia, North Carolina, begins. Textile mill owners brutally put this down with help from the North Carolina National Guard and roaming bands of vigilantes.

81. **October 29, 1929**—Black Tuesday on Wall Street starts the Great Depression. Widespread unemployment followed, reaching 25 percent by the winter of 1933.

82. **March 7, 1932**—Communist-led march of unemployed workers on Ford's River Rouge Complex in Dearborn, Michigan, is met with deadly violence from Henry Ford's personal thugs and the Dearborn police.

83. **July 28, 1932**—Encampment of the Bonus Army, a group of impoverished World War I veterans demanding their government pensions early to help them through the Great Depression, is burned by General Douglas MacArthur. This

incident helps seal the image of President Herbert Hoover as uncaring in the public mind and he loses the presidency to Franklin Delano Roosevelt that fall.

84. **May 17, 1933**—National Industrial Recovery Act introduced in the House. This bill attempts to reduce competition among industries to alleviate the Great Depression. It also contains a clause assuring workers they can unionize. The government has no way to enforce this, but for workers, it tells them that President Roosevelt wants them to form unions.

85. **April 12, 1934**—The first great strike of 1934 begins when Toledo Electric Auto-Lite workers walk off the job, winning union recognition and starting the most militant year for workers in American history.

86. **May 9, 1934**—Longshoremen strike begins in San Francisco and expands up and down the West Coast. Led by the radical Australian immigrant Harry Bridges, the longshoremen lose the strike after an epic battle that includes a brief general strike in San Francisco, but they win most of their demands through government arbitration.

87. **May 16, 1934**—Teamsters in Minneapolis strike. Led by communist organizers, the union local defeats organized employers to establish union power in that city, even though it is despised by politically conservative national Teamsters leadership.

88. **July 11, 1934**—Southern Tenant Farmers' Union forms to organize sharecroppers, mostly African American but some whites, being pushed off their land by federal agricultural policies.

89. **September 5, 1934**—North Carolina governor calls out National Guard to bust textile strike, one of many states to use state violence to suppress this strike that has spread from Rhode Island to Georgia.

90. **May 6, 1935**—Works Progress Administration is created as part of the New Deal, a series of programs hiring millions of

unemployed Americans to work for the federal government building dams, schools, roads, and other infrastructure.

91. **July 5, 1935**—Franklin Roosevelt signs the National Labor Relations Act, guaranteeing workers the right to organize for the first time in American history and ushering in the regulatory regime required to establish collective bargaining between employers and unions.

92. **August 14, 1935**—Roosevelt signs the Social Security Act, creating old-age insurance and fulfilling the demands of millions of American workers for a dignified old age.

93. **November 9, 1935**—Committee for Industrial Organization is formed within the American Federation of Labor to organize industrial workers. Headed by United Mine Workers of America president John L. Lewis, it would soon leave the AFL and become the Congress of Industrial Organizations, organizing millions of American workers in the next few years in auto, steel, rubber, and electric plants.

94. **June 17, 1936**—Steel Workers Organizing Committee forms within the CIO to organize the steel plants.

95. **February 11, 1937**—Flint sit-down strike, in which workers with the CIO-affiliated United Auto Workers sit down on their jobs and halt production at General Motors, ends. This titanic victory led to the organizing of the auto industry, stabilized the CIO, and transformed the American labor movement.

96. **May 30, 1937**—Memorial Day Massacre in Chicago, when police open fire on workers organizing Republic Steel, killing ten workers. The so-called Little Steel companies would violently resist unions until 1941.

97. **June 25, 1938**—Franklin Roosevelt signs Fair Labor Standards Act, establishing as national law the eight-hour day and forty-hour week, overtime pay, and minimum wage, and banning child labor.

98. **January 25, 1941**—Brotherhood of Sleeping Car Porters' head A. Philip Randolph announces his plan for a March on Washington to protest segregation in defense plants. This

leads Franklin Roosevelt to desegregate hiring in the defense industry in June.

99. **August 4, 1942**—Bracero Program is created to bring guest workers from Mexico to the United States on short-term contracts, mostly to work on farms under highly exploitative conditions.

100. **May 1, 1943**—Franklin Roosevelt orders the seizure of coal mines after the United Mine Workers of America refuses National War Labor Board arbitration. This federal action demonstrates the limits of the Roosevelt administration's tolerance for union radicalism during World War II.

101. **May 29, 1943**—*Saturday Evening Post* publishes Norman Rockwell's Rosie the Riveter cover, representing the millions of women who work industrial jobs during World War II.

102. **June 3, 1943**—Detroit hate strike begins when autoworkers at a Packard plant walk off the job to protest the hiring of black workers.

103. **September 19, 1945**—Twenty-four women picket the Lindstrom Tool and Toy Company in Bridgeport, Connecticut, after they are fired from their wartime jobs.

104. **September 22, 1946**—Tobacco workers win contract in early victory for Operation Dixie campaign, the ultimately failed CIO attempt to organize the South.

105. **December 3, 1946**—Oakland General Strike begins. In the most important moment in the huge strike wave of 1945–46, workers shut down the city for two days, demanding higher wages and attempting to build political power. Undermined by conservative elements within organized labor, it also spurred a backlash against union power among the nation's politicians.

106. **June 20, 1947**—President Harry Truman vetoes the Taft-Hartley Act, which bans most of the radical tactics unions used to organize in the 1930s, forces union leaders to sign anticommunist affidavits, and allows states to pass so-called right-to-work laws that allow workers to opt out of their

unions and still receive their benefits. Congress overwhelmingly overrides Truman's veto, demonstrating the weakness of political support for unions.

107. **May 23, 1950**—The Treaty of Detroit between the United Auto Workers and General Motors brings long-term stability for the auto industry and grants large wage and benefit increases in exchange for the UAW no longer challenging the fundamental power of the auto industry.

108. **April 8, 1952**—President Truman nationalizes the steel industry in order to forestall a strike, outraging employers who had sought to beat back their unions by forcing them off the job. When the Supreme Court rules that Truman overstepped his authority, a strike happens and the United Steelworkers of America win a major victory.

109. **March 14, 1954**—*Salt of the Earth* premieres, a film produced by the International Union of Mine, Mill, and Smelter Workers, a union evicted from the CIO for its communist leadership, about a strike of New Mexico zinc miners that used innovative tactics such as miners' wives leading the picketing to win a major victory. The film is red-baited and remains largely unseen for years.

110. **December 5, 1955**—AFL and CIO merge, ending the great period of American organizing and bringing the two labor federations back into one organization.

111. **May 8, 1959**—Local 1199 begins the New York hospital strike, a critical strike they did not win but which went far to expand the bargaining rights of hospital workers and laid the groundwork for building service worker unionism in coming decades.

112. **September 14, 1959**—President Dwight Eisenhower signs the Landrum-Griffin Act, expanding the anticommunist provisions of the Taft-Hartley Act and creating new regulations to fight corruption in unions.

113. **January 16, 1961**—Lettuce workers go on strike in the Imperial Valley of California, beginning the modern farmworker organizing movement.

114. **January 17, 1962**—President John F. Kennedy issues Executive Order 10988, authorizing collective bargaining for public workers. Public sector unionization would explode over the next decade.

115. **August 28, 1963**—The March on Washington for Jobs and Freedom takes place. Although the economic justice portion of the March of Washington is largely forgotten today, it had a strong labor agenda, demanding a $2 minimum wage and emphasizing the civil rights movement's emphasis on economic justice.

116. **April 4, 1968**—Martin Luther King Jr. is assassinated while supporting striking sanitation workers in Memphis.

117. **May 21, 1968**—The Poor People's Campaign, King's final campaign to unite the poor of all races to demand economic justice, starts its camp construction in Washington, D.C. Without King's leadership, the campaign did not succeed in pressuring politicians to craft antipoverty legislation.

118. **November 17, 1968**—New York State education commissioner reasserts state control over Ocean Hill–Brownsville school district in Brooklyn, ending major conflict between United Federation of Teachers and local Black Power activists over school control.

119. **September 23, 1969**—President Richard Nixon announces Philadelphia Plan to desegregate Philadelphia's construction unions, hoping to break union and African American support of the Democratic Party.

120. **December 30, 1969**—Nixon signs the Federal Coal Mine Health and Safety Act, the first comprehensive law to protect the health of coal miners, which only happened after a grassroots effort by angry coal miners in the face of opposition from their own union leadership.

121. **March 18, 1970**—Postal workers go on strike, an illegal action by federal employees but one that leads to a massive victory.

122. **May 8, 1970**—Hard Hat Riot takes place when building

trades unionists in New York beat up antiwar protesters. This and other similar incidents drove a wedge between organized labor and other social movements of the era.

123. **July 29, 1970**—United Farm Workers win first union contract in history of California agricultural labor.

124. **August 26, 1970**—National Organization for Women leads the Women's Strike for Equality, with a strong economic justice agenda demanding equal pay for equal work.

125. **April 28, 1971**—Occupational Safety and Health Administration, a federal agency dedicated to workplace safety, opens its doors.

126. **March 5, 1972**—Workers at a General Motors plant in Lordstown, Ohio, go on strike. This strike received national attention because it was an expression of great frustration by a young workforce over the dissatisfaction they felt on the assembly line and with both their employer and their own union, whom they felt did not take their interests seriously. The Lordstown strike defined an era of dissatisfaction among the rank and file.

127. **July 19, 1972**—AFL-CIO refuses to endorse George McGovern for president because his anti–Vietnam War position clashes with that of union head George Meany, continuing to divide organized labor from other social movements.

128. **January 23, 1973**—Oil, Chemical and Atomic Workers go on strike against Shell Oil after building alliances with environmentalists, who provide critical grassroots support against the company.

129. **March 23, 1974**—Coalition of Labor Union Women holds its founding conference, demanding economic justice for women, including equal and fair treatment within the labor movement, where they face widespread discrimination.

130. **April 14, 1975**—Bunker Hill Mining Company in Idaho announces sterilization policy for women working in its lead smelter, an example of the continued discrimination women face on the job even after the government forced companies to hire them.

131. **June 4, 1975**—California creates Agricultural Labor Relations Act, granting the state's farmworkers collective bargaining rights for the first time, a major victory for the United Farm Workers.

132. **June 5, 1976**—Teamsters for a Democratic Union forms, demanding reforms within the union.

133. **March 29, 1977**—American Federation of State, County, and Municipal Employees members go on strike in Atlanta. After AFSCME helps Maynard Jackson become one of the first black mayors of a major city in the United States, Jackson turns his back on the union and defeats workers' attempt to rise out of poverty.

134. **September 19, 1977**—Black Monday in Youngstown, Ohio, when Youngstown Sheet and Tube Company shuts its doors, laying off 4,100 workers. This moment was repeated over and over again during the next thirty years, leading to the deindustrialization of the United States' manufacturing cities and decimation of the industrial unions that made up the core of the CIO.

135. **October 31, 1978**—President Jimmy Carter signs the Pregnancy Discrimination Act, which states that pregnant workers "shall be treated the same for all employment-related purposes . . . as other persons not so affected but similar in their ability or inability to work."

136. **October 19, 1980**—Amalgamated Clothing and Textile Workers Union forces J.P. Stevens to sign a union contract for the first time, a major victory in the long struggle to organize southern textile mills. However, globalization soon draws textile companies to close their southern mills, union or nonunion, and move production to Latin America and Asia.

137. **August 3, 1981**—Professional Air Traffic Controllers Organization goes on strike. President Ronald Reagan fires all the strikers, even after PATCO endorsed him in 1980. The greatest defeat in American labor history, the PATCO strike opened the door to a new era of union busting from employers.

138. **June 30, 1983**—The Phelps Dodge mining company forces their miners in Arizona to go on strike by offering them an insulting contract as a ploy to destroy the union entirely. The company succeeds and private sector employers begin eliminating unions from their workplaces.

139. **April 11, 1986**—Police teargas strikers at the Hormel plant in Austin, Minnesota, who are fighting against an employer seeking to eliminate the union and union leadership unwilling to support them.

140. **September 17, 1989**—Ninety-eight miners and one minister engage in a peaceful takeover of the Pittston Moss 3 coal preparation plant, leading to a rare union victory in this era when the United Mine Workers of America wins a strike that focuses on the company eliminating health care benefits.

141. **June 15, 1990**—Los Angeles police beat members of the Service Employees International Union who are organizing as part of the Justice for Janitors campaign, a largely immigrant-led workers' movement demanding union contracts to clean office buildings.

142. **January 1, 1994**—North American Free Trade Agreement between the United States, Mexico, and Canada goes into effect, codifying the era of free trade that sent millions of American jobs to Mexico and other nations in the decades before and after this treaty.

143. **October 23, 1995**—AFL-CIO convention begins that leads to election of John Sweeney as federation president, overturning decades of staid leadership that watched the labor movement decline. A new emphasis on organizing follows, but the AFL-CIO is unable to stop the continued corporate and government attacks that undermine organized labor.

144. **April 7, 2000**—Worker Rights Consortium is founded as part of the antisweatshop movement that unions and college activists coordinated to fight against the exploitation of overseas workers making apparel for import into the United States.

145. **September 11, 2001**—Seventy-three restaurant workers are killed in the 9/11 attacks. Restaurant Opportunities Center, formed in aftermath, fights to end the tipped minimum wage that exploits restaurant workers.

146. **September 16, 2004**—Farm Labor Organizing Committee signs a contract with the Mount Olive Pickle Company, a major victory for the national farmworker organizing movement.

147. **September 17, 2011**—Occupy Wall Street begins, a grassroots protest against income inequality that starts in Manhattan and spreads around the nation that fall.

148. **November 29, 2012**—One hundred fast-food workers engage in a one-day strike, beginning the Fight for $15 movement that galvanizes Americans to demand higher wages.

149. **March 9, 2015**—Wisconsin governor Scott Walker signs a draconian "right-to-work" bill that decimates public sector unions in his state, allowing workers to opt out of their union and also drastically limiting the issues around which unions can bargain, a sign of the new aggression of the Republican Party against unions.

150. **November 8, 2016**—Donald Trump is elected president of the United States, using populist rhetoric to tap into the economic and racial fears of the white working class. Despite his rhetoric, his presidency proceeds to eviscerate labor protections.

Notes

Introduction: Strikes and American History

1. Caroline O'Donovan, "Facebook Played a Pivotal Role in the West Virginia Teachers' Strike," *Buzzfeed*, March 7, 2018, https://www.buzzfeed.com/carolineodonovan/facebook-group-west-virginia-teachers-strike.

2. Dave Jamieson, "West Virginia Teachers Plan Nationwide Strike," *Huffington Post*, February 20, 2018, https://www.huffingtonpost.com/entry/west-virginia-teachers-plan-statewide-strike_us_5a8c8a8ae4b00a30a2503bcc.

3. Jess Bidgood, "West Virginia Raises Teachers' Pay to End State-wide Strike," *New York Times*, March 6, 2018.

4. Jane McAlevey, "The West Virginia Teachers Strike Shows That Winning Big Requires Creating a Crisis," *The Nation*, March 12, 2018, https://www.thenation.com/article/the-west-virginia-teachers-strike-shows-that-winning-big-requires-creating-a-crisis.

5. Josiah Bartlett Lambert, *"If the Workers Took a Notion": The Right to Strike and American Political Development* (Ithaca, NY: Cornell University Press, 2005),

1: Lowell Mill Girls and the Development of American Capitalism

1. William Cronon, *Changes in the Land: Indians, Colonists, and the Ecology of New England* (New York: Hill and Wang, 1983); Brian Donahue, *The Great Meadow: Farmers and the Land in Colonial Concord* (New Haven, CT: Yale University Press, 2004); W. Jeffrey Bolster, *The Mortal Sea: Fishing the Atlantic in the Age of Sail* (Cambridge, MA: Harvard University Press, 2012).

2. E.P. Thompson, *The Making of the English Working Class* (New York: Vintage Books, 1963); R.M. Hartwell, *The Causes of the Industrial Revolution in England* (London: Methuen, 1967); E.A. Wrigley, *Continuity, Chance and Change: The Character of the Industrial Revolution in England* (New York: Cambridge University Press, 1988).

3. Jonathan Prude, *The Coming of Industrial Order: Town and Factory Life in Rural Massachusetts, 1810–1860* (Amherst: University of Massachusetts Press, 1999), 34–64.

4. Sven Beckert, *Empire of Cotton: A Global History* (New York: Knopf, 2014).

5. Carl Chinn, *Poverty Amidst Prosperity: The Urban Poor in England, 1834–2014* (Manchester, UK: Manchester University Press, 1995); Rachel G. Fuchs, *Gender and Poverty in Nineteenth-Century Europe* (New York: Cambridge University Press, 2005); Teresa Anne Murphy, *Ten Hours' Labor: Religion, Reform, and Gender in Early New England* (Ithaca, NY: Cornell University Press, 1992).

6. Jonathan Prude, "The Social System of Early New England Textile Mills: A Case Study, 1812–40," in *The New England Working Class and the New Labor History*, ed. Herbert G. Gutman and Donald H. Bell (Urbana: University of Illinois Press, 1987), 106.

7. Murphy, *Ten Hours' Labor*, 9–31, 47–48.

8. Daniel Walker Howe, *What Hath God Wrought: The Transformation of America, 1815–1848* (New York: Oxford University Press, 2007).

9. Carol Sheriff, *The Artificial River: The Erie Canal and the Paradox of Progress, 1817–1862* (New York: Hill and Wang, 1997), 44–45.

10. Ibid., 43.

11. Tyler Anbinder, *Nativism and Slavery: The Northern Know Nothings and the Politics of the 1850s* (New York: Oxford University Press, 1992).

12. Mark Aldrich, *Death Rode the Rails: American Railroad Accidents and Safety, 1828–1965* (Baltimore: Johns Hopkins University Press, 2006).

13. Jonathan Levy, *Freaks of Fortune: The Emerging World of Capitalism and Risk in America* (Cambridge, MA: Harvard University Press, 2012), 7–9.

14. H. Marlow Green, "Common Law, Property Rights and the Environment: A Comparative Analysis of Historical Developments in the United States and England and a Model for the Future," *Cornell International Law Journal* 30, no. 2 (1997): 541–86; Jouni Paavola, "Water Quality as Property: Industrial Water Pollution and Common Law in the Nineteenth Century United States," *Environment and History* 8, no. 3 (August 2002): 295–318.

15. Aldrich, *Death Rode the Rails*, 159.

16. Maurice F. Neufeld, "The Size of the Jacksonian Labor Movement: A Cautionary Account," *Labor History* 23, no. 4 (1982): 599–607.

17. Paul Kahan, *The Homestead Strike: Labor, Violence, and American Industry* (New York: Routledge, 2014), 30.

18. Troy Rondinone, *The Great Industrial War: Framing Class Conflict in the Media, 1865–1950* (New Brunswick, NJ: Rutgers University Press, 2010), 13–37.

19. Prude, "The Social System of Early New England Textile Mills," 107–8.

20. Murphy, *Ten Hours' Labor*, 33–46.

21. Bruce Laurie, *Working People of Philadelphia, 1800–1850* (Philadelphia: Temple University Press, 1980), 90–92; Howe, *What Hath God Wrought*, 548.

22. Joshua R. Greenberg, *Advocating the Man: Masculinity, Organized Labor, and the Household in New York, 1800–1840* (New York: Columbia University Press, 2008).

23. Timothy J. Gilfoyle, *City of Eros: New York City, Prostitution, and the Commercialization of Sex, 1790–1920* (New York: Norton, 1992).

24. John F. Kasson, *Civilizing the Machine: Technology and Republican Values in America, 1776–1900* (New York: Penguin, 1976), 55–60.

25. Wendy M. Gordon, *Mill Girls and Strangers: Single Women's Independent Migration in England, Scotland, and the United States, 1850–1881* (Albany: State University of New York Press, 2002), 57–100.

26. Thomas Dublin, *Women at Work: The Transformation of Work and Community in Lowell, Massachusetts, 1826–1860* (New York: Columbia University Press, 1979), 24–25, 36–38.

27. Chad Montrie, *Making a Living: Work and Environment in the United States* (Chapel Hill: University of North Carolina Press, 2008), 13–34.

28. Dublin, *Women at Work*, 104–5.

29. Ibid., 89–95.

30. Harriet Hanson Robinson, *Loom and Spindle* (New York: Thomas Y. Crowell, 1898), 83–86.

31. Quoted in Dublin, *Women at Work*, 98–103

32. Quoted in Charles Patrick Neill, *Report on Condition of Women and Child Wage-Earners in the United States*, vol. 8–10 (Washington, D.C.: Government Printing Office, 1911), 31.

33. Murphy, *Ten Hours' Labor*, 156.

34. Dublin, *Women at Work*, 109.

35. Quoted in Benjamin Kline Hunnicutt, *Free Time: The Forgotten American Dream* (Philadelphia: Temple University Press, 2013), 33–34.

36. Gordon, *Mill Girls and Strangers*, 86.

37. Quoted in Murphy, *Ten Hours' Labor*, 204.

38. Ibid., 205.

39. Dublin, *Women at Work*, 109–20.

40. Quoted in Nancy F. Cott, Jeanne Boydston, Ann Braude, Lori Ginzburg, and Molly Ladd-Taylor, eds., *Root of Bitterness: Documents of the Social History of American Women*, 2nd ed. (Lebanon, NH: University Press of New England, 1996), 158.

41. Murphy, *Ten Hours' Labor*, 206.

42. Ibid., 208.

43. Ibid., 223.

44. Gordon, *Mill Girls and Strangers*, 60–61.

45. Ibid., 81.

46. Howe, *What Hath God Wrought*.

47. Suellen Hoy, *Chasing Dirt: The American Pursuit of Cleanliness* (New York: Oxford University Press, 1995), 19–27; Kathryn Kish Sklar, *Catharine Beecher: A Study in American Domesticity* (New York: Norton, 1976).

48. Eric Foner, *Free Soil, Free Labor, Free Men: The Ideology of the Republican Party Before the Civil War* (New York: Oxford University Press, 1970).

49. David R. Roediger, *The Wages of Whiteness: Race and the Making of the American Working Class*, rev. ed. (London: Verso, 1999), 65–92; Josiah Bartlett Lambert, *"If the Workers Took a Notion": The Right to Strike and American Political Development* (Ithaca, NY: Cornell University Press, 2005), 23–38; Foner, *Free Soil, Free Labor, Free Men*, 42.

50. Eric Foner, *Reconstruction: America's Unfinished Revolution, 1863–1877* (New York: Harper and Row, 1988), 29.

51. Ibid., 30–31.

52. Robert H. Zieger, *For Jobs and Freedom: Race and Labor in America Since 1865* (Lexington: University Press of Kentucky, 2007), 25–26.

53. Carole Turbin, *Working Women of Collar City: Gender, Class, and*

Community in Troy, New York, 1864–86 (Urbana: University of Illinois Press, 1994).

2: Slaves on Strike

1. W.E.B. DuBois, *Black Reconstruction in America: An Essay Toward a History of the Part Which Black Folk Played in the Attempt to Reconstruct Democracy in America, 1860–1880* (New York: Oxford University Press, 2007).

2. Andrés Reséndez, *The Other Slavery: The Uncovered Story of Indian Enslavement in America* (Boston: Houghton Mifflin Harcourt, 2016); Alan Gallay, *Indian Slavery in Colonial America* (Lincoln: University of Nebraska Press, 2009); Frank T. Proctor, *Damned Notions of Liberty: Slavery, Culture, and Power in Colonial Mexico, 1640–1769* (Albuquerque: University of New Mexico Press, 2010).,

3. Edmund S. Morgan, *American Slavery, American Freedom: The Ordeal of Colonial Virginia* (New York: Norton, 1975).

4. Morgan, *American Slavery, American Freedom*; Thomas D. Morris, *Southern Slavery and the Law, 1619–1860* (Chapel Hill: University of North Carolina Press, 2004); Richard S. Dunn, *A Tale of Two Plantations: Slave Life and Labor in Jamaica and Virginia* (Cambridge, MA: Harvard University Press, 2014); Ira Berlin, *Many Thousands Gone: The First Two Centuries of Slavery in North America* (Cambridge, MA: Harvard University Press, 2009).

5. Jill Lepore, *New York Burning: Liberty, Slavery, and Conspiracy in Eighteenth-Century Manhattan* (New York: Knopf, 2005); Christy Clark-Pujara, *Dark Work: The Business of Slavery in Rhode Island* (New York: New York University Press, 2016); Philip D. Morgan, *Slave Counterpoint: Black Culture in the Eighteenth-Century Chesapeake and Lowcountry* (Chapel Hill: University of North Carolina Press, 1998).

6. Peter Wood, *Black Majority: Negroes in Colonial South Carolina from 1670 Through the Stono Rebellion* (New York: Norton, 1974).

7. Ira Berlin, *The Long Emancipation: The Demise of Slavery in the United States* (Cambridge, MA: Harvard University Press, 2015); Allen Carden, *Freedom's Delay: America's Struggle for Emancipation, 1776–1865* (Knoxville: University of Tennessee Press, 2015); Annette Gordon-Reed, *Thomas Jefferson and Sally Hemings: An American Controversy* (Charlottesville: University of Virginia Press, 1997).

8. Alan Taylor, *The Internal Enemy: Slavery and War in Virginia, 1772–1832* (New York: Norton, 2013).

9. Sven Beckert, *Empire of Cotton: A Global History* (New York: Knopf, 2014); Walter Johnson, *River of Dark Dreams: Slavery and Empire in the Cotton Kingdom* (Cambridge, MA: Harvard University Press, 2013);

Edward E. Baptist, *The Half Has Never Been Told: Slavery and the Making of American Capitalism* (New York: Basic Books, 2014).

10. Mark Fiege, *The Republic of Nature: An Environmental History of the United States* (Seattle: University of Washington Press, 2012), 100–155.

11. Quote from Jennifer Hildebrand, "Uncovering the True Relationship Between Masters and Slaves," in *African Americans in the Nineteenth Century: People and Perspectives*, ed. Dixie Ray Haggard (Santa Barbara, CA: ABC-CLIO, 2010), 72.

12. Harriet Jacobs, *Incidents in the Life of a Slave Girl* (Cambridge, MA; Harvard University Press, 1987), 48–49.

13. Daniel Rasmussen, *American Uprising: The Untold Story of America's Largest Slave Revolt* (New York: Harper, 2011).

14. David Robertson, *Denmark Vesey: The Buried Story of America's Largest Slave Rebellion and the Man Who Led It* (New York: Knopf, 1999); David F. Allmendinger Jr., *Nat Turner and the Rising in Southampton County* (Baltimore: Johns Hopkins University Press, 2014).

15. James Sidbury, *Ploughshares into Swords: Race, Rebellion, and Identity in Gabriel's Virginia, 1730–1810* (New York: Cambridge University Press, 1997), 25–26.

16. Thavolia Glymph, *Out of the House of Bondage: The Transformation of the Plantation Household* (New York: Cambridge University Press, 2008).

17. Melton A. McLaurin, *Celia, a Slave* (Athens: University of Georgia Press, 1991).

18. Michael Todd Landis, *Northern Men with Southern Loyalties: The Democratic Party and the Sectional Crisis* (Ithaca, NY: Cornell University Press, 2014); Leonard L. Richards, *The Slave Power: The Free North and Southern Domination, 1780–1860* (Baton Rouge: Louisiana State University Press, 2000); Joel H. Sibley, *Storm over Texas: The Annexation Controversy and the Road to the Civil War* (New York: Oxford University Press, 2005).

19. Eric Foner, *The Fiery Trial: Abraham Lincoln and American Slavery* (New York: Norton, 2010); Charles B. Dew, *Apostles of Disunion: Southern Secession Commissioners and the Causes of the Civil War* (Charlottesville: University of Virginia Press, 2001).

20. Quoted in DuBois, *Black Reconstruction*, 61–62.

21. Quoted in Bruce Levine, *The Fall of the House of Dixie: The Civil War and the Social Revolution That Transformed the South* (New York: Random House, 2013), 57.

22. Allen C. Guelzo, *Lincoln's Emancipation Proclamation: The End of Slavery in America* (New York: Simon and Schuster, 2005), 13–66.

23. Adam Goodheart, "How Slavery Really Ended in America," *New York Times Magazine*, April 1, 2011.

24. DuBois, *Black Reconstruction*, 67.

25. Cate Lineberry, *Be Free or Die: The Amazing Story of Robert Smalls' Escape from Slavery to Union Hero* (New York: St. Martin's Press, 2017).

26. David Roediger, *Seizing Freedom: Slave Emancipation and Liberty for All* (London: Verso, 2014), 2.

27. Glymph, *Out of the House of Bondage*, 109.

28. Jeffrey R. Kerr-Ritchie, *Freedpeople in the Tobacco South: Virginia, 1860–1900* (Chapel Hill: University of North Carolina Press, 1999), 28–29.

29. Levine, *Fall of the House of Dixie*, 101.

30. Eric Foner, *Reconstruction: America's Unfinished Revolution, 1863–1877* (New York: Harper and Row, 1988), 4.

31. Levine, *Fall of the House of Dixie*, 103.

32. Quoted in Roediger, *Seizing Freedom*, 30.

33. Phillip W. Magness and Sebastian N. Page, *Colonization After Emancipation: Lincoln and the Movement for Black Resettlement* (Columbia: University of Missouri Press, 2011).

34. Foner, *Reconstruction*, 35–50; Victor B. Howard, *Black Liberation in Kentucky: Emancipation and Freedom, 1862–1884* (Lexington: University Press of Kentucky, 2013).

35. Levine, *Fall of the House of Dixie*, 137.

36. John David Smith, ed., *Black Soldiers in Blue: African American Troops in the Civil War Era* (Chapel Hill: University of North Carolina Press, 2005); Bruce Tap, *The Fort Pillow Massacre: North, South, and the Status of African-Americans in the Civil War Era* (New York: Routledge, 2013).

37. Glymph, *Out of the House of Bondage*, 106; Leslie A. Schwalm, "'Sweet Dreams of Freedom': Freedwomen's Reconstruction of Life and Labor in Lowcountry South Carolina," in *The Black Worker: A Reader*, ed. Eric Arnesen (Urbana: University of Illinois Press, 2007), 11.

38. Quoted in John David Smith, *Black Voices from Reconstruction, 1865–1877* (Brookfield, CT: Millbrook Press), 28.

39. Foner, *Reconstruction*, 69–71.

40. Schwalm, "'Sweet Dreams of Freedom,'" 17–19.

41. Willie Lee Rose, *Rehearsal for Reconstruction: The Port Royal Experiment* (New York: Oxford University Press, 1976); Kevin Dougherty, *The Port Royal Experiment: A Case Study in Development* (Jackson: University Press of Mississippi, 2014); Foner, *Reconstruction*, 55.

42. Quoted in Smith, *Black Voices from Reconstruction*, 42.

43. Ibid., 59.

44. Robert H. Zieger, *For Jobs and Freedom: Race and Labor in America Since 1865* (Lexington: University Press of Kentucky, 2007), 20–21.

45. Foner, *Reconstruction*, 77–123.

46. Foner, *Reconstruction*, 199–201, 208–9; David M. Oshinsky, *"Worse Than Slavery": Parchman Farm and the Ordeal of Jim Crow Justice* (New York: Free Press, 1996), 20–22.

47. Foner, *Reconstruction*, 155–70.

48. Quoted in Kerr-Ritchie, *Freedpeople in the Tobacco South*, 38.

49. Tera W. Hunter, *To 'Joy My Freedom: Southern Black Women's Lives and Labors After the Civil War* (Cambridge, MA: Harvard University Press, 1997), 27–31, 75–76.

50. Paul Ortiz, *Emancipation Betrayed: The Hidden History of Black Organizing and White Violence in Florida from Reconstruction to the Bloody Election of 1920* (Berkeley: University of California Press, 2005), 34–37, 53–54; Scott Reynolds Nelson, *Steel Drivin' Man: John Henry, the Untold Story of an American Legend* (New York: Oxford University Press, 2006).

51. Kerr-Ritchie, *Freedpeople in the Tobacco South*, 211–12.

52. Edward Royce, *The Origins of Southern Sharecropping* (Philadelphia: Temple University Press, 2010); Foner, *Reconstruction*, 392–411.

53. Rebecca J. Scott, *Degrees of Freedom: Louisiana and Cuba After Slavery* (Cambridge, MA: Harvard University Press, 2009), 61–93

54. Ibid.

55. Daniel H. Usner Jr., *Indian Work: Language and Livelihood in Native American History* (Cambridge, MA: Harvard University Press, 2009); Brian Hosmer and Colleen O'Neill, eds., *Native Pathways: American Indian Culture and Economic Development in the Twentieth Century* (Boulder: University Press of Colorado, 2004).

3: The Eight-Hour-Day Strikes

1. Ari Kelman, *A Misplaced Massacre: Struggling Over the Memory of Sand Creek* (Cambridge, MA: Harvard University Press, 2013); Andrew R. Graybill, *The Red and the White: A Family Saga of the American West* (New York: Norton, 2013); Richard White, *Railroaded: The Transcontinentals and the Making of Modern America* (New York: Norton, 2011); James M. McPherson, *Battle Cry of Freedom: The Civil War Era* (New York: Oxford University Press, 1988).

2. Melinda Lawson, *Patriot Fires: Forging a New American Nationalism in the Civil War North* (Lawrence: University Press of Kansas, 2002), 40–64; Ron Chernow, *Titan: The Life of John D. Rockefeller, Sr.* (New York: Knopf, 2007).

3. James R. Green, *The World of the Worker: Labor in Twentieth-Century America* (New York: Hill and Wang, 1980), 3–6; Ruth Rosen, *The Lost Sisterhood: Prostitution in America, 1900–1918* (Baltimore: Johns Hopkins University Press, 1982); Andrew B. Arnold, *Fueling the Gilded Age: Railroads, Miners, and Disorder in Pennsylvania Coal Country* (New York: New York University Press, 2014).

4. Robert C. Bannister, *Social Darwinism: Science and Myth in Anglo-American Social Thought* (Philadelphia: Temple University Press, 1979). For a broad overview of the Gilded Age, see Rebecca Edwards, *New Spirits: America in the "Gilded Age," 1865–1905*, 3rd ed. (New York: Oxford University Press, 2015).

5. Mark Wahlgren Summers, *The Ordeal of the Reunion: A New History of Reconstruction* (Chapel Hill: University of North Carolina Press, 2014), 179–203, 273–97.

6. Elmus Wicker, *Banking Panics of the Gilded Age* (New York: Cambridge University Press, 2000); M. John Lubetkin, *Jay Cooke's Gamble: The Northern Pacific Railroad, the Sioux, and the Panic of 1873* (Norman: University of Oklahoma Press, 2006).

7. Samuel Gompers, *Seventy Years of Life and Labor: An Autobiography*, vol. 1 (New York: E.P. Dutton & Company, 1925), 96.

8. See Richard Schneirov, "Chicago's Great Upheaval of 1877: Class Polarization and Democratic Politics," in *The Great Strikes of 1877*, ed. David O. Stowell (Urbana: University of Illinois Press, 2008), 76–104, for how the Panic of 1873 led to bubbling upheaval in that city.

9. Robert Michael Smith, *From Blackjacks to Briefcases: A History of Commercialized Strikebreaking and Unionbusting in the United States* (Athens: Ohio University Press, 2003).

10. Kevin Kenny, *Making Sense of the Molly Maguires* (New York: Oxford University Press, 1998).

11. *Baltimore Sun*, July 14, 1877.

12. Patricia A. Cooper, *Once a Cigar Maker: Men, Women, and Work Culture in American Cigar Factories, 1900–1919* (Urbana: University of Illinois Press, 1987), 20–21.

13. Quoted in Philip Dray, *There Is Power in a Union: The Epic Story of Labor in America* (New York: Doubleday, 2010), 117.

14. Quoted in Melvyn Dubofsky, *The State and Labor in Modern America* (Chapel Hill; University of North Carolina Press, 1994), 11.

15. On the Great Railroad Strike of 1877, see Philip S. Foner, *The Great Labor Uprising of 1877* (New York: Monad Press, 1977); David O. Stowell, *Streets, Railroads, and the Great Strike of 1877* (Chicago: University of Chicago Press, 1999); David O. Stowell, ed., *The Great Strikes of 1877.*

16. Daniel Walker Howe, *What Hath God Wrought: The Transformation of America, 1815–1848* (New York: Oxford University Press, 2007), 540. On the idea of wage slavery, see Lawrence B. Glickman, *A Living Wage: American Workers and the Making of a Consumer Society* (Ithaca, NY: Cornell University Press, 1997).

17. David Brundage, *The Making of Western Labor Radicalism: Denver's Organized Workers, 1878–1905* (Urbana: University of Illinois Press, 1994), 33.

18. Edward T. O'Donnell, *Henry George and the Crisis of Inequality: Progress and Poverty in the Gilded Age* (New York: Columbia University Press, 2015); Matthew Hild, *Greenbackers, Knights of Labor, and Populists: Farmer-Labor Insurgency in the Late-Nineteenth-Century South* (Athens: University of Georgia Press, 2010); John L. Thomas, *Alternative America: Henry George, Edward Bellamy, Henry Demarest Lloyd and the American Adversary Tradition* (Cambridge, MA: Harvard University Press, 1983).

19. David R. Roediger, *The Wages of Whiteness: Race and the Making of the American Working Class*, rev. ed. (London: Verso, 1999).

20. David R. Roediger and Elizabeth D. Esch, *The Production of Difference: Race and the Management of Labor in U.S. History* (New York: Oxford University Press, 2012).

21. Michael Kazin, "The July Days in San Francisco, 1877: Prelude to Kearneyism," in *The Great Strikes of 1877*, ed. David O. Stowell (Urbana: University of Illinois Press, 2008), 136–63.

22. Alexander Saxton, *The Indispensable Enemy: Labor and the Anti-Chinese Movement in California* (Berkeley: University of California Press, 1971); Roger Daniels, *Asian America: Chinese and Japanese in the United States Since 1850* (Seattle: University of Washington Press, 1988).

23. Tomás Almaguer, *Racial Fault Lines: The Historical Origins of White Supremacy in California* (Berkeley: University of California Press, 1994), 183–204.

24. James Green, *Death in the Haymarket: A Story of Chicago, the First Labor Movement and the Bombing That Divided Gilded Age America* (New York: Pantheon Books, 2006), 85–101.

25. Kim Voss, *The Making of American Exceptionalism: The Knights of Labor and Class Formation in the Nineteenth Century* (Ithaca, NY: Cornell University Press, 1993), 73.

26. Troy Rondinone, *The Great Industrial War: Framing Class Conflict in the Media, 1865–1950* (New Brunswick, NJ: Rutgers University Press, 2010), 66.

27. Clayton Sinyai, *Schools of Democracy: A Political History of the American Labor Movement* (Ithaca, NY: Cornell University Press, 2006), 22.

28. Peter Rachleff, *Black Labor in the South: Richmond, Virginia, 1865–1890* (Philadelphia: Temple University Press, 1984)

29. Robert H. Zieger, *For Jobs and Freedom: Race and Labor in America Since 1865* (Lexington: University Press of Kentucky, 2007), 37.

30. Paul Ortiz, *Emancipation Betrayed: The Hidden History of Black Organizing and White Violence in Florida from Reconstruction to the Bloody Election of 1920* (Berkeley: University of California Press, 2005), 46; Daniel Letwin, *The Challenge of Interracial Unionism: Alabama Coal Miners, 1878–1921* (Chapel Hill: University of North Carolina Press, 1998); Henry M. McKiven Jr., *Iron and Steel: Class, Race, and Community in Birmingham, Alabama, 1875–1920* (Chapel Hill: University of North Carolina Press, 1995).

31. Elizabeth Jameson, *All That Glitters: Class, Conflict, and Community in Cripple Creek* (Urbana: University of Illinois Press, 1998, 114–39; Voss, *The Making of American Exceptionalism*, 81.

32. Joseph Gerteis, *Class and the Color Line: Interracial Class Coalition in the Knights of Labor and the Populist Movement* (Durham, NC: Duke University Press, 2007).

33. Clark D. Halker, *For Democracy, Workers, and God: Labor Song-Poems and Labor Protest, 1865–95* (Urbana: University of Illinois Press, 1991), 34–35.

34. Josiah Bartlett Lambert, *"If the Workers Took a Notion": The Right to Strike and American Political Development* (Ithaca, NY: Cornell University Press, 2005), 38.

35. Benjamin Kline Hunnicutt, *Free Time: The Forgotten American Dream* (Philadelphia: Temple University Press, 2013), 72–73.

36. Leon Fink, *Workingmen's Democracy: The Knights of Labor and American Politics* (Urbana: University of Illinois Press, 1983).

37. Quoted in Rondinone, *The Great Industrial War*, 71.

38. Theresa A. Case, *The Great Southwest Railroad Strike and Free Labor* (College Station: Texas A&M Press, 2010).

39. Ibid.

40. Quoted in, among other places, Allan Ornstein, *Class Counts: Education, Inequality, and the Shrinking Middle Class* (Lanham, MD: Rowman & Littlefield, 2007), 143.

41. Rondinone, *The Great Industrial War*, 70–78.

42. Paul Avrich, *The Haymarket Tragedy* (Princeton, NJ: Princeton University Press, 1984), 1–52.

43. Ibid., 61.

44. Richard Schneirov, *Labor and Urban Politics: Class Conflict and the Origin of Modern Liberalism in Chicago, 1864–97* (Urbana: University of Illinois Press, 1998), 183.

45. Green, *Death in the Haymarket*, 145–59. On Spies, see Avrich, *The Haymarket Tragedy*, 120–30.

46. Green, *Death in the Haymarket*, 114–17, 169–71.

47. Ibid., 1–8.

48. Quoted in ibid., 9.

49. Avrich, *The Haymarket Tragedy*, 159.

50. Albert R. Parsons, "Autobiography of Albert R. Parsons," in *The Autobiographies of the Haymarket Martyrs*, ed. Philip S. Foner (New York: Humanities Press, 1969), 51.

51. Green, *Death in the Haymarket*, 209–73.

52. Ibid., 20–21.

53. Voss, *The Making of American Exceptionalism*, 185–228. See also Cedric de Leon, *The Origins of Right to Work: Antilabor Democracy in Nineteenth-Century Chicago* (Ithaca, NY: Cornell University Press, 2015).

54. Lambert, *"If the Workers Took a Notion,"* 57.

55. Green, *The World of the Worker*, 32–33.

56. Zieger, *For Jobs and Freedom*, 65; Green, *The World of the Worker*, 43.

57. Paul Kahan, *The Homestead Strike: Labor, Violence, and American Industry* (New York: Routledge, 2014), 46.

58. Ibid., 19.

59. Paul Krause, *The Battle for Homestead, 1880–1892: Politics, Culture, and Steel* (Pittsburgh: University of Pittsburgh Press, 1992).

60. David Nasaw, *Andrew Carnegie* (New York: Penguin, 2007), 451.

61. Elmus Wicker, *Banking Panics of the Gilded Age* (New York: Cambridge University Press, 2000).

62. Howard R. Lamar, *Charlie Siringo's West: An Interpretative Biography* (Albuquerque: University of New Mexico Press, 2005), 173–90.

63. Cynthia M. Blair, "'We Must Live Anyhow': African American Women and Sex Work in Chicago, 1880–1900," in *The Black Worker: A Reader*, ed. Eric Arnesen (Urbana: University of Illinois Press, 2007), 122–46; Rosen, *The Lost Sisterhood*; Timothy J. Gilfoyle, *City of Eros: New York City, Prostitution, and the Commercialization of Sex, 1790–1920* (New York: Norton, 1992).

64. Eric Rauchway, *Murdering McKinley: The Making of Theodore Roosevelt's America* (New York: Hill and Wang, 2003).

4: The Anthracite Strike and the Progressive State

1. Daniel R. Ernst, *Lawyers Against Labor: From Individual Rights to Corporate Liberalism* (Urbana: University of Illinois Press, 1995).

2. William H. Carwardine, *The Pullman Strike* (Chicago: Charles H. Kerr and Company, 1894), 25, 49.

3. A good overview of the Pullman strike is in Carl Smith, *Urban Disorder and the Shape of Belief: The Great Chicago Fire, the Haymarket Bomb, and the Model Town of Pullman*, 2nd ed. (Chicago: The University of Chicago Press, 2007).

4. Nick Salvatore, *Eugene V. Debs: Citizen and Socialist* (Urbana: University of Illinois Press, 1982), 114–26.

5. Quoted in Troy Rondinone, *The Great Industrial War: Framing Class Conflict in the Media, 1865–1950* (New Brunswick, NJ: Rutgers University Press, 2010), 82–83.

6. Eugene V. Debs, "Liberty," November 22, 1895, reprinted in *The Pullman Strike*, ed. Leon Stein (New York: Arno and New York Times, 1969), 14.

7. Salvatore, *Eugene V. Debs*, 126–39.

8. Elizabeth Jameson, *All That Glitters: Class, Conflict, and Community in Cripple Creek* (Urbana: University of Illinois Press, 1998); Mark Wyman, *Hard Rock Epic: Western Miners and the Industrial Revolution, 1860–1910* (Berkeley: University of California Press, 1989).

9. Melvyn Dubofsky, *We Shall Be All: A History of the Industrial Workers of the World*, 2nd ed. (Urbana: University of Illinois Press, 1988), 19–56.

10. Charles Postel, *The Populist Vision* (New York: Oxford University Press, 2007).

11. Bruno Ramirez, *When Workers Fight: The Politics of Industrial Relations in the Progressive Era, 1898–1916* (Westport, CT: Greenwood Press, 1978), 9–10.

12. Rondinone, *The Great Industrial War*, 96–97.

13. Perry K. Blatz, *Democratic Miners: Work and Labor Relations in the Anthracite Coal Industry, 1875–1925* (Albany: State University of New York Press, 1994), 10.

14. William Graebner, *Coal-Mining Safety in the Progressive Period: The Political Economy of Reform* (Lexington: University Press of Kentucky, 1976); Andrew B. Arnold, *Fueling the Gilded Age: Railroads, Miners, and Disorder in Pennsylvania Coal Country* (New York: New York University Press, 2014); James Whiteside, *Regulating Danger: The Struggle for Mine Safety in the Rocky Mountain Coal Industry* (Lincoln: University of Nebraska Press, 1990); Daniel J. Curran, *Dead Laws for Dead Men: The Politics of Federal Coal Mine Health and Safety Legislation* (Pittsburgh: University of Pittsburgh Press, 1993).

15. Andrew E. Kersten, *Clarence Darrow: American Iconoclast* (New York: Hill and Wang, 2011), 108.

16. Craig Phelan, *Divided Loyalties: The Public and Private Life of Labor Leader John Mitchell* (Albany: State University of New York Press, 1994).

17. Thomas Keil and Jacqueline M. Keil, *Anthracite's Demise and the Post-Coal Economy of Northeastern Pennsylvania* (Bethlehem, PA: Lehigh University Press, 2015), 23–51.

18. Elliott J. Gorn, *Mother Jones: The Most Dangerous Woman in America* (New York: Hill and Wang, 2001), 77; Blatz, *Democratic Miners*, 55–63.

19. Quoted in Kersten, *Clarence Darrow*, 108.

20. Ibid., 109.

21. Thomas Dublin and Walter Licht, *The Face of Decline: The Pennsylvania Anthracite Region in the Twentieth Century* (Ithaca, NY: Cornell University Press, 2005), 36.

22. Ibid., 37.

23. For overviews of the Anthracite strike, see Robert J. Cornell, *The Anthracite Coal Strike of 1902* (Washington, D.C.: Catholic University of America Press, 1957) and Jonathan Grossman, "The Coal Strike of 1902—Turning Point in U.S. Policy," *Monthly Labor Review* 98, no. 10 (October 1975): 21–28.

24. Quoted in Rondinone, *The Great Industrial War*, 102.

25. Lewis L. Gould, *The Presidency of Theodore Roosevelt*, 2nd ed. (Lawrence: University Press of Kansas, 2011), 63–67.

26. Quoted in Ron Chernow, *The House of Morgan: An American Banking Dynasty and the Rise of Modern Finance* (New York: Atlantic Monthly Press, 1990), 107.

27. Blatz, *Democratic Miners*, 121–40.

28. Quoted in Kersten, *Clarence Darrow*, 110.

29. Keil and Keil, *Anthracite's Demise*, 45–49.

30. Kersten, *Clarence Darrow*, 110.

31. Quoted in Walter Nugent, *Progressivism: A Very Short Introduction* (New York: Oxford University Press, 2009), 38.

32. Blatz, *Democratic Miners*, 141–69.

33. Dublin and Licht, *The Face of Decline*, 39; Blatz, *Democratic Miners*, 171–204.

34. Quoted in Bernard Schwartz, *A History of the Supreme Court* (New York: Oxford University Press, 1995), 194.

35. Nancy Woloch, *A Class by Herself: Protective Laws for Women Workers, 1890s–1990s* (Princeton, NJ: Princeton University Press, 2015).

36. Nancy Woloch, *Muller v. Oregon: A Brief History with Documents* (Boston: Bedford/St. Martin's, 1996).

37. Woloch, *A Class by Herself.*

38. Quoted in Richard A. Greenwald, *The Triangle Fire, the Protocols of Peace, and Industrial Democracy in Progressive Era New York* (Philadelphia: Temple University Press, 2011), 32.

39. Nan Enstad, *Ladies of Labor, Girls of Adventure: Working Women, Popular Culture, and Labor Politics at the Turn of the Twentieth Century* (New York: Columbia University Press, 1999), 84–160; Maxine Schwartz Seller, "The Uprising of the Twenty Thousand: Sex, Class, and Ethnicity in the Shirtwaist Makers' Strike of 1909," in *"Struggle a Hard Battle": Essays on Working-Class Immigrants*, ed. Dirk Hoerder (DeKalb: Northern Illinois Press, 1986), 254–79.

40. Greenwald, *The Triangle Fire.*

41. Quoted in Ibid., 132.

42. Quoted in David von Drehle, *Triangle: The Fire That Changed America* (New York: Atlantic Monthly Press, 2003), 177.

43. Von Drehle, *Triangle*: Jo Ann E. Argersinger, *The Triangle Fire: A Brief History with Documents* (Boston: Bedford/St. Martin's, 2009).

44. Thomas White and Louis Murphy, "Eight Days in a Burning Mine," *The World*, October 1911; State of Illinois Bureau of Labor Statistics, *Report on the Cherry Mine Disaster* (Springfield: Illinois State Journal Co., 1910).

45. Donald W. Rogers, *Making Capitalism Safe: Work Safety and Health Regulation in America, 1880–1940* (Urbana: University of Illinois Press, 2009).

46. Eric Arnesen, "The Quicksands of Economic Insecurity: African Americans, Strikebreaking, and Labor Activism in the Industrial Era," in *The Black Worker: A Reader*, ed. Eric Arnesen (Urbana: University of Illinois Press, 2007), 41–71.

47. Upton Sinclair, *The Jungle* (New York: Modern Library, 2002); James Harvey Young, *Pure Food: Securing the Federal Food and Drugs Act of 1906* (Princeton, NJ: Princeton University Press, 1989).

48. Quoted in Carlos Schwantes, *Hard Traveling: A Portrait of Work Life in the New Northwest* (Lincoln: University of Nebraska Press, 1999), xii.

49. Quoted in Joseph A. McCartin, *Labor's Great War: The Struggle of Industrial Democracy and the Origins of Modern American Labor Relations, 1912–1921* (Chapel Hill: University of North Carolina Press, 1997), 12; see also Frank Tobias Higbie, *Indispensable Outcasts: Hobo Workers and Community in the American Midwest, 1880–1930* (Urbana: University of Illinois Press, 2003), 66–97; Erik Loomis, *Empire of Timber: Labor Unions and the Pacific Northwest Forests* (New York: Cambridge Press, 2016), 18–53.

50. Robert Michael Smith, *From Blackjacks to Briefcases: A History of Commercialized Strikebreaking and Unionbusting in the United States* (Athens: Ohio University Press, 2003), 29–31.

51. Quoted in Robert H. Zieger, Timothy J. Minchin, and Gilbert J. Gall, *American Workers, American Unions: The 20th and Early 21st Centuries*, 4th ed. (Baltimore: Johns Hopkins University Press, 2014), 23.

52. Thomas G. Andrews, *Killing for Coal: America's Deadliest Labor War* (Cambridge, MA: Harvard University Press, 2008); Zeese Papanikolas, *Buried Unsung: Louis Tikas and the Ludlow Massacre* (Salt Lake City: University of Utah Press, 1982).

53. Howard M. Gitelman, *Legacy of the Ludlow Massacre: A Chapter in American Industrial Relations* (Philadelphia: University of Pennsylvania Press, 1988); Fawn-Amber Montoya, ed., *Making an American Workforce: The Rockefellers and the Legacy of Ludlow* (Boulder: University Press of Colorado, 2014).

5: The Bread and Roses Strike

1. For a good short summary of IWW intellectual beliefs, see Sharon Smith, *Subterranean Fire: A History of Working-Class Radicalism in the United States* (Chicago: Haymarket Books, 2006), 78–80.

2. Quoted in Melvyn Dubofsky, *We Shall Be All: A History of the Industrial Workers of the World*, 2nd ed. (Urbana: University of Illinois Press, 1988), 50.

3. Elizabeth Jameson, *All That Glitters: Class, Conflict, and Community in Cripple Creek* (Urbana: University of Illinois Press, 1998).

4. Quoted in Ralph Darlington, *Syndicalism and the Transition to Communism: An International Comparative Analysis* (Burlington, VT: Ashgate Publishing, 2013), 22.

5. William Trautmann, "Why Strikes Are Lost," in *Rebel Voices: An IWW Anthology*, ed. Joyce Kornbluh (Ann Arbor: University of Michigan Press, 1964), 22.

6. Dubofsky, *We Shall Be All*, 81–87.

7. Frank Fletcher, "The 'American Dream' and the 1912 Lawrence Textile Strike," in *The Great Lawrence Textile Strike of 1912: New Scholarship on the Bread & Roses Strike*, ed. Robert Forrant and Jurg Siegenthaler (Amityville, NY: Baywood Publishing, 2014), 130–31.

8. William D. Haywood, *Bill Haywood's Book: The Autobiography of William D. Haywood* (New York: International Publishers, 1929), 186.

9. Dubofsky, *We Shall Be All*, 91–119, 131–45; J. Anthony Lukas, *Big Trouble: A Murder in a Small Western Town Sets Off a Struggle for the Soul of America* (New York: Simon and Schuster, 1997); L. Glen Seretan, *Daniel*

DeLeon: The Odyssey of an American Marxist (Cambridge, MA: Harvard University Press, 1979).

10. Carlos A. Schwantes, *Radical Heritage: Labor, Socialism, and Reform in Washington and British Columbia, 1885–1917* (Seattle: University of Washington Press, 1979).

11. Mark Wyman, *Hard Rock Epic: Western Miners and the Industrial Revolution, 1860–1910* (Berkeley: University of California Press, 1979).

12. David R. Berman, *Radicalism in the Mountain West, 1890–1920: Socialists, Populists, Miners, and Wobblies* (Boulder: University Press of Colorado, 2007).

13. Dubofsky, *We Shall Be All*, 120–31.

14. Robert L. Tyler, *Rebels of the Woods: The I.W.W. in the Pacific Northwest* (Eugene: University of Oregon Press, 1967), 33–39.

15. David M. Rabban, *Free Speech in Its Forgotten Years* (New York: Cambridge University Press, 1997), 77–127.

16. Matthew S. May, *Soapbox Rebellion: The Hobo Orator Union and the Free Speech Fights of the Industrial Workers of the World, 1909–1916* (Tuscaloosa: University of Alabama Press, 2013).

17. Dubofsky, *We Shall Be All*, 199–209; Cliff Brown, *Racial Conflict and Violence in the Labor Market: Roots in the 1919 Steel Strike* (New York: Garland, 1998), 48–49.

18. Haywood, *Bill Haywood's Book*, 241–42.

19. Howard Kimeldorf, *Battling for American Labor: Wobblies, Craft Workers, and the Making of the Union Movement* (Berkeley: University of California Press, 1999), quote on p. 31. On the Philadelphia dockworkers, see Peter Cole, *Wobblies on the Waterfront: Interracial Unionism in Progressive-Era Philadelphia* (Urbana: University of Illinois Press, 2007).

20. Robert Forrant and Jurg Siegenthaler, eds., introduction to *The Great Lawrence Textile Strike of 1912*, 2–3.

21. Bruce Watson, *Bread & Roses: Mills, Migrants, and the Struggle for the American Dream* (New York: Penguin, 2005), 9, 27.

22. Ardis Cameron, *Radicals of the Worst Sort: Laboring Women in Lawrence, Massachusetts, 1860–1912* (Urbana: University of Illinois Press, 1993), 17–72.

23. Joyce Kornbluh, "Bread and Roses: The 1912 Lawrence Textile Strike," in *Rebel Voices: An IWW Anthology*, ed. Joyce Kornbluh (Ann Arbor: University of Michigan Press, 1964), 159; Watson, *Bread & Roses*, 50–54, 62–74; Janelle Bourgeois, "'Believe Comrades . . . the Day Is Coming When Those at the End Their Rope Will Require Struggle. It Will Be, Perhaps, Tomorrow.' Franco-Belgian Immigrants and the 1912

Strike," in *The Great Lawrence Textile Strike of 1912: New Scholarship on the Bread & Roses Strike*, 23–25.

24. Quoted in Watson, *Bread & Roses*, 103.

25. Chad Pearson, *Reform or Repression: Organizing America's Anti-Union Movement* (Philadelphia: University of Pennsylvania Press, 2015), 80.

26. Watson, *Bread & Roses*, 110–13.

27. Elizabeth Gurley Flynn, *The Rebel Girl: An Autobiography* (New York: International Publishers, 1973), 131.

28. Cameron, *Radicals of the Worst Sort*, 117–69.

29. Quoted in Kornbluh, "Bread and Roses", 160.

30. Watson, *Bread & Roses*, 114–16.

31. Ibid., 129.

32. Quoted in ibid., 152.

33. Ibid., 147–49.

34. Ibid., 131–32.

35. Quoted in ibid., 143

36. Ibid., 150.

37. Ibid., 178–98; quote on p. 179.

38. Ibid., 217–40.

39. Ibid., 241–46.

40. Steve Golin, *The Fragile Bridge: Paterson Silk Strike, 1913* (Philadelphia: Temple University Press, 1998).

41. Golin, *The Fragile Bridge*; Anne Huber Tripp, *The I.W.W. and the Paterson Silk Strike of 1913* (Urbana: University of Illinois Press, 1987).

42. Elizabeth Gurley Flynn, "The Truth About the Patterson Strike," in *Rebel Voices: An IWW Anthology*, ed. Joyce Kornbluh (Ann Arbor: University of Michigan Press, 1964), 222.

43. Golin, *The Fragile Bridge*.

44. Dubofsky, *We Shall Be All*, 294–300; Don Mitchell, *The Lie of the Land: Migrant Workers and the California Landscape* (Minneapolis: University of Minnesota Press, 1996), 36–57.

45. Norman H. Clark, *Mill Town: A Social History of Everett, Washington, from Its Earliest Beginnings on the Shores of Puget Sound to the Tragic and Infamous Event Known as the Everett Massacre* (Seattle: University of Washington Press, 1970).

46. Flynn, *The Rebel Girl*, 164.

47. Eric Thomas Chester, *The Wobblies in Their Heyday: The Rise and Destruction of the Industrial Workers of the World During the World War I Era* (Santa Barbara, CA: Praeger, 2014).

48. Erik Loomis, *Empire of Timber: Labor Unions and the Pacific Northwest Forests* (New York: Cambridge University Press, 2016), 18–53. Quotations from page 39.

49. Dubofsky, *We Shall Be All*, 313–33.

50. Randi Storch, *Working Hard for the American Dream: Workers and Their Unions, World War I to the Present* (Malden, MA: Wiley-Blackwell, 2013), 12–13.

51. Leon Fink, *Sweatshops at Sea: Merchant Seamen in the World's First Globalized Industry, from 1812 to the Present* (Chapel Hill: University of North Carolina Press, 2011).

52. Chester, *The Wobblies in Their Heyday*, 117–32.

53. James W. Byrkit, *Forging the Copper Collar: Arizona's Labor-Management War of 1901–1921* (Tucson: University of Arizona Press, 2016).

54. Jane Little Botkin, *Frank Little and the IWW: The Blood That Stained an American Family* (Norman: University of Oklahoma Press, 2017); Arnold Stead, *Always on Strike: Frank Little and the Western Wobblies* (Chicago: Haymarket Books, 2014).

55. Loomis, *Empire of Timber*, 54–88.

56. Meg Jacobs, *Pocketbook Politics: Economic Citizenship in Twentieth-Century America* (Princeton, NJ: Princeton University Press, 2005), 53–92.

57. Nan Elizabeth Woodruff, "The Organizing Tradition Among African American Plantation Workers in the Arkansas Delta in the Age of Jim Crow," in *The Black Worker: A Reader*, ed. Eric Arnesen (Urbana: University of Illinois Press, 2007), 178–94; Cole, *Wobblies on the Waterfront*, 111–27, 148–65; Tom Copeland, *The Centralia Tragedy of 1919: Elmer Smith and the* Wobblies (Seattle: University of Washington Press, 1993); Ernest Freeberg, *Democracy's Prisoner: Eugene V. Debs, the Great War, and the Right to Dissent* (Cambridge, MA: Harvard University Press, 2010); Robert Whitaker, *On the Laps of Gods: The Red Summer of 1919 and the Struggle for Justice That Remade a Nation* (New York: Crown, 2008).

6: The Flint Sit-Down Strike and the New Deal

1. Randi Storch, *Working Hard for the American Dream: Workers and Their Unions, World War I to the Present* (Malden, MA: Wiley-Blackwell, 2013), 3–4.

2. Dana Frank, *Purchasing Power: Consumer Organizing, Gender, and the Seattle Labor Movement, 1919–1929* (New York: Cambridge University Press, 1994).

3. Josiah Bartlett Lambert, *"If the Workers Took a Notion": The Right to Strike and American Political Development* (Ithaca, NY: Cornell University

Press, 2005), 82; James Green, *The Devil Is Here in These Hills: West Virginia's Coal Miners and Their Battle for Freedom* (New York: Atlantic Monthly Press, 2015).

4. Nikki Mandell, *The Corporation as Family: The Gendering of Corporate Welfare, 1890–1930* (Chapel Hill: University of North Carolina Press, 2002); Jonathan H. Rees, *Representation and Rebellion: The Rockefeller Plan at the Colorado Fuel and Iron Company, 1914–1942* (Boulder: University Press of Colorado, 2010).

5. Eric Rauchway, *The Great Depression and the New Deal: A Very Short Introduction* (New York: Oxford University Press, 2008), 8–22.

6. Robert H. Zieger, Timothy J. Minchin, and Gilbert J. Gall, *American Workers, American Unions: The 20th and Early 21st Centuries*, 4th ed. (Baltimore: Johns Hopkins University Press, 2014), 50.

7. Ibid., 52–53.

8. Stephen H. Norwood, *Strikebreaking and Intimidation: Mercenaries and Masculinity in Twentieth-Century America* (Chapel Hill: University of North Carolina Press, 2002), 171–93. On radicalism, see Robin D.G. Kelley, *Hammer and Hoe: Alabama Communists During the Great Depression* (Chapel Hill: University of North Carolina Press, 1990); Randi Storch, *Red Chicago: American Communism at Its Grassroots, 1928–35* (Urbana: University of Illinois Press, 2007); James J. Lorence, *Palomino: Clinton Jencks and Mexican-American Unionism in the American Southwest* (Urbana: University of Illinois Press, 2013).

9. Jennifer Luff, *Commonsense Anticommunism: Labor and Civil Liberties Between the World Wars* (Chapel Hill: University of North Carolina Press, 2012).

10. Quoted in Zieger, Minchin, and Gall, *American Workers, American Unions*, 63.

11. Steven Ortiz, "Rethinking the Bonus March: Federal Bonus Policy, the Veterans of Foreign Wars, and the Origins of a Protest Movement," *Journal of Policy History* 18, no. 3 (July 2006): 275–303.

12. Ellis W. Hawley, *The New Deal and the Problem of Monopoly: A Study in Economic Ambivalence* (Princeton, NJ: Princeton University Press, 1996); Jason Scott Smith, *Building New Deal Liberalism: The Political Economy of Public Works, 1933–1956* (New York: Cambridge University Press, 2006).

13. Colin Gordon, *New Deals: Business, Labor, and Politics in America, 1920–1935* (New York: Cambridge University Press, 1994).

14. Quoted in Ira Katznelson, *Fear Itself: The New Deal and the Origins of Our Time* (New York: Liveright, 2013), 230.

15. Zaragosa Vargas, *Labor Rights Are Civil Rights: Mexican American Workers in Twentieth-Century America* (Princeton, NJ: Princeton University Press, 2005), 83–89.

16. Irving Bernstein, *The Turbulent Years: A History of the American Worker, 1933–1941* (Boston: Houghton Mifflin, 1970), 218–29; Peter A. Korth and Margaret R. Beegle, *I Remember Like Today: The Auto-Lite Strike of 1934* (East Lansing: Michigan State University Press, 1988).

17. Bernstein, *The Turbulent Years*, 255.

18. Bruce Nelson, *Workers on the Waterfront: Seaman, Longshoremen, and Unionism in the 1930s* (Urbana: University of Illinois Press, 1988); Bernstein, *The Turbulent Years*, 252–98; Harvey Schwartz, *Solidarity Stories: An Oral History of the ILWU* (Seattle: University of Washington Press, 2009).

19. Bernstein, *The Turbulent Years*, 229–52; Philip A. Korth, *The Minneapolis Teamsters Strike of 1934* (East Lansing: Michigan State University Press, 1995); Barry Eidlin, "'Upon This (Foundering) Rock: Minneapolis Teamsters and the Transformation of American Business Unionism, 1934–1941," *Labor History* 50, no. 3 (August 2009): 249–67.

20. Elizabeth Faue, *Community of Suffering and Struggle: Women, Men, and the Labor Movement in Minneapolis, 1915–1945* (Chapel Hill: University of North Carolina Press, 1991), 100–125.

21. Beth English, *A Common Thread: Labor, Politics, and Capital Mobility in the Textile Industry* (Athens: University of Georgia Press, 2006).

22. Janet Irons, *Testing the New Deal: The General Textile Strike of 1934 in the American South* (Urbana: University of Illinois Press, 2000); Bernstein, *The Turbulent Years*, 298–315; Landon R.Y. Storrs, *Civilizing Capitalism: The National Consumers' League, Women's Activism, and Labor Standards in the New Deal Era* (Chapel Hill: University of North Carolina Press, 2000), 130.

23. Meg Jacobs, *Pocketbook Politics: Economic Citizenship in Twentieth-Century America* (Princeton, NJ: Princeton University Press, 2005), 145–49.

24. Katznelson, *Fear Itself*, 257–60.

25. Robert H. Zieger, *The CIO, 1935–1955* (Chapel Hill: University of North Carolina Press, 1995).

26. Fraser M. Ottanelli, *The Communist Party of the United States: From the Depression to World War II* (New Brunswick, NJ: Rutgers University Press, 1991).

27. Steven Fraser, *Labor Will Rule: Sidney Hillman and the Rise of American Labor* (Ithaca, NY: Cornell University Press, 1993), 356–78; Lizabeth Cohen, *Making a New Deal: Industrial Workers in Chicago, 1919–1939* (New York: Cambridge University Press, 1990), 253–61.

28. Sidney Fine, *Sit-Down: The General Motors Strike of 1936–1937* (Ann Arbor: University of Michigan Press, 1969), 14–53; Walter Galenson, *The CIO Challenge to the AFL: A History of the American Labor Movement, 1935–1941* (Cambridge, MA: Harvard University Press, 1960), 129–30.

29. Quoted in Jerold S. Auerbach, *Labor and Liberty: The La Follette Committee and the New Deal* (Indianapolis: Bobbs-Merrill, 1966), 109.

30. Quoted in Dray, *There Is Power in a Union: The Epic Story of Labor in America* (New York: Doubleday, 2010), 460.

31. Fine, *Sit-Down*, 60.

32. Quoted in ibid., 111.

33. Auerbach, *Labor and Liberty*.

34. Fine, *Sit-Down*, 63–99.

35. Frances Fox Piven and Richard A. Cloward, *Poor People's Movements: Why They Succeed, How They Fail* (New York: Vintage Books, 1979), 137.

36. Fine, *Sit-Down*, 174–77.

37. Daniel Nelson, *American Rubber Workers and Organized Labor, 1900–1941* (Princeton, NJ: Princeton University Press, 1988), 170–233.

38. Quoted in Sharon Smith, *Subterranean Fire: A History of Working-Class Radicalism in the United States* (Chicago: Haymarket Books, 2006), 140.

39. Quoted in Fine, *Sit-Down*, 201.

40. Sol Dollinger and Genora Johnson Dollinger, *Not Automatic: Women and the Left in the Forging of the Auto Workers' Union* (New York: Monthly Review Press, 2000).

41. Quoted in Philip Dray, *There Is Power in a Union*, 464.

42. Art Preis, *Labor's Giant Step: Twenty Years of the CIO* (New York: Pioneer Publishers, 1964), 54–55; Fine, *Sit-Down*, 1–13.

43. Reuther, *The Brothers Reuther*, 157.

44. Fine, *Sit-Down*, 154.

45. Galenson, *The CIO Challenge to the AFL*, 135.

46. Quoted in Galenson, *The CIO Challenge to the AFL*, 139

47. Quoted in Dray, *There Is Power in a Union*, 463.

48. Quoted in Fine, *Sit-Down*, 228.

49. Quoted in ibid., 172.

50. Quoted in Preis, *Labor's Giant Step*, 60.

51. Fine, *Sit-Down*, 233–36; quote from Melvyn Dubofsky and Warren R. van Tine, *John L. Lewis: A Biography* (Urbana: University of Illinois Press, 1986), 195.

52. Fine, *Sit-Down*, 279–86.

53. Nelson Lichtenstein, *The Most Dangerous Man in Detroit: Walter Reuther and the Fate of American Labor* (New York: Basic Books, 1995), 75.

54. Reuther, *The Brothers Reuther*, 170–71.

55. Jacobs, *Pocketbook Politics*, 154.

56. Howard Zinn, Dana Frank, and Robin D.G. Kelley, *Three Strikes: Miners, Musicians, Salesgirls, and the Fighting Spirit of Labor's Last Century* (Boston: Beacon Press, 2001), 59–118.

57. Quoted in Steven P. Dandaneau, *A Town Abandoned: Flint, Michigan, Confronts Deindustrialization* (Albany: State University of New York Press, 1996), 3.

58. Galenson, *The CIO Challenge to the AFL*, 178–84; B.J. Widick, *Detroit: City of Race and Class Violence* (Chicago: Quadrangle Books, 1972), 73–87.

59. Ahmed White, *The Last Great Strike: Little Steel, the CIO, and the Struggle for Labor Rights in New Deal America* (Oakland: University of California Press, 2016); John Hinshaw, *Steel and Steelworkers: Race and Class Struggle in Twentieth-Century Pittsburgh* (Albany: State University of New York Press, 2002), 1–6.

60. Quoted in Joseph G. Rayback, *History of American Labor* (New York: MacMillan, 1959), 343.

61. Quoted in Storch, *Working Hard for the American Dream*, 59. For overall view of strike, see White, *The Last Great Strike.*

62. Michael Dennis, *Blood on Steel: Chicago Steelworkers and the Strike of 1937* (Baltimore: Johns Hopkins University Press, 2014). Quoted on p. 71.

63. White, *The Last Great Strike*, 269–81.

64. Rick Halpern, *Down on the Killing Floor: Black and White Workers in Chicago's Packinghouses, 1904–54* (Urbana: University of Illinois Press, 1997).

65. Katznelson, *Fear Itself.*

66. Jacobs, *Pocketbook Politics*, 168.

67. Katznelson, *Fear Itself*, 267–72; Jonathan Grossman, "Fair Labor Standards Act of 1938: Maximum Struggle for a Minimum Wage," United States Department of Labor, Office of the Assistant Secretary for Administration and Management, dol.gov/oasam/programs/history/flsa1938.htm.

68. Kelley, *Hammer and Hoe*, 34–56.

69. Donald H. Grubbs, *Cry from the Cotton: The Southern Tenant Farmers' Union and the New Deal* (Chapel Hill: University of North Carolina Press, 1971); Mark D. Naison, "The Southern Tenant Farmers' Union and the CIO," in *"We Are All Leaders": The Alternative Unionism of the Early 1930s*, ed. Staughton Lynd (Urbana: University of Illinois Press, 1996), 102–16.

70. Cletus E. Daniel, *Bitter Harvest: A History of California Farmworkers, 1870–1941* (Berkeley: University of California Press, 1982), 222–57;

Camille Guerin-Gonzales, *Mexican Workers and American Dreams: Immigration, Repatriation, and California Farm Labor, 1900–1939* (New Brunswick, NJ: Rutgers University Press, 1994), 111–38.

7: The Oakland General Strike and Cold War America

1. Nelson Lichtenstein, *Labor's War at Home: The CIO in World War II*, (New York: Cambridge University Press, 1982), 46.

2. Nancy A. Hewitt and Steven F. Lawson, *Exploring American Histories: A Brief Survey with Sources* (New York: Bedford/St. Martin's, 2013), 734.

3. Steven Fraser, *Labor Will Rule: Sidney Hillman and the Rise of American Labor* (Ithaca, NY: Cornell University Press, 1993).

4. Philip Yale Nicholson, *Labor's Story in the United States* (Philadelphia: Temple University Press, 2004), 230; Ruth Milkman, *Gender at Work: The Dynamics of Job Segregation by Sex During World War II* (Urbana: University of Illinois Press, 1987), 85–86.

5. Gerald Mayer, "Union Membership Trends in the United States," Congressional Research Service, Cornell University ILR School, August 31, 2004, digitalcommons.ilr.cornell.edu/cgi/viewcontent.cgi?article=1176&context=key_workplace.

6. Lichtenstein, *Labor's War at Home*, 8–43.

7. David Kennedy, *The American People in World War II: Freedom from Fear, Part II* (New York: Oxford University Press, 2003), 217.

8. Alonzo L. Hamby, *Man of Destiny: FDR and the Making of the American Century* (New York: Basic Books, 2015), 363–65.

9. Lichtenstein, *Labor's War at Home*, 112.

10. Ibid., 121–27; Randi Storch, *Working Hard for the American Dream: Workers and Their Unions, World War I to the Present* (Malden, MA: Wiley-Blackwell, 2013), 91.

11. George Lipsitz, *Rainbow at Midnight: Labor and Culture in the 1940s* (Urbana: University of Illinois Press, 1994), 22.

12. Gwen Sharp, "Myth-Making and the 'We Can Do It!' Poster," *Society Pages*, January 4, 2011, thesocietypages.org/socimages/2011/01/04/myth-making-and-the-we-can-do-it-poster.

13. Lichtenstein, *Labor's War at Home*, 124.

14. William H. Harris, *Keeping the Faith: A. Philip Randolph, Milton P. Webster, and the Brotherhood of Sleeping Car Porters, 1925–37* (Urbana: University of Illinois Press, 1991); Melinda Chateauvert, *Marching Together: Women of the Brotherhood of Sleeping Car Porters* (Urbana: University of

Illinois Press, 1998); Beth Tompkins Bates, "Mobilizing Black Chicago: The Brotherhood of Sleeping Car Porters and Community Organizing, 1925–35," in *The Black Worker: A Reader*, ed. Eric Arnesen (Urbana: University of Illinois Press, 2007), 195–221.

15. Aimin Zhang, *The Origins of the African-American Civil Rights Movement, 1865–1956* (New York: Routledge, 2002), 108–22; Andrew Edmund Kersten, *Race, Jobs, and the War: The FEPC in the Midwest, 1941–46* (Urbana: University of Illinois Press, 2000); Merl E. Reed, *Seedtime for the Modern Civil Rights Movement: The President's Committee on Fair Employment Practice, 1941–1946* (Baton Rouge: Louisiana State University Press, 1991).

16. Manning Marable, *Race, Reform, and Rebellion: The Second Reconstruction of Black America*, 3rd ed. (Jackson: University Press of Mississippi, 2007), 14.

17. Lipsitz, *Rainbow at Midnight*, 77; Thomas J. Sugrue, *The Origins of the Urban Crisis: Race and Inequality in Postwar Detroit* (Princeton, NJ: Princeton University Press, 1996), 28–31; Matthew L. Basso, *Meet Joe Copper: Masculinity and Race on Montana's World War II Home Front* (Chicago: University of Chicago Press, 2013).

18. Lipsitz, *Rainbow at Midnight*, 99.

19. Ibid., 51–52.

20. Zaragosa Vargas, *Labor Rights Are Civil Rights: Mexican American Workers in Twentieth-Century America* (Princeton, NJ: Princeton University Press, 2005), 265–70.

21. Lichtenstein, *Labor's War at Home*, 221–30.

22. Lipsitz, *Rainbow at Midnight*, 100.

23. Ira Katznelson, *Fear Itself: The New Deal and the Origins of Our Time* (New York: Liveright, 2013), 184.

24. Michael K. Honey, "Operation Dixie, the Red Scare, and the Defeat of Southern Labor Organizing," in *American Labor and the Cold War: Grassroots Politics and Postwar Political Culture*, ed. Robert W. Cherny, William Issel, and Kieran Walsh Taylor (New Brunswick, NJ: Rutgers University Press, 2004), 216–44.

25. William Powell Jones, "'Simple Truths of Democracy': African Americans and Organized Labor in the Post–World War II South," in *The Black Worker: A Reader*, ed. Eric Arnesen (Urbana: University of Illinois Press, 2007), 254.

26. Robin D.G. Kelley, *Hammer and Hoe: Alabama Communists During the Great Depression* (Chapel Hill: University of North Carolina Press, 1990).

27. Quoted in Katznelson, *Fear Itself,* 190.

28. Michelle Brattain, *The Politics of Whiteness: Race, Workers, and Culture in the Modern South* (Princeton NJ: Princeton University Press, 2001), 132–62, quote on p. 142.

29. Robert Rodgers Korstad, *Civil Rights Unionism: Tobacco Workers and the Struggle for Democracy in the Mid-Twentieth-Century South* (Chapel Hill: University of North Carolina Press, 2003); Landon R.Y. Storrs, *Civilizing Capitalism: The National Consumers' League, Women's Activism, and Labor Standards in the New Deal Era* (Chapel Hill: University of North Carolina Press, 2000). On capital mobility, see Jefferson Cowie, *Capital Moves: RCA's Seventy-Year Quest for Cheap Labor* (New York: The New Press, 1999); Tami J. Friedman, "'How Can Greenville Get New Industry to Come Here if We Get the Label of a C.I.O. Town': Capital Migration and the Limits of Unionism in the Postwar South," in *Life and Labor in the New New South,* ed. Robert H. Zieger (Gainesville: University Press of Florida, 2012), 16–44.

30. Alan Draper, *Conflict of Interests: Organized Labor and the Civil Rights Movement in the South, 1954–1968* (Ithaca, NY: ILR Press, 1994).

31. Albert Vetere Lannon, *Fight or Be Slaves: The History of the Oakland–East Bay Labor Movement* (Lanham, MD: University Press of America, 2000), 105.

32. Dana Frank, *Purchasing Power: Consumer Organizing, Gender, and the Seattle Labor Movement, 1919–1929* (New York: Cambridge University Press, 1994); Harvey O'Connor, *Revolution in Seattle: A Memoir* (New York: Monthly Review Press, 1964).

33. Lipsitz, *Rainbow at Midnight,* 120–53.

34. Marilynn S. Johnson, *The Second Gold Rush: Oakland and the East Bay in World War II* (Berkeley: University of California Press, 1993), quote on 30; Chris Rhomberg, *No There There: Race, Class, and Political Community in Oakland* (Berkeley: University of California Press, 2004), 97–100.

35. Quoted in Rhomberg, *No There There,* 104. See also Robert O. Self, *American Babylon: Race and the Struggle for Postwar Oakland* (Princeton, NJ: Princeton University Press, 2003), 36–40.

36. Quoted in Rhomberg, *No There There,* 107.

37. Lannon, *Fight or Be Slaves,* 105–11.

38. Quoted in Lipsitz, *Rainbow at Midnight,* 149.

39. Stan Weir, "American Labor on the Defensive: A 1940's Odyssey," *Radical America* 9, no. 4–5 (July–August 1975): 179.

40. Ibid., 178–81.

41. Quoted in Lipsitz, *Rainbow at Midnight,* 150.

42. Ibid., 102–8.

43. Elizabeth A. Fones-Wolf, *Selling Free Enterprise: The Business Assault on Labor and Liberalism, 1945–60* (Urbana: University of Illinois Press, 1994).

44. Meg Jacobs, *Pocketbook Politics: Economic Citizenship in Twentieth-Century America* (Princeton, NJ: Princeton University Press, 2005), 182.

45. Judith Stepan-Norris and Maurice Zeitlin, *Left Out: Reds and America's Industrial Unions* (New York: Cambridge University Press, 2003), 274–75.

46. Robert A. Caro, *Means of Ascent* (New York: Alfred A. Knopf, 1990), 223–28, 283; quote from Elizabeth Tandy Shermer, *Sunbelt Capitalism: Phoenix and the Transformation of American Politics* (Philadelphia: University of Pennsylvania Press, 2013), 109.

47. Katznelson, *Fear Itself*, 333–34.

48. Ahmed White, *The Last Great Strike: Little Steel, the CIO, and the Struggle for Labor Rights in New Deal America* (Oakland: University of California Press, 2016), 275–80.

49. Quoted in Jeffrey S. Ashley and Marla J. Jarmer, eds., *The Bully Pulpit, Presidential Speeches, and the Shaping of Public Policy* (Lanham, MD: Lexington Books, 2015), 96.

50. Kim Scipes, *AFL-CIO's Secret War Against Developing Country Workers: Solidarity or Sabotage?* (Lanham, MD: Lexington Books, 2011).

51. Ronald L. Filippelli and Mark D. McColloch, *Cold War in the Working Class: The Rise and Decline of the United Electrical Workers* (Albany: State University of New York Press, 1985); Jennifer Luff, *Commonsense Anticommunism: Labor and Civil Liberties Between the World Wars* (Chapel Hill: University of North Carolina Press, 2012); Jerry Lembcke and William Tattam, *One Union in Wood: A Political History of the International Woodworkers of America* (New York: International Publishers, 1984).

52. James J. Lorence, *Palomino: Clinton Jencks and Mexican-American Unionism in the American Southwest* (Urbana: University of Illinois Press, 2013); James J. Lorence, *The Suppression of Salt of the Earth: How Hollywood, Big Labor, and Politicians Blacklisted a Movie in Cold War America* (Albuquerque: University of New Mexico Press, 1999); Vargas, *Labor Rights Are Civil Rights*, 162–74.

53. Ellen Schrecker, "Labor and the Cold War: The Legacy of McCarthyism," in *American Labor and the Cold War: Grassroots Politics and Postwar Political Culture*, ed. Robert W. Cherny, William Issel, and Kieran Walsh Taylor, eds. (New Brunswick, NJ: Rutgers University Press, 2004), 7–24; Randi Storch, "The United Packinghouse Workers of America, Civil Rights, and the Communist Party in Chicago," in Cherny, Issel, and Taylor, *American Labor and the Cold War*, 72–84; Rick Halpern, *Down on the Killing Floor: Black and White Workers in Chicago's Packinghouses, 1904–54* (Urbana: University of Illinois Press, 1997).

54. Maeva Marcus, *Truman and the Steel Seizure Case: The Limits of Presidential Power* (Durham, NC: Duke University Press, 1994).

55. Judith Stein, *Pivotal Decade: How the United States Traded Factories for Finance in the Seventies* (New Haven, CT: Yale University Press, 2010), 1–3.

56. Erik Loomis, *Empire of Timber: Labor Unions and the Pacific Northwest Forests* (New York: Cambridge University Press, 2016), 120.

8: Lordstown and Workers in a Rebellious Age

1. Todd Gitlin, *The Sixties: Years of Hope, Days of Rage* (New York: Bantam Books, 1987); Alice Echols, *Shaky Ground: The Sixties and Its Aftershocks* (New York: Columbia University Press, 2002); Daniel T. Rodgers, *Age of Fracture* (Cambridge, MA: Harvard University Press, 2011); James J. Farrell, *The Spirit of the Sixties: The Making Postwar Radicalism* (New York: Routledge University Press, 1997).

2. Jefferson Cowie, *Stayin' Alive: The 1970s and the Last Days of the Working Class* (New York: The New Press, 2010); James Morton Turner, *The Promise of Wilderness: American Environmental Politics Since 1964* (Seattle: University of Washington Press, 2012); Gretchen Lemke-Santangelo, *Daughters of Aquarius: Women of the Sixties Counterculture* (Lawrence: University Press of Kansas, 2009); Edward D. Berkowitz, *Something Happened: A Political and Cultural Overview of the Seventies* (New York: Columbia University Press, 2006); Joseph Crespino, *In Search of Another Country: Mississippi and the Conservative Counterrevolution* (Princeton, NJ: Princeton University Press, 2007).

3. Kim Scipes, *AFL-CIO's Secret War Against Developing Country Workers: Solidarity or Sabotage?* (Lanham, MD: Lexington Books, 2011); Robert H. Zieger, Timothy J. Minchin, and Gilbert J. Gall, *American Workers, American Unions: The 20th and Early 21st Centuries*, 4th ed. (Baltimore: Johns Hopkins University Press, 2014), 168–92.

4. Peter B. Levy, *The New Left and Labor in the 1960s* (Urbana: University of Illinois Press, 1994), 15–16.

5. The calculation of the $2 minimum wage was made using the Bureau of Labor Statistics' inflation calculator, data.bls.gov/cgi-bin/cpicalc.pl.

6. Quoted in William P. Jones, "The 'Void at the Center of the Story': The Negro American Labor Council and the Long Civil Rights Movement," in *Reframing Randolph: Labor, Black Freedom, and the Legacies of A. Philip Randolph*, ed. Andrew E. Kersten and Clarence Lang (New York: New York University Press, 2015), 23; John Nichols, *The S Word: A Short History of an American Tradition . . . Socialism* (London: Verso, 2015), 221.

7. William P. Jones, *The March on Washington: Jobs, Freedom, and the Forgotten History of Civil Rights* (New York: Norton, 2013); Thomas J.

Sugrue, *Sweet Land of Liberty: The Forgotten Struggle for Civil Rights in the North* (New York: Random House, 2008) 305–8.

8. Timothy J. Minchin, *The Color of Work: The Struggle for Civil Rights in the Southern Paper Industry, 1945–1980* (Chapel Hill: University of North Carolina Press, 2001); Timothy J. Minchin, *Hiring the Black Worker: The Racial Integration of the Southern Textile Industry, 1960–1980* (Chapel Hill: University of North Carolina Press, 1999).

9. Nelson Lichtenstein, *The Most Dangerous Man in Detroit: Walter Reuther and the Fate of American Labor* (New York: Basic Books 1995), 374.

10. Bruce Nelson, *Divided We Stand: American Workers and the Struggle for Black Equality* (Princeton, NJ: Princeton University Press, 2001), 219–50.

11. Cowie, *Stayin' Alive*, 242–43.

12. Michelle Brattain, *The Politics of Whiteness: Race, Workers, and Culture in the Modern South* (Princeton, NJ: Princeton University Press, 2001), 260–61.

13. Levy, *The New Left and Labor in the 1960s*, 65–83.

14. Quoted in ibid., 82.

15. Andrew Hartman, *A War for the Soul of America: A History of the Culture Wars* (Chicago: University of Chicago Press, 2015), 59–62

16. Levy, *The New Left and Labor in the 1960s*, 10–15, 30–37.

17. Penny Lewis, *Hardhats, Hippies, and Hawks: The Vietnam Antiwar Movement as Myth and Memory* (Ithaca, NY: Cornell University Press, 2013).

18. Levy, *The New Left and Labor in the 1960s*, 1–2.

19. Gerald Hunt and Monica Bielski Boris, "The Lesbian, Gay, Bisexual, and Transgender Challenge to American Labor," in *The Sex of Class: Women Transforming American Labor*, ed. Dorothy Sue Cobble (Ithaca, NY, NY: Cornell University Press, 2007), 95.

20. Marcia Walker-McWilliams, *Reverend Addie Wyatt: Faith and the Fight for Labor, Gender, and Racial Equality* (Urbana: University of Illinois Press, 2016).

21. Quoted in "Myra. K. Wolfgang, Feminist Leader, 61," *New York Times*, April 13, 1976.

22. Silke Roth, *Building Movement Bridges: The Coalition of Labor Union Women* (Westport, CT: Greenwood Publishing, 2003).

23. Sara Dubow, *Ourselves Unborn: A History of the Fetus in Modern America* (New York: Oxford University Press, 2011), 123–26.

24. 24.to5.org/about-us/our-story-2.

25. "Crystal Lee Sutton," oral history, in Victoria Byerly, *Hard Times Cotton Mill Girls: Personal Histories of Womanhood and Poverty in the South* (Ithaca, NY: Cornell University Press, 1986), 201–18.

26. Miriam Frank, *Out in the Union: A Labor History of Queer America* (Philadelphia: Temple University Press, 2014).

27. Studs Terkel, *Working: People Talk About What They Do All Day and How They Feel About What They Do* (New York: Ballantine Books, 1972), 263.

28. Lynne Page Snyder, "'The Death-Dealing Smog over Donora, Pennsylvania': Industrial Air Pollution, Public Health Policy, and the Politics of Expertise, 1948–1949," *Environmental History Review* 18, no. 1 (Spring 1994): 117–39.

29. Daniel M. Berman, *Death on the Job: Occupational Health and Safety Struggles in the United States* (New York: Monthly Review Press, 1978).

30. Robert Gordon, "'Shell No!' OCAW and the Labor-Environmental Alliance," *Environmental History* 3, no. 4 (October 1998): 460–87; Les Leopold, *The Man Who Hated Work and Loved Labor: The Life and Times of Tony Mazzocchi* (White River Junction, VT: Chelsea Green Publishing, 2007).

31. Quoted in Robyn Muncy, *Relentless Reformer: Josephine Roche and Progressivism in Twentieth-Century America* (Princeton, NJ: Princeton University Press, 2014), 275.

32. Richard Fry, "Making Amends: Coal Miners, the Black Lung Association, and Federal Compensation Reform, 1969–1972," *Federal History* 5 (January 2013): 35–56.

33. Richard Fry, "Dissent in the Coalfields: Miners, Federal Politics, and Union Reform in the United States, 1968–1973," *Labor History* 55, no. 2 (May 2014): 173–88.

34. Cowie, *Stayin' Alive*, 38–42.

35. Dan La Botz, "The Tumultuous Teamsters of the 1970s," in *Rebel Rank and File: Labor Militancy and Revolt from Below During the Long 1970s*, ed. Aaron Brenner, Robert Brenner, and Cal Winslow (London: Verso, 2010), 199–226.

36. Randi Storch, *Working Hard for the American Dream: Workers and Their Unions, World War I to the Present* (Malden, MA: Wiley-Blackwell, 2013), 149.

37. Quoted in "The Spreading Lordstown Syndrome," *Business Week*, March 4, 1972, 69–70.

38. Lichtenstein, *The Most Dangerous Man in Detroit*, 271–98.

39. Levy, *The New Left and Labor in the 1960s*, 153–54; John Barnard, *American Vanguard: The United Auto Workers During the Reuther Years, 1935–1970* (Detroit: Wayne State University, 2004), 451–76.

40. Quoted in Cowie, *Stayin' Alive*, 45.

41. Quoted in "The Spreading Lordstown Syndrome."

42. Stanley Aronowitz, *False Promises: The Shaping of American Working Class Consciousness* (New York: McGraw-Hill, 1973), 21.

43. Agis Salpukas, "Young Workers Disrupt Key G.M. Plant," *New York Times*, January 23, 1972.

44. See Ben Hamper, *Rivethead: Tales from the Assembly Line* (New York: Warner Books, 1991) for a firsthand account of the rough-and-tumble life on a GM assembly line in Flint in the 1970s and early 1980s.

45. Aronowitz, *False Promises*, 37.

46. Quoted in Cowie, *Stayin' Alive*, 48.

47. Terkel, *Working*, 257–59.

48. Ibid., 262.

49. Quoted in Aronowitz, *False Promises*, 43.

50. Ibid.

51. James M. Rubenstein, *Making and Selling Cars: Innovation and Change in the U.S. Automotive Industry* (Baltimore: Johns Hopkins University Press, 2001), 156–57; Aronowitz, *False Promises*, 21–50; Cowie, *Stayin' Alive*, 42–49.

52. Cowie, *Stayin' Alive*, 42–43.

53. Quoted in James R. Green, *The World of the Worker: Labor in Twentieth-Century America* (New York: Hill and Wang, 1980), 221.

54. Quoted in Cowie, *Stayin' Alive*, 46.

55. Ibid., 250–60.

56. Judith Stein, *Pivotal Decade: How the United States Traded Factories for Finance in the Seventies* (New Haven, CT: Yale University Press, 2010).

57. Quoted in Cowie, *Stayin' Alive*, 261–312.

58. Robert Bruno, *Steelworker Alley: How Class Works in Youngstown* (Ithaca, NY: Cornell University Press, 1999). 10.

59. John Russo and Sherry Lee Linkon, "Collateral Damage: Deindustrialization and the Uses of Youngstown," in *Beyond the Ruins: The Meanings of Deindustrialization*, ed. Jefferson Cowie and Joseph Heathcott (Ithaca, NY: Cornell University Press, 2003), 201–18; Steven High and David W. Lewis, *Corporate Wasteland: The Landscape and Memory of Deindustrialization* (Ithaca, NY: Cornell University Press, 2007), 65–86.

60. Stein, *Pivotal Decade*, 38; Ruth Milkman, *Farewell to the Factory: Auto Workers in the Late Twentieth Century* (Berkeley: University of California Press, 1997).

61. George Lipsitz, *Rainbow at Midnight: Labor and Culture in the 1940s* (Urbana: University of Illinois Press, 1994), 8.

9: Air Traffic Controllers and the New Assault on Unions

1. Joseph E. Slater, *Public Workers: Government Employee Unions, the Law, and the State, 1900–1962* (Ithaca, NY: Cornell University Press, 2004); Francis Russell, *A City in Terror: Calvin Coolidge and the 1919 Boston Police Strike* (Boston: Beacon Press, 1975).

2. John F. Lyons, *Teachers and Reform: Chicago Public Education, 1929–1970* (Urbana: University of Illinois Press, 2008), 164; Slater, *Public Workers*, 190.

3. Philip F. Rubio, *There's Always Work at the Post Office: African American Postal Workers and the Fight for Jobs, Justice, and Equality* (Chapel Hill: University of North Carolina Press, 2010).

4. Joan Turner Beifuss, *At the River I Stand: Memphis, the 1968 Strike, and Martin Luther King* (Brooklyn: Carlson Publishing, 1989), 24. See Francis Ryan, *AFSCME's Philadelphia Story: Municipal Workers and Union Power in the Twentieth Century* (Philadelphia: Temple University Press, 2011) for a deep look at AFSCME's rise in one city.

5. Beifuss, *At the River I Stand*; Michael K. Honey, *Going Down Jericho Road: The Memphis Strike, Martin Luther King's Last Campaign* (New York: W.W. Norton, 2011); quote from Honey, p. 297.

6. Gerald D. McKnight, *The Last Crusade: Martin Luther King, Jr., the FBI, and the Poor People's Campaign* (Boulder, CO: Westview Press, 1998).

7. John Walsh and Garth Mangum, *Labor Struggle in the Post Office: From Selective Lobbying to Collective Bargaining* (Armonk, NY: M.E. Sharpe, 1992), 3–12, 23.

8. Quoted in Aaron Brenner, "Postal Workers' Strikes" in *The Encyclopedia of Strikes in American History*, ed. Aaron Brenner, Benjamin Day, and Immanuel Ness (New York: Routledge, 2015), 269.

9. Peter B. Levy, *The New Left and Labor in the 1960s* (Urbana: University of Illinois Press, 1994), 151–53; Walsh and Mangum, *Labor Struggle in the Post Office*, 13–27; Rubio, *There's Always Work at the Post Office*, 233–61.

10. Storch, *Working Hard for the American Dream: Workers and Their Unions, World War I to the Present* (Malden, MA: Wiley-Blackwell, 2013), 137.

11. On the rise of post-1965 black political power in the South, see George Derek Musgrove, *Rumor, Repression, and Racial Politics: How the Harassment of Black Elected Officials Shaped Post–Civil Rights America*

(Athens: University of Georgia Press, 2012); David R. Colburn and Jeffrey S. Adler, eds., *African-American Mayors: Race, Politics, and the American City* (Urbana: University of Illinois Press, 2005).

12. Pearl K. Ford, ed., *African Americans in Georgia: A Reflection of Politics and Policy in the New South* (Macon, GA: Mercer University Press, 2010), 130–32; Jessica Ann Levy, "Selling Atlanta: Black Mayoral Politics from Protest to Entrepreneurism, 1973 to 1990," *Journal of Urban History* 41, no. 3 (May 2015): 420–43.

13. Joseph McCartin, "Managing Discontent: The Life and Career of Leamon Hood, Black Public Employee Union Activist," in *The Black Worker: A Reader,* Eric Arnesen (Urbana: University of Illinois Press, 2007), 271–99; Manning Marable, *How Capitalism Underdeveloped Black America: Problems in Race, Political Economy, and Society* (Boston: South End Press, 1983); David Andrew Harmon, *Beneath the Image of the Civil Rights Movement and Race Relations: Atlanta, Georgia, 1946–1981* (New York: Garland Publishing, 1996), 240–42, 298–300.

14. Charles Noble, *Liberalism at Work: The Rise and Fall of OSHA*, (Philadelphia: Temple University Press, 1986), 176–206.

15. Joseph A. McCartin, *Collision Course: Ronald Reagan, the Air Traffic Controllers, and the Strike That Changed America* (New York: Oxford University Press, 2011), 49.

16. Ibid., 50–51.

17. Quoted in Willis J. Nordlund, *Silent Skies: The Air Traffic Controllers' Strike* (Westport, CT: Praeger, 1998), 63.

18. McCartin, *Collision Course*, 102.

19. Ibid., 57.

20. Ibid., 79–87.

21. Ibid., 90–119.

22. Ibid., 120–44.

23. Ibid., 145.

24. Ibid., 145–59.

25. Ibid., 176–201.

26. "Thanksgiving Travelers Face Possible Airline, Bus Strikes," *Washington Post*, November 19, 1977.

27. McCartin, *Collison Course*, 163–75.

28. Ibid., 227–33.

29. Mike Causey, "Reagan Is Endorsed by PATCO's Board," *Washington Post*, October 24, 1980.

30. McCartin, *Collision Course*, 227–49.

31. Ibid., 238.

32. Quoted in ibid., 270.

33. Ibid., 250–77.

34. Nordlund, *Silent Skies*, 2.

35. "Controlling the Air Controllers," *Washington Post*, July 20, 1978.

36. Warren Brown, "The Air Controllers: At First, Frustration, Then Risky Defiance," *Washington Post*, August 3, 1981.

37. McCartin, *Collision Course*, 283–84.

38. Quoted in ibid., 289.

39. Lee Hockstader, "For Workers and Strikers, Controllers Walkout Hits Home" *Washington Post*, August 5, 1981.

40. Quoted in McCartin, *Collision Course*, 294.

41. Quoted in ibid., 291.

42. Ibid., 310.

43. Quoted in Jeremy Brecher, *Strike!*, rev. ed. (New York: South End Press, 1997), 311–12.

44. Quoted in Warren Brown, "U.S. Rules Out Rehiring Striking Air Controllers," *Washington Post*, August 7, 1981.

45. McCartin, *Collision Course*, 340–41.

46. Barbara Kingsolver, *Holding the Line: Women in the Great Arizona Mine Strike of 1983* (Ithaca, NY: ILR Press, 1996); Jonathan D. Rosenblum, *Copper Crucible: How the Arizona Miners' Strike of 1983 Recast Labor-Management Relations in America* (Ithaca, NY: ILR Press, 1995).

47. Ibid.

48. Peter Rachleff, *Hard-Pressed in the Heartland: The Hormel Strike and the Future of the Labor Movement* (Boston: South End Press, 1993); Neala J. Schleuning, *Women, Community, and the Hormel Strike of 1985–86* (Westport, CT: Greenwood Press, 1994).

49. Ibid.

50. Ibid.

51. Robert Michael Smith, *From Blackjacks to Briefcases: A History of Commercialized Strikebreaking and Unionbusting in the United States* (Athens: Ohio University Press, 2003), 119–30.

52. A.H. Raskin, "Lane Kirkland: New Style," *New York Times*, October 28, 1979.

53. Gerald Mayer, *Union Membership Trends in the United States*, Congressional Research Service, Cornell University ILR School, August 31, 2004, digitalcommons.ilr.cornell.edu/cgi/viewcontent.cgi?article=1176&context=key_workplace..

54. Steven K. Ashby and C.J. Hawking, *Staley: The Fight for a New American Labor Movement* (Urbana: University of Illinois Press, 2009).

55. Richard A. Brisbin Jr., *A Strike Like No Other Strike: Law and Resistance During the Pittston Coal Strike of 1989–1990* (Baltimore: Johns Hopkins University Press, 2002); Tom Juravich and Kate Bronfenbrenner, *Ravenswood: The Steelworkers' Victory and the Revival of American Labor* (Ithaca, NY: Cornell University Press, 1999).

56. Erik Loomis, "Democrats and Labor: Frenemies Forever?" *Boston Review*, April 18, 2017, bostonreview.net/politics/erik-loomis-democrats-and-labor-frenemies-forever.

57. Kim Moody, *Workers in a Lean World: Unions in the International Economy* (London: Verso, 1997), 129.

58. Erik Loomis, *Out of Sight: The Long and Disturbing Story of Corporations Outsourcing Catastrophe* (New York: The New Press, 2015).

10: Justice for Janitors and Immigrant Unionism

1. Erik Loomis, "The Perils of a Partisan NLRB," *Democracy: A Journal of Ideas*, October 11, 2016, democracyjournal.org/arguments/the-perils-of-a-partisan-nlrb.

2. Bureau of Labor Statistics, "Union Members—2016," new release, www.bls.gov/news.release/pdf/union2.pdf.

3. Monica Davey, "Unions Suffer Latest Defeat in Midwest with Signing of Wisconsin Measure," *New York Times*, March 9, 2015.

4. Jonathan Oosting, "Michigan Union Membership Dropped Significantly in 2014, First Full Year Under Right-to-Work Law," *Michigan Live*, January 23, 2015, mlive.com/lansing-news/index.ssf/2015/01/michigan_union_membership_down.html.

5. Shaun Richman, "Labor's Bill of Rights," *Century Foundation*, July 18, 2017, tcf.org/content/report/labors-bill-rights.

6. Clifford Krauss, "Texas Oil Fields Rebound from Price Lull, but Jobs Are Left Behind," *New York Times*, February 19, 2017; Brian Baskin, "Next Leap for Robots: Picking Out and Boxing Your Online Order," *Wall Street Journal*, July 25, 2017.

7. Chris Arnade, "Mocked and Forgotten: Who Will Speak for the American White Working Class?" *The Guardian*, March 24, 2016, theguardian.com/politics/2016/mar/24/white-working-class-issues-free-trade-american-south; Benjamin Wallace-Wells, "The Despair of Learning That Experience No Longer Matters," *New Yorker*, April 10, 2017.

8. Erik Loomis, *Out of Sight: The Long and Disturbing Story of Corporations Outsourcing Catastrophe* (New York: The New Press, 2015).

9. Mae M. Ngai, *Impossible Subjects: Illegal Aliens and the Making of Modern America* (Princeton, NJ: Princeton University Press, 2004).

10. Francisco E. Balderrama and Raymond Rodríguez, *Decade of Betrayal: Mexican Repatriation in the 1930s* (Albuquerque: University of New Mexico Press, 2006).

11. Vicki L. Ruiz, *Cannery Women, Cannery Lives: Mexican Women, Unionization, and the California Food Processing Industry, 1930–1950* (Albuquerque: University of New Mexico Press, 1987); Zaragosa Vargas, *Labor Rights Are Civil Rights: Mexican American Workers in Twentieth-Century America* (Princeton, NJ: Princeton University Press, 2013).

12. Deborah Cohen, *Braceros: Migrant Citizens and Transnational Subjects in the Postwar United States and Mexico* (Chapel Hill: University of North Carolina Press, 2011).

13. Frank Bardacke, *Trampling Out the Vintage: Cesar Chavez and the Two Souls of the United Farm Workers* (New York: Verso, 2011); Matt Garcia, *From the Jaws of Victory: The Triumph and Tragedy of Cesar Chavez and the Farm Worker Movement* (Berkeley: University of California Press, 2012).

14. Silvia Giagnoni, *Fields of Resistance: The Struggle of Florida's Farmworkers for Justice* (Chicago: Haymarket Books, 2011).

15. W.K. Barger and Ernesto M. Reza, *The Farm Labor Movement in the Midwest: Social Change and Adaptation Among Migrant Farmworkers* (Austin: University of Texas Press, 1994).

16. Mario Jimenez Sifuentez, *Of Forests and Fields: Mexican Labor in the Pacific Northwest* (New Brunswick, NJ: Rutgers University Press, 2016).

17. Margaret Gray, "The Dark Side of Local," *Jacobin*, August 21, 2016, jacobinmag.com/2016/08/farmworkers-local-locavore-agriculture-exploitation; Margaret Gray, *Labor and the Locavore: The Making of a Comprehensive Food Ethic* (Berkeley: University of California Press, 2013).

18. Eileen Boris and Jennifer Klein, "'We Were the Invisible Workforce': Unionizing Home Care," in *The Sex of Class: Women Transforming American Labor*, ed. Dorothy Sue Cobble (Ithaca, NY: Cornell University Press, 2007), 177–93.

19. Frederick Douglass Opie, *Upsetting the Apple Cart: Black-Latino Coalitions in New York City from Protest to Public Office* (New York: Columbia University Press, 2015), 13–48, quote on p. 29.

20. Boris and Klein, "'We Were the Invisible Workforce.'" .

21. Robert Gottlieb, *Environmentalism Unbound: Exploring New Pathways for Change* (Cambridge, MA: MIT Press, 2001), 147–80.

22. Richard Mines and Jeffrey Avina, "Immigrants and Labor Standards: The Case of California Janitors," in *U.S.-Mexico Relations: Labor*

Market Interdependence, ed. Jorge A. Bustamante, Clark W. Reynolds, and Raúl A. Hinojosa Ojeda (Stanford, CA: Stanford University Press, 1992), 429–48.

23. Fred B. Glass, *From Mission to Microchip: A History of the California Labor Movement* (Berkeley: University of California Press, 2016), 398–99; National Commission for Employment Policy, *Employment Effects of the North American Free Trade Agreement: Recommendations and Background Studies* (Collingdale, PA: DIANE Publishing, 1994), 49.

24. Mines and Avina, "Immigrants and Labor Standards"; Lydia A. Savage, "Geographies of Organizing: Justice for Janitors in Los Angeles," in *Organizing the Landscape: Geographical Perspectives on Labor Unionism*, ed. Andrew Herod (Minneapolis: University of Minnesota Press, 1998), 238–39.

25. Savage, "Geographies of Organizing," 236.

26. Randy Shaw, *Beyond the Fields: Cesar Chavez, the UFW, and the Struggle for Justice in the 21st Century* (Berkeley: University of California Press, 2008), 97–100.

27. Gottlieb, *Environmentalism Unbound*, 176.

28. John Howley, "Justice for Janitors: The Challenge of Organizing in Contract Services," *Labor Research Review* 15, no. 1 (Spring 1990): 61.

29. Christian Zlolniski, *Janitors, Street Venders, and Activists: The Lives of Mexican Immigrants in Silicon Valley* (Berkeley: University of California Press, 2006), 60–61.

30. Richard W. Hurd and William Rouse, "Progressive Union Organizing: The SEIU Justice for Janitors Campaign," *Review of Radical Political Economics* 21, no. 3 (Fall 1989): 70–75.

31. Roger Waldinger et al., "Justice for Janitors: Organizing in Difficult Times," *Dissent* (Winter 1997): 37–44.

32. Glass, *From Mission to Microchip*, 400–401.

33. Quoted in Waldinger et al., "Justice for Janitors," 43.

34. Ibid., 40.

35. Glass, *From Mission to Microchip*, 401–6.

36. John H. M. Laslett, *Sunshine Was Never Enough: Los Angeles Workers, 1880–2010* (Berkeley: University of California Press, 2012), 299–301.

37. Waldinger et al., "Justice for Janitors," 41.

38. Savage, "Geographies of Organizing," 244.

39. Ruth Milkman, *L.A. Story: Immigrant Workers and the Future of the U.S. Labor Movement* (New York: Russell Sage Foundation, 2006).

40. Edmund F. Wehrle, *Between a River and a Mountain: The AFL-CIO and the Vietnam War* (Ann Arbor: University of Michigan Press, 2005).

41. Timothy J. Minchin, *Labor Under Fire: A History of the AFL-CIO Since 1979* (Chapel Hill: University of North Carolina Press, 2017), 48–72.

42. Ibid., 214–36.

43. Savage, "Geographies of Organizing,"225–26.

44. Richard A. Brisbin Jr., *A Strike Like No Other Strike: Law and Resistance During the Pittston Coal Strike of 1989–1990* (Baltimore: Johns Hopkins University Press, 2002).

45. Minchin, *Labor Under Fire*, 214–36.

46. Ibid., 237–63.

47. Liza Featherstone and United Students Against Sweatshops, *Students Against Sweatshops* (New York: Verso, 2002).

48. Vernon M. Briggs Jr., *Immigration and American Unionism* (Ithaca, NY: Cornell University Press, 2001).

49. James P. Kraft, *Vegas at Odds: Labor Conflict in a Leisure Economy, 1960–1985* (Baltimore: Johns Hopkins University Press, 2010.); Culinary Workers Union Local 226," "Our Union/History," culinaryunion226.org/union/history.

50. Saru Jayaraman, *Behind the Kitchen Door* (Ithaca, NY: Cornell University Press, 2013); "ROC United Applauds Maine and Flagstaff, AZ for Eliminating Tipped Minimum Wage," November 9, 2016, rocunited.org/2016/11/roc-united-applauds-maine-flagstaff-az-eliminating-tipped-minimum-wage.

51. Leon Fink, *The Maya of Morganton: Work and Community in the Nuevo New South* (Chapel Hill: University of North Carolina Press, 2003), quote on p. 54.

52. Ibid.

53. Laura Grattan, *Populism's Power: Radical Grassroots Democracy in America* (New York: Oxford University Press, 2016), 101–4; Ned Resnikoff, "Auto Union Walks Back Major Concession to One of Detroit's Big Three," *Al Jazeera America*, October 9, 2015, america.aljazeera.com/articles/2015/10/9/union-walks-back-major-concession-to-big-three.html.

54. See, for example, Gregg Shotwell, *Autoworkers Under the Gun: A Shop-Floor View of the End of the American Dream* (Chicago: Haymarket Books, 2011).

55. Steven P. Dandaneau, *A Town Abandoned: Flint, Michigan, Confronts Deindustrialization* (Albany: State University of New York Press, 1996); Bryce Covert, "Flint Activist Who Fought Poisoned Water Now Faces Foreclosure for Overdue Water Bill," *ThinkProgress*, May 4, 2017, thinkprogress.org/flint-water-bills-foreclosure-melissa-mays-3ef5b59bd50a.

56. John Nichols, *Uprising: How Wisconsin Renewed the Politics of Protest, from Madison to Wall Street* (New York: Nation Books, 2012); Daniel Katz and Richard Greenwald, eds., *Labor Rising: The Past and Future of Working People in America* (New York: The New Press, 2012); Emmett Rensin and Lucy Schiller, "Republicans Are Set to Destroy Iowa's Labor Unions," *New Republic*, February 7, 2017, newrepublic.com/article/140485/republicans-set-destroy-iowas-labor-unions.

57. Todd Gitlin, *Occupy Nation: The Roots, the Spirit, and the Promise of Occupy Wall Street* (New York: HarperCollins, 2012).

58. Sarah Jaffe, *Necessary Trouble: Americans in Revolt* (New York: Nation Books, 2016).

59. Mary Anne Trasciatti, "The Fighting Tradition," *Jacobin*, June 9, 2016, jacobinmag.com/2016/06/verizon-cwa-strike-iww-wobblies-scabs-pickets-contract-union.

60. Quoted in Michael McCormack, "Verizon Workers' Victory Is a Win for All Working Americas," *Century Foundation*, June 8, 2016, tcf.org/content/commentary/verizon-workers-victory-win-working-americans.

Conclusion: Take Back Power

1. Erik Loomis, "8 Ways America's Headed Back to the Robber-Baron Era," *AlterNet*, July 2, 2012, alternet.org/story/156111/8_ways_america%27s_headed_back_to_the_robber-baron_era.

2. Jefferson Cowie, *The Great Exception: The New Deal and the Limits of American Politics* (Princeton, NJ: Princeton University Press, 2016).

Index

Publishing in the Public Interest

Thank you for reading this book published by The New Press. The New Press is a nonprofit, public interest publisher. New Press books and authors play a crucial role in sparking conversations about the key political and social issues of our day.

We hope you enjoyed this book and that you will stay in touch with The New Press. Here are a few ways to stay up to date with our books, events, and the issues we cover:

- Sign up at www.thenewpress.com/subscribe to receive updates on New Press authors and issues and to be notified about local events
- Like us on Facebook: www.facebook.com/newpress books
- Follow us on Twitter: www.twitter.com/thenewpress

Please consider buying New Press books for yourself; for friends and family; or to donate to schools, libraries, community centers, prison libraries, and other organizations involved with the issues our authors write about.

The New Press is a 501(c)(3) nonprofit organization. You can also support our work with a tax-deductible gift by visiting www.thenewpress.com/donate.